DESPERATE HUNGER GETS GOD'S ATTENTION

ALSO BY DR. DEBBIE RICH

Resurrected

Giving

Desperate HUNGER Gets God's Attention

DESPERATE HUNGER GETS GOD'S ATTENTION

DR. DEBBIE RICH

Foreword by
DRS. RODNEY AND ADONICA HOWARD-BROWNE

Without limiting the rights under copyright(s) reserved below, no part of this publication may be reproduced, stored in, introduced into a retrieval system, or transmitted in any form or by any means (electronic, mechanical, photocopying, recording, or otherwise) without the prior permission of the publisher and the copyright owner.

The content of this book is provided "AS IS." The publisher and the author make no guarantees or warranties as to the accuracy, adequacy, or completeness of or results to be obtained from using the content of this book, including any information that can be accessed through hyperlinks or otherwise, and expressly disclaim any warranty expressed or implied, including but not limited to implied warranties of merchantability or fitness for a particular purpose. This limitation of liability shall apply to any claim or cause whatsoever, whether such claim or cause arises in contract, tort, or otherwise. In short, you, the reader, are responsible for your choices and the results they bring.

The scanning, uploading, and distributing of this book via the internet or any other means without the permission of the publisher and copyright owner is illegal and punishable by law. Please purchase only authorized copies, and do not participate in or encourage piracy of copyrighted materials. Your support of the author's rights is appreciated.

Copyright © 2024 by Debra K. Rich. All rights reserved.

Released December 2024
ISBN: 978-1-64457-770-7 (Paperback)
ISBN: 978-1-64457-771-4 (Hardcover)

Rise UP Publications
644 Shrewsbury Commons Ave
Ste 249
Shrewsbury PA 17361
United States of America
www.riseUPpublications.com
Phone: 866-846-5123

Unless otherwise noted, all scriptures are from the KING JAMES VERSION, public domain.

Scripture quotations marked (NKJV) are taken from the NEW KING JAMES VERSION®. Copyright© 1982 by Thomas Nelson, Inc. Used by permission. All rights reserved.

Scripture quotations marked (AMP) or (AMPC) are taken from the AMPLIFIED® BIBLE, Copyright© 1954, 1958, 1962, 1964, 1965, 1987 by the Lockman Foundation Used by Permission. (www.Lockman.org)

Scripture quotations marked (NASB) are taken from the NEW AMERICAN STANDARD BIBLE®, Copyright© 1960, 1962, 1963, 1968, 1971, 1972, 1973, 1975, 1977, 1995 by The Lockman Foundation. Used by permission.

Scripture quotations marked MSG are taken from THE MESSAGE, copyright © 1993, 2002, 2018 by Eugene H. Peterson. Used by permission of NavPress, represented by Tyndale House Publishers. All rights reserved.

Scripture quotations marked (ESV) are taken from THE HOLY BIBLE, ENGLISH STANDARD VERSION®, Copyright© 2001 by Crossway, a publishing ministry of Good News Publishers. Used by permission.

Scripture quotations marked (NIV) are taken from THE HOLY BIBLE, NEW INTERNATIONAL VERSION®. Copyright© 1973, 1978, 1984, 2011 by Biblica, Inc.™. Used by permission of Zondervan

CONTENTS

Foreword	9
Introduction	11
Chapter 1 *What Is Spiritual Hunger and Spiritual Thirst?*	15
Chapter 2 *Cultivating Hunger*	25
Chapter 3 *People in The Bible Who Had an Encounter*	61
Chapter 4 *Hunger Throughout Church History*	115
Chapter 5 *Things That Kill Hunger*	159
Chapter 6 *Hunger Will Cause You to Experience Him*	179
Chapter 7 *The Cost of Carrying the Anointing*	241
Chapter 8 *Get Hungry Enough to Get Your Dreams Back*	273
About Debbie Rich	277

FOREWORD

DRS. RODNEY AND ADONICA HOWARD-BROWNE

Debbie's newest book, "Desperate Hunger, Gets God's Attention", explains why spiritual hunger is a prerequisite for obtaining everything God has for you.

Debbie Rich had the call of God on her life from an early age, but through various circumstances, she was not able to fulfill that call for many years. However, her hunger for God would not let her give up. She never lost her faith and determination to serve God and be used by Him, no matter how many obstacles were in her way. That faith and perseverance stemmed from a spiritual desire to know God and a love for Him that would not be denied. Her spiritual hunger for God has taken her into over fifty nations.

When we met Debbie, she was a single mom of three boys with no money, no home, and driving a car that had already been written off by an insurance company after it went down the side of a mountain into a tree. She had a call on her life, but no one believed in her or expected her to make it —and they told her so. Many tried to persuade her to quit ministry and go back to where she came from.

Debbie's hunger brought her to our meetings in Anchorage, Alaska, in the middle of the Alaskan winter. She had to brave mountain passes and icy

FOREWORD

roads to come to those meetings. When she heard what was happening, her hunger for God was greater than the reasons and excuses to not attend. God gave us a word for her—that it was not the end, but only the beginning and every promise that God had made her, from a child, would indeed come to pass! Her hunger for God caused her to grab everything that God had for her in those meetings; the fire of God, the anointing of The Holy Spirit, and the teaching on giving and being a blessing. She purposed in her heart to boldly act on the Word.

As Debbie has now traveled to over fifty nations and crisscrossed the United States, preaching the gospel of Jesus Christ, her hunger has never diminished. It has only increased, as she has witnessed the faithfulness of God to her time and time again. As you read this book, you will become convinced that God is no respecter of persons. What He does for one, He will do for another, if that one will develop a spiritual hunger that will not be denied.

As you read, "Desperate Hunger", you will be inspired to develop a relationship with God and to know Him in a very personal and intimate way. This will cause you to press into the things of God as never before. Spiritual hunger will take you places in God that nothing else will, as it has Debbie, and every other person who has hungered for God. If you grab onto the truth of God's Word, the way Debbie has, you will be blessed beyond your imagination.

It is a privilege and an honor for us to know Debbie, have her base out of our church, The River at Tampa Bay, and to watch God's grace in her life. We pray that you will read this book and receive its message. As you pursue God with a holy passion, He has promised to fill you. You will never be the same.

Drs. Rodney and Adonica Howard-Browne

INTRODUCTION

If you're holding this book, it means you're ready to begin a journey that will challenge, inspire, and transform your spiritual life. This book will ignite a desperate hunger and thirst within you that only God can satisfy.

> Blessed are those who hunger and thirst for righteousness,
> For they shall be filled.
>
> MATTHEW 5:6 (NKJV)

This powerful promise is the core message of this book. If you're comfortable where you are spiritually, this book isn't for you. But if you're desperate for more of God, if you're willing to cry out and press in until you're overflowing with His presence, then you're in the right place.

I wrote this book because I believe with all my heart that God responds to our desperation. Just as a starving person will do anything to find food, you must approach your spiritual life with the same hunger. Think of a baby crying relentlessly until it's fed; that's the kind of desperate hunger that gets God's attention. He hears the cries of the hungry and the thirsty, and He promises to fill them.

INTRODUCTION

In today's world, many of us have lost touch with what it means to be desperately hungry or thirsty. We've become so accustomed to instant gratification that we've forgotten how to yearn deeply for something. But spiritual hunger and thirst are not just casual metaphors; they are the driving forces that propel us into the depths of God's heart. This book is a call to awaken that longing within you, to stir up a passion and desperation that cannot be quenched by anything less than His presence.

Throughout these pages, I will share stories and testimonies of how God has moved mightily in my life and the lives of others who have dared to seek Him with all their hearts. You will read about miraculous healings, divine encounters, and the unmistakable power of the Holy Spirit. These stories are not just meant to inspire you but to challenge you to believe that what God has done for others, He can do for you.

We will explore together the Biblical foundations of spiritual hunger and thirst. You'll learn why Jesus used these physical sensations to describe our need for Him and how they relate to our spiritual well-being. You'll also find practical steps to cultivate this holy desire, such as immersing yourself in the Word, spending time in prayer, and fasting.

As you read, I encourage you to open your heart and let the Holy Spirit take your spiritual temperature. Are you hot, cold, or lukewarm? Wherever you find yourself, know that there is always more of God to experience. Hunger is the true measure that determines how much of God you'll receive. As Smith Wigglesworth said, "The only thing I'm satisfied with is my dissatisfaction." Let that dissatisfaction drive you deeper into God's presence.

Desperate Hunger Get's God's Attention isn't just about your spiritual growth, it's also about becoming a vessel through which God's Spirit can flow to others. We are called to be carriers of revival, to let our hunger for God create an atmosphere where His presence can move powerfully. By the end of this book, I pray you will be filled to overflowing and equipped to carry His fire wherever you go.

INTRODUCTION

Join me on this journey with an expectant heart. Let these words ignite a desperate hunger and thirst within you. I want you to whole-heartedly seek God's righteousness and experience the ultimate fulfillment that comes from being filled with His Spirit. This is your moment. Don't let it pass by. Get ready to be filled!

ONE

WHAT IS SPIRITUAL HUNGER AND SPIRITUAL THIRST?

If you don't want to have your spiritual temperature taken, you need to put this book down immediately. The Holy Spirit will be your doctor for the next few hours. He is about to take your temperature to see if you are spiritually hot, cold, or lukewarm. It should be taken now because when you face God, there will be no rescheduling of your appointment.

Why do we need to be hungry?

> Blessed are those who hunger and thirst for righteousness,
> for they shall be filled.
>
> MATTHEW 5:6 (NKJV)

God is attracted to our desperation and our holy appetite.

> And Jesus said unto them, I am the bread of life: he that cometh to me shall never hunger; and he that believeth on me shall never thirst.
>
> JOHN 6:35

Jesus promised that anyone who came to Him would not hunger but would be satisfied. Many times, we are waiting for God to come to us, but He wants us to come to Him.

Hunger is the greatest driving force on the face of the earth. A certain spirit of desperation accompanies hunger, and desperate people do desperate things. A man who has never stolen before will steal food when his family has none. When people get hungry enough for natural food, others better beware. Starving people will break through barricades when they hear the rumor of a bread truck in the area. Nothing will stop them.

When a baby is hungry, he will cry and scream until someone responds. He knows that his survival depends on his ability to demonstrate hunger. He doesn't care about others' opinions. He isn't concerned about manners. He may disrupt a church service to display his hunger. A nursing mom cannot refuse a baby's hunger, and neither can God. God responds to the cries of the hungry when someone cries out and says, "Somebody feed me." You must get desperate enough to cry out and get God's attention.

Matthew 5:6 speaks of hunger and thirst. Why? Both sustain life. A person can live about three months without food and only three days without water. Likewise, we can't survive spiritually without eating His Word and drinking His new wine.

The definition of hunger is to crave, to demand, to have an appetite. When we speak of spiritual things, God wants us to desire Him, crave Him, and press into Him, like you would press in for your natural life. Hunger will take you places in God that nothing else can. Hunger will push you to do more than the natural, ordinary man could do.

Very few people understand hunger or thirst in the modern Western world. When we go to someone's house, they ask, "Are you hungry?" Many times, we answer, "Yes, I guess I am." Usually, that means that we haven't eaten in the last five minutes and can probably squeeze something else into our already half-full stomach.

William Barclay, in his Daily Study Bible commentary on Matthew, provides a brief description.

DESPERATE HUNGER GETS GOD'S ATTENTION

"In the ancient world, it was very different. A working man's wage was the equivalent of threepence a day, and, even making every allowance for the difference in the purchasing power of money, no man can ever go far on that wage. A working man in Palestine ate meat only once a week, and in Palestine, the working man and the day laborer were never very far from the borderline of real hunger and actual starvation.

"It was still more so in the case of thirst. It was not possible for the vast majority of people to turn on a tap and find the clear, cold water pouring into their house. A man might be on a journey, and in the midst of it, the hot wind which brought the sandstorm might begin to blow. There was nothing for him to do but to wrap his head in this burnous and turn his back to the wind, and wait, while the swirling sand filled his nostrils and his throat until he was likely to suffocate, and until he was parched with an imperious thirst. In the conditions of modern Western life, there is no parallel at all to that."

> Now on the final and most important day of the Feast, Jesus stood, and He cried in a loud voice, If any man is thirsty, let him come to Me and drink!
> He who believes in Me [who cleaves to and trusts in and relies on Me] as the Scripture has said, From his innermost being shall flow [continuously] springs and rivers of living water.
>
> JOHN 7:37-38 (AMPC)

Finis Dake tells us in his Annotated Bible:

> "It was the eighth and last day of the feast. It was known as a day of the great assembly and the offering of sacrifices for Israel. The first seven days professed to offer sacrifices for other nations but on this day a priest drew water from the Pool of Siloam in a golden vessel and brought it to the temple. At the time of the morning sacrifice, while it was on the altar, he poured this water mingled with wine upon it, and the people were singing with great joy. It was at the

moment when joy was flowing among the crowd and the wine was being drunk that Jesus said 'if any man thirsts (you think this is good?) *Let him come to me and drink and out of his belly shall flow rivers of living water.'* He's equating spiritual hunger and thirst with joy and the move of The Holy Ghost."

Thirst means an eager, famishing, all-consuming craving and involves the passion of the soul for union with God. It means the fullness of spirit. Thirst doesn't mean that I could drink some more water if it is offered. It means, "Whatever it takes, I must have that kind of intimacy with You, God."

We see then that Jesus is not using hunger or thirst as we would describe the emptiness or dryness we feel between meals, but a hunger or thirst that seemingly can never be satisfied. Barclay describes it this way, "It is the hunger of the man who is starving for food and the thirst of the man who will die unless he drinks."

If a person goes long enough without eating, they lose their appetite. Somehow, starvation breaks the hunger mechanism. The same is true of drinking water. If a person goes a long time without drinking water, by the time he or she finally recognizes thirst, he is usually extremely dehydrated. I know from first-hand experience. I don't do it spiritually, but I tend to not drink enough water. When I finally recognize that I am thirsty, there is already a detrimental effect on my body. If you quit eating or drinking spiritually, revival will be over for you.

Extraordinary results require extraordinary effort. If you want to see something you've never seen before, you must do something that you've never done before. You cannot remain in the status quo. We are to become thermostats for society and set the temperature, not thermometers where we register what is going on in the world. We must get hot enough to create an atmosphere that God wants to move in. You will be criticized, but it would be worse to get to Heaven and see what you could have done. I don't want to imagine what it would be like for God to let down a screen in Heaven to show us what we could have done if we had hungered for Him more.

Hunger is the only thing that can predetermine how much of God you'll receive. Smith Wigglesworth, the notable English preacher, said this; "The only thing I'm satisfied with is my dissatisfaction." Wigglesworth loved the fact that he couldn't get enough of God.

When you become hungry for God, others will call you a fanatic. The definition of a fanatic is someone who has more of Jesus than you do. You must be consumed with revival until all you eat and breathe is revival. You must allow God to become a holy obsession until you have a supernatural encounter with the manifested presence of God. Then, you will be revived and become a carrier of revival.

Divine deposits are preceded by divine desire. Those divine desires are birthed out of the heart of God.

David said:

> One thing have I desired of the Lord, that will I seek after;
> that I may dwell in the house of the Lord all the days of
> my life, to behold the beauty of the Lord, and to enquire
> in his temple.
>
> PSALM 27:4

Desire is *a* deep-seated longing. It is intense but narrow. It wants a few things and wants them badly. David did not yearn for everything. Desire cannot spread itself over a wide area. We must let God become a holy obsession. We must become Holy Ghost-possessed and expect miracles. Miracles are divine interventions of God.

The problem is that we've allowed the things of this world to satisfy our hunger. Good things are the enemy of the best things. In the natural realm, those who satisfy their hunger with junk food are not hungry for wholesome, nutritious food. That's what many in the church have done. They've eaten fast food that is not good for them. Others act like they are on a spiritual diet of God-lite food. Don't be one of those who is satisfied with where you are spiritually. You must keep your heart hungry. That will propel you to new levels of Holy Ghost fire, which will, in turn, cause you to receive everything else from God. We have a job to do on this earth. We must plunder Hell and populate Heaven. To do so, we must get desperate.

Desperation involves panting for God in your way and refusing to be denied. When you begin to hunger for God more than anything else, He will lead you into truth and revelation, the gifts of the Spirit, your miracle, healing, and breakthrough. You'll operate in the fruit of The Spirit. People will hear and see Jesus in you. You must get hungry for revival; to see nations shaken, lives changed, people saved, healed, delivered, and restored to their first love.

A spiritually healthy person not only hungers, but thirsts after righteousness.

The definition of thirst is a feeling of needing or wanting to drink something. (Definitions from Webster's American Dictionary of the English Language, 1828.)

KJV Dictionary Definition of thirst: "A vehement desire of drink. Feeling pain for want of drink." It does not mean that I could use some more water. Spiritual thirst means, "Whatever it takes, I'm going to have that kind of intimacy with You, God, until I'm filled."

In John Chapter 7, Jesus is equating hunger and thirst with joy and the move of The Holy Ghost. It was the last day of the feast, and it was called the great day of the feast. The first seven days were about Israel offering sacrifices for other nations. On this day, a priest drew water from the Pool of Siloam in a golden vessel. He then brought it to the temple. At the time of the morning sacrifice, while it was on the altar, he poured this water mingled with wine upon it. The people were singing with great joy. It was at the moment when joy was flowing among the crowd, the wine was being drunk, that Jesus said, "If any man thirsts, Let him come to me and drink, and out of his belly shall flow rivers of living water."

Your belly speaks of your innermost being where The Spirit of God dwells on the inside of you if you have been born again. Rivers of living water refers to the flow of The Spirit of God. The head-waters are from the throne room of God. They bring refreshing to each individual and then to anyone we get around. We are vessels of that living water. He pours into us, and He pours through us. Always remember that God will get His gifts to you if He can get them through you.

We each must learn how to yield to The Holy Spirit to better enable those Rivers of God to bubble out from the inside of us. We can be a fountain of His goodness to those in need. We can allow those rivers to bubble out of us in the middle of any circumstances.

> As the hart panteth after the water brooks, so panteth my
>   soul after thee, O God.
> My soul thirsteth for God, for the living God...
>
> PSALM 42:1-2

David is thirsting and panting after God. He did that because he was thirsty for God. Panting does not refer to the quiet longing of an inward desire, but it refers to an audible panting produced by the agony of the heart. You can see a dog panting, his sides heaving in and out. His tongue hangs out of his mouth. He makes the sound of panting. It is obvious that he is thirsty.

Everyone pants differently. The woman with the issue of blood panted by pressing past the opinions of others who said she should not be in public. She was in agony because of her disease and probably groaned as she was crawling to Jesus. It could be a shout like Blind Bartimaeus when he called for Jesus. It could be a hoarse cry, a whisper, a laugh, a dance, or a run around the building, but you are audibly and visibly letting God know that you are panting.

My pastor, Dr. Rodney Howard-Browne, gives a testimony of when the fire came upon him dramatically. Pastor Rodney became so hungry and desperate for God that he began to call out, "God, come down here and touch me with Your fire, or take me home to be with You. I have to have more of You." He called out like that for about twenty minutes until he lost his voice. Some would say that is unnecessary because God is not deaf. No,

He's not, but He doesn't get nervous either. He loves people making a demand on the anointing and panting in their way. God answered by fire and that is the fire that Pastors Rodney and Adonica Howard-Browne have taken into over ninety nations now. It is the fire that reached me and that I have now taken into fifty-three nations.

There are many reasons that a deer takes to the water. He goes there because he is thirsty. He gets clean as he bathes in the river. It refreshes him when he is exhausted. The deer feeds near the water. When hunted, he will take to the river and stay submerged as long as breath permits, with only his nose sticking out. He will then swim downstream in the river while being extremely careful not to touch the branches of trees on either side. By doing so, he prevents hounds from finding his scent. He's never left the river.

Do you know we're being hunted by the enemy? We are being hunted and chased. There is only one way to keep him from getting our scent. We must stay in the river, with only the tip of our noses out of the river of God. We must stay submerged. We cannot ever go back to land. We must be careful never to touch earthly things and never give our whereabouts. Avoid whatever will pull us out of the river: TV, movies, wrong friends, frequenting old places where we indulged in sin, etc.

A spiritually hungry person realizes that things can be changed by prayer. He is so desperate to see God move. Things can be changed when a spiritually hungry person prays. John G. Lake said in his book, *The Flow of The Spirit, Secrets of a Real Christian Life,* that Daniel said that he was convinced by the study of the books of prophecy that the time had come when they ought to be delivered from captivity in Babylon. The seventy years were fulfilled, but yet there was no deliverance. So he diligently set his face to pray it into being. If it was going to come to pass mechanically by a certain date, it would not have been necessary.

John G. Lake also says in the same book:

> "Daniel fasted and prayed in sackcloth and ashes that deliverance might come. God's purposes come to pass when our hearts get the

real God cry, the supreme cry, not the secondary or third. When all the powers and energies of your spirit, soul, and body are reaching out and crying to God for the answer, it is going to come."

John G. Lake also told the story of a man named Dan Von Vurren. "He had tuberculosis and had a few months to live. He decided that he was going to develop a farm so that his family would have a way to live after he was gone.

> "He was sent a letter about all the people who were saved, healed, and filled with The Holy Ghost. He crawled under an African thorn tree and put his face to the ground and cried out to God. 'God, you can do something for me too.' He was instantly healed of tuberculosis. He had prayed for his wife's salvation for eighteen years to no avail. When he came home she could see that he was healed. She cried out for him to pray for her and she was saved.
> "Dan Von Vurren had eleven children. In just one week, this man, his children, and his wife were baptized in the Holy Ghost. He also had a brother on a nearby farm. He went to see him and within weeks, nineteen were saved and filled with The Holy Ghost.
> "One morning, God spoke to him and said, 'Go to Pretoria. I'm going to send you to different members of parliament.' He obeyed and first went to Premier Louis Botha, who had known him since he was a boy. Botha said, 'I knew him as a reckless rollicking fella but that man who came into my office and stood about ten feet from my desk was not him. Before he commenced to speak, I began to shake and rattle in my chair. I knelt down. I had to put my head under my desk and cried to God.' The Premier said that Dan Von Vurren looked like God, and he talked like God. He added that he was superhumanly wonderful. Next, Von Vurren went to the secretary of the state treasury and the same thing happened.
> "For eighteen days, God kept him going to lawyers, judges, and officials in the land until every high official knew there was a God and a Savior and they received the baptism of The Holy Ghost. It was a result of his hunger for God.

"Von Vurren went up and down the land like a burning fire. Everywhere he went, sinners were saved, healed, and baptized in the Holy Ghost. He set the districts on fire with the power of God. Because one man hungered and thirsted for God and His righteousness, the nation of South Africa was set ablaze."

TWO

CULTIVATING HUNGER

There are levels in God. We see in the Bible in the story of Ezekiel's river that there are ankle-high waters, knee-high waters, waist-high waters, and water too deep to swim in. Why settle for barely getting by or the shallow waters of religion when God wants to submerge you in His glory? Charles Spurgeon wrote: "Some Christians sail their boat in such low spiritual waters that the keel scrapes on the gravel all the way to Heaven, instead of being carried on a flood tide."

Deep must call unto deep. We cannot be complacent, apathetic, or lethargic. There is a difference between knowing about God and knowing Him intimately. Some could win a Bible trivia game, and He will say to them on that Day, "I never knew you." I can't think of anything worse than that. We must know Him as never before. We must have a passionate love for Him, not just know some facts about Him. This will require intimacy and communion with Him and spending time in His presence. Extraordinary results require extraordinary effort.

You must stir yourself up to greater hunger. A radical and uncommon harvest requires an uncommon seed. It requires you to do something you've never done before, say something you never said before, go someplace you never have gone before, and worship as you never have before. It all depends on where you want to go in your experience. What kind of encounter do you want to have? Where do you want to go, and what do you want to do with it? It may require you to turn up the heat. Extraordinary results require extraordinary effort.

I love the story of Evangelist Richard Moore, a good friend of mine. Richard is also a Rhema graduate. After he graduated, he had posters printed that advertised Miracles, Healings, Signs, and Wonders crusades. He says that the posters were great. The only problem was that there were no signs and wonders. He ended up meeting Dr. Rodney Howard-Browne, who hired him to come on the road with him and help him with driving, taking care of the book table, and helping to usher and catch people in the prayer lines. Revival broke out in upstate New York not long after Richard started working for Dr. Rodney. Richard witnessed people being touched in dramatic ways. He saw people overcome with joy, stuck to the floor, crying, laughing, and unable to speak in English for hours. Richard desired that and could not figure out why he could not get it. He was desperate and decided to get in the line for prayer.

When Pastor Rodney came to him, he said, "What are you doing in the line, Richard?" "Why can't I get this? I am hungry." "Then, get hungrier." When Richard did not receive, he became more desperate. He got back in the line. "What are you doing in the line, Richard?' "Why can't I get this?" Pastor Rodney replied, "Get hungrier. Get thirstier." Richard stood in every prayer line for four and a half months. After some time, he began to wonder if he was even saved. He went to his hotel room and said the sinner's prayer again. He got back in the line, and still nothing. So, he decided that maybe he wasn't really baptized in the Holy Ghost. He re-read Brother Hagin's Book *Seven Vital Steps to Receiving the Holy Spirit*. He finished the book and spoke in tongues and got back in the line. He still couldn't seem to get touched the way that others were being touched in the meetings. He refused to give up. He did not get offended at God. He just kept pressing in.

After four and one-half months, he was sitting in the front row of Dr. Rodney's morning meeting. Dr. Rodney recognized that The Holy Spirit fell on Richard. Dr. Rodney was sensitive to The Holy Spirit and could recognize what was happening. However, at the time, Richard was not yet sensitive to The Holy Spirit and didn't realize that anything had happened to him spiritually. Dr. Rodney asked Richard to come to the pulpit and greet the people. Richard thought to himself, "Why would he want me to greet the people? I don't have anything. If I greet the people, they will not get anything." So, he shook his head that he didn't want to come up. You don't do that with Pastor Rodney. He looked at Evangelist Richard and said, "Come here, Richard." Richard obeyed and walked to the pulpit. He decided that he would just give some ordinary, religious greeting, such as "Hello, God bless you. Have a good meeting." But when Richard reached the platform, the power of The Holy Ghost hit him, and the fire of God engulfed him. He couldn't speak. He was a changed man. That experience turned him upside down and changed his ministry forever. He ministers out of that fire today. When Pastor Rodney calls him up to testify about it, he never can get the testimony out. He begins to relive that moment and steps right back into it. I've seen him try to give the testimony many times. Sometimes, he turns red and his entire body gets stiff and ushers come and carry him off. At other times, he gets stuck on the word fire and can only get the consonant f out. He stutters while saying, "The F, F, F, F" (trying to say the word fire). Pastor Rodney has to translate what he is saying. The entire audience is hit with the fire at that point. It is a powerful word from a man who refused to be denied.

Many people helped cultivate spiritual hunger inside of me. The two most important were my maternal grandparents, Floyd and Esther Bates. From the time I was a toddler, both of my grandparents were telling me about Jesus and His Bible. They also talked of great revival meetings that they attended in person. They told of the miracles and healings, the excitement and joy, and the presence of God. I wanted to experience that for myself. Testimonies have great power to stir hunger in others. They also remind us of what we have experienced so that it never grows old.

My parents were not serving God at the time, and my grandparents made sure that their grandchildren knew of the saving grace of Christ Jesus. I can remember saying the sinner's prayer to receive Jesus Christ as my personal Savior at the young age of three. I wanted to see the same miracles my grandparents saw. I got hungrier and hungrier to experience all that God would have for me. I hung onto every word spoken to me by my Sunday school teachers. I also listened intently when my children's church teacher told the same stories over and over about Jonah in the belly of a big fish, Daniel in the lion's den, Esther becoming queen, and Peter walking on the water.

I couldn't get enough of God or church. My parents allowed my grandparents to pick me up and take me to church every time the doors were open. Our church had Sunday night services, mid-week services, and one-week revival meetings quite frequently. I longed for the day when I could be baptized in water, but it was not allowed until we were twelve years old.

I also was hungry to be baptized in The Holy Spirit. Many of my friends received it before I did. I so wanted it to be all God, that I made the mistake of trying to figure it out with my head and did not understand how to yield and cooperate with The Holy Spirit. I started seeking that experience from about five years old, but did not receive it until I was twelve years old. We were not taught about how to yield to The Holy Spirit. When my grandpa dropped me off at my house that night after church, I must have looked a mess. I had cried, laughed, and spoken in tongues for quite some time at the altar. My dad was reading a newspaper when I arrived home. He looked up briefly and said, "Maybe we shouldn't let your grandparents take you to church so much. A little religion is o.k., but you don't want to go off the deep end." I knew that I never wanted to be in the shallow end of God's deep presence. I wanted to be upside down with only my toenails sticking out.

I remember a time when our youth group was invited to go to a youth camp with several other church's youth. After the counselors went to sleep, some of them snuck alcohol into the tents. Some of the boys went into some of the girl's tents. I walked off by myself down a country road and asked The Lord what made me different. I wrote my first song that night, "Which Side of The Road Shall I Take." I was very aware of how holy He is, how sacred the call upon my life was, and that I could not presume on the blood of Jesus Christ. I could not understand why the rest of the youth group did not feel the same way. They chose to taunt me by calling me Reverend Rich when I tried to encourage them to live a Godly lifestyle. I knew only one thing, that I couldn't get enough of God and would pursue Him with everything within me.

I attended a public high school. There were about six hundred students in my school. Everyone there knew my testimony. They also knew that I would not compromise my relationship with God. I was in most of the activities that were offered. I was part of the school choir and the drama club, and I loved acting in the school plays. I was on the drill team and became a cheerleader. I refused to attend parties because I knew what took place at them. I would not date anyone in the school because I knew what The Bible said about being unequally yoked together.

> Be ye not unequally yoked together with unbelievers: for what fellowship hath righteousness with unrighteousness? and what communion hath light with darkness?
>
> 2 CORINTHIANS 6:14

I was determined to wait for God's man of faith and power. It was the hunger in me that helped me live a holy life. I wrote articles for the school newspaper about The Bible and Christianity. In speech class, I gave sermons. I refused to go to my prom, school dances, or parties. My hunger for God was greater than the temptation to compromise. Classmates respected my faith and voted for me to read Scripture at our high school Vesper graduation service.

We had very few young men in our youth group at church. The ones that did attend our church were living a compromising lifestyle. I knew that no one of the opposite sex in my high school was living for God. That was narrowing the field.

Our youth group had a roller-skating party one evening with another Pentecostal youth group. I attended. A young man from the other church asked me to skate. Most of the time, the other girls from church were asked out. I was the girl everyone thought of having a Bible study with. I was flattered to be asked. He was pleasant and asked me to go for pizza after the party. I did, and we had an enjoyable evening. He asked if he could start dating me. I agreed and nine months later, one month after I graduated from high school, we were married.

Before we were married, I told my youth leader that there were a couple of things that concerned me. He didn't seem to be as spiritually hungry as I was. I loved to talk about the things of God after church, and he seemed to change the subject. I noticed that he seldom lifted his hands in worship. I also noticed that he got very angry one evening when I went to church with my grandfather instead of waiting for him to take me. He was running an hour late and it was in the days before cell phones. I couldn't reach him. We were having a revival at our church, and I thought something must have come up on his job, so my grandfather offered to take me to church. Later, after he arrived, he told me that I better never do that again. The handwriting was on the wall, but I was blinded by the fact that I had not dated anyone and felt that there were almost no Christian men available in our small town. I felt that I should be thankful that one wanted to marry me.

My youth leader wondered if I was just being a bit too picky. He said that sometimes guys aren't as emotional as women and that he would probably grow more responsive to the things of God later.

I had made my calling very clear to him and he said that he understood and would go to Bible school with me. He said that he was not called to preach but understood that I was called and promised that he would support me in that calling. I had kept myself pure, waited for a Christian man, made my calling clear, and I thought everything would be all right. I had no idea that the enemy was trying to steal my hunger and my calling.

The night of my wedding is forever etched in my memory. My parents borrowed money to give me as nice a wedding as they could afford. We had about three hundred guests, and the wedding march started. As I walked down the aisle, I suddenly knew that something was wrong. I even stopped for a moment as tears ran down my face. I heard someone on the aisle seat say, "Look at her. She's so happy she's crying." I wanted to call out, "That's not why I am crying. Someone help me." However, I did not want to humiliate him, his family, or my family. I tried to tell myself that maybe this was just prenuptial jitters. "Maybe every bride feels this way." I proceeded down the aisle and woke up the next morning to abuse that lasted the next eighteen years.

I am not going to go into detail about the abuse or what I endured over the next several years. I have those details in another book called *Resurrected*. My only reason for mentioning it at all is for you to understand that the more the Devil tries to put out your hunger, the more important it is to press into God as never before. You still have a choice. Even though we've all made some less-than-great choices in life, we don't have to continue the pattern. We can say, "Enough is enough." I refused to give into depression, feeling sorry for myself, spiritual apathy, or lukewarmness. My hunger remained intact, even when I felt there was no way that I could ever fulfill the call of God. I had to work at cultivating that hunger as never before.

Through a series of events, I eventually attended Rhema Bible Training Center in Broken Arrow, Oklahoma. We had three sons by then: ages eleven, nine, and six. I was going to Bible school full-time, working at a doughnut shop until midnight every night, at minimum wage, and getting three sons off to school each day. We did not have the money for a dryer, so I hung our clothes on the line to dry. We did not have air conditioning in our apartment. It was located beside the railroad tracks. The hot, muggy Tulsa summer was overwhelming as the temperatures climbed to over one hundred degrees for about a solid month. Eventually, we acquired a small window air conditioner unit for one bedroom. We ate nothing but oatmeal for a week during this time. We did not have the finances for anything else.

The abuse was continuing despite multiple promises that it would end. After a quarrel one night, I was locked out of my house. I was forced to walk around the town in a downpour of rain, with tears running down my face faster. My sons were inside the house crying and unable to help me. I was tempted to go back to Nebraska to family but was so hungry for what I was receiving in Bible school that I told myself that I could go on by the grace of God. Thank God that I did.

The burning hunger for the things of God enabled me to graduate from Rhema at the top of my class. I felt like a Superwoman walking down that aisle in my cap and gown. I knew that the Devil had tried his best to get me to give up on the call of God and go home, but the grace of God prevailed. What I learned in those classes, combined with what I had overcome, made me stronger and produced an even greater hunger for God.

While listening to Reverend Kenneth E. Hagin preach at his Winter Bible Seminar one night, I was challenged to find somewhere to preach. He made the statement to the graduates of Rhema Bible Training Center, who were still in the Tulsa area, "You must not be called to preach like I was called to preach. If you were, you would find yourself a place to preach, whether on a street corner or wherever. Either get to preaching or quit lying by saying that you are called to preach." He wasn't speaking to me. I was a first-year student. He was speaking to those who came to Bible school, got comfortable in a good church that had a nice youth group for their children, and forgot why they initially came to Bible school. They came because they felt they had a call of God upon their life. However, life keeps going and it is easier to accept the status quo than to walk on the water to witness God's miraculous power take place.

Even though I realized that Brother Hagin was not speaking to me, I am very sensitive to the conviction and direction of The Holy Spirit as someone is preaching. I take it very personally. I thought to myself, 'That's right. I have to find somewhere to preach, even while going to Bible school and working a job.' The next day, I started calling nursing homes to see who would let me have a service once a week. The first place that I called,

DESPERATE HUNGER GETS GOD'S ATTENTION

which also was near my apartment, agreed to let me come once a week. I played the piano, sang, and preached my heart out every Monday between school and work. In the summertime, when my sons were on summer vacation from school, I brought them with me and had them sing as well.

I preached my heart out every week. However, it seemed that no one was paying attention and that I had absolutely no fruit from that ministry. It looked like no one had even one piece of their mind intact. One of the patients walked up and down the space in front of me while clapping her hands. Another flashed her blouse up and down in the service. Another one kept shouting, "Shut up and turn the television on." Needless to say, I had to fight discouragement. Then, one day, when I gave the altar call, a lady looked straight at me, raised her hand, and I decided everything was worth it. I rushed over to her and asked her again if she wanted to receive Christ into her heart as her savior. She replied sternly, "No, I want a cigarette." Talk about being deflated! I mumbled that what she requested was not my job, but I would try to find someone to help her.

As I walked out of that nursing facility that day, my shoulders slumped forward. I fought back tears and told The Lord that I was through with nursing home ministry. I decided that it was not my calling. If I had no fruit, I was wasting everyone's time, including mine. Then, I heard the still, small voice of The Holy Spirit on the inside of me, "Did I call you to be successful, or did I call you to be obedient? These people have no witness here and no one to share the love of God. My Word will not return unto me void. Just keep sowing The Word." Tears streamed down my face as I surrendered and told The Lord that I would keep doing all that I knew to do until He gave me further instruction.

The very next week brought about a miraculous breakthrough. The nurses wheeled a young man who was sitting in a wheelchair into my service. He was tied in by a strap. He was slumped forward in the wheelchair, his tongue hung out of his mouth, and his eyes were cloudy and non-focused. He was hollering profanities of the worst kind. His slobber was falling to the floor. I wondered if they brought him into the meeting just to antagonize me. It had been noticeable for quite some time that most of the employees were atheists, and they purposely interrupted me. They frequently stood in front of me while I was preaching, calling across the room to each other. "Gladys, bring me some gauze over here." I wondered why they couldn't simply walk over to the person they were communicating with and ask the question. Now, they brought someone to the meeting in a vegetative state who only swore at me.

I finished my teaching and, as my custom was, walked around the room, shook hands with people, and told them, "Goodbye, and God bless you." When I came to the young man in the wheelchair, I almost skipped over him. I could feel a demonic spirit of lust coming from him and knew that he couldn't comprehend much of anything. I also thought, 'Why take the chance of him pulling me into the chair with him?' As I walked past him, much to my surprise, he called out to me. "Can you please help me?" I was almost in shock to realize that he could speak something other than profanity. I asked him if he had ever accepted Jesus Christ as his Savior. He replied, "No, those things inside of me won't let me. Do you know what I mean?" I answered, "Yes, sir, I do know what you mean."

At that moment, he looked up, and our eyes met. I knew that the management was just waiting for an opportunity and excuse to justify terminating my ministry. I knew that I could not have demonic manifestations taking place. I looked up to Heaven and used one of the most theological prayers that I have ever petitioned God with. "H-E-L-P". Immediately, I was flooded with a gift of faith that I have only known on that magnitude a couple of times since. I knew that he was about to be delivered and healed. I bent over and barely touched his head and whispered, "Be free, in Jesus' name." Immediately, his tongue went back into his mouth, those glazed eyes cleared, he broke out in a smile, held his head up, and started crying and laughing at the same time. He declared, "Freedom, I've never known it before now." I gave another altar call, and many hands went up. From that day forward, I witnessed many salvations, healings, and people baptized in The Holy Ghost. I continued there until after graduation from Bible School.

DESPERATE HUNGER GETS GOD'S ATTENTION

What does this story have to do with hunger? Everything. No one knew that I was ministering in that place. I did not receive extra credit in Bible school for ministering there. Brother Kenneth Hagin nor any other teacher knew that I was there. I was not getting famous. There was no ulterior motive. I was simply hungry for God, for people to be saved, and for me to be used by God. I was not just spiritually hungry as a child and teenager. I wasn't just hungry enough to get me to Bible school. I knew that I had to continue to hunger while at Bible school. I knew that I needed to be stretched, stay sensitive to the voice of The Holy Spirit, and be obedient to anything He asked me to do. What it takes to get, it takes to keep.

I went to every service that I could, even though I was exhausted from going to work and school, as well as taking care of my family. The marital abuse continued while I was in Bible school. I could have had many excuses to do the bare minimum or to even quit school. However, I continued to cultivate that hunger through prayer, Bible reading, being in good meetings, and staying around people of the Holy Ghost fire, who challenged me.

After graduation, I worked for Kenneth Hagin Ministries for a little over a year. Eventually, my husband decided that he wanted to move to Alaska. We met a couple from Alaska who asked me to take over the church that they pioneered. They were going to Russia as missionaries. We put our three boys and a very large Newfoundland dog in the back of a pickup truck as we headed four thousand miles up the Alcan highway in September of 1990. I so wanted to believe that we were leaving our troubles behind us, but what does not get fixed follows you.

The winter of 1990 was an especially rough one in Sutton, Alaska, in the Matanuska Valley. My husband and worship leader had an affair that finished our eighteen-year marriage. I found myself without a husband, living in a trailer that was too cold for me to heat, and driving a totaled car that my son had driven off a mountain while learning to drive. I was a long way from the home I grew up in, located in Dakota City, Nebraska. The boys were hurting, and we had to make plans to move in with another family, which meant giving up their pets and their rooms. I began to feel sorry for myself.

I knew that I had a choice; I could continue to feel sorry for myself, develop a victim mentality, get mad at God and backslide, or press into God more than I had ever before. Do you know what made the choice very easy? My spiritual hunger. I was hungrier than I was sad. I was hungrier than I was bitter. I was hungrier than I was angry. Spiritual hunger will not let you stay down, even if it looks like you were temporarily knocked down. Hunger will cause you to bounce back again because you can't keep a hungry man or woman down very long. It was as though I heard the ten-count in boxing and knew that I had to get back up. I don't care if your nose is broken and over to one side of your face with blood pouring out. You must get up before that ten-count is over. Shock the Devil and stand to your feet.

Instead of backsliding or retreating, I pressed into God. I told God that I wanted to experience what people in the Bible had experienced. I reminded Him of the fact that I read all the revival books on my library shelf countless times. I heard my grandparent's stories of revival all of my life. I asked The Lord if the book of Acts was just in my Bible to make me drool. Then, I wrote a song about how much I needed and wanted His anointing.

These are the words of the song I wrote:

"I Ask For Fresh Oil From Heaven"

> I Ask for fresh oil from Heaven once again
> A double portion of your spirit upon me
> The hand of the Lord, the mantle from Heaven
> The anointing to set every captive free
> Oh it's the anointing of the Holy Ghost
> It's the anointing that I cherish the most
> It's the anointing, so I have heard

Gives you power to preach the Word
The anointing oh, they have said,
Gives you power to raise the dead
The anointing upon the mind
Gives revelation to the blind
The anointing upon the sad
Will make them laugh, dance, and be glad
The anointing upon the weak
Will give them strength that they can leap
For the sick, it will heal
For the confused, point out His will
For the broken it will mend
And for the called, it will send
Oh, the anointing, that precious power
Is what we need in this great hour
So I ask for fresh oil from Heaven once again

Oh, like Jacob of old
Of this blessing, I won't let go
Like Elisha on that day
A double portion shall be my stay
Like Peter on Pentecost
Power and utterance to win the lost
Like Paul and Silas in the midnight hour
Everything will shake under His great power
Off their necks, the bondage will break
For the anointing is all it will take
So I ask for fresh oil from Heaven once again.

The next Sunday, I sang that song in our church. When I finished, you could hear a pin drop. The anointing blanketed the church service as well as every individual in the building. I knew that I needed to sing one more song. I felt led by The Holy Spirit to sing "On Holy Ground." Suddenly, the power of The Holy Ghost enveloped me and knocked me off the piano bench. I found out later that when I went to the floor, so did the rest of my congregation.

I was so drunk in the Holy Ghost for the first time in my Pentecostal life. I saw it happen to others occasionally. I knew that it was real and that people have been that way in past revivals and throughout church history.

However, I thought those people had a certain kind of personality and that I could never respond in such a way. I was wrong. That day was the turning point in my life and ministry. I was on the floor for a long time, as God was burning out scars from years of abuse and rejection, and then He replaced that with filling me to overflowing with His love and glory.

When you get enough of the oil from Heaven, and enough fire of The Holy Ghost engulfs you, and enough of His Holy Ghost's new wine, you will have an experience in Him like you never had before. That is the fresh oil, fresh wine, and fresh fire that I minister out of. Yes, spiritual hunger and thirst make all the difference.

People have asked me if I have ever been tempted to quit. Of course. It's not a sin to be tempted. Everyone is. It's only a sin when you dwell on it, give into it, and act on it. I shake it off immediately when it comes to my mind. My spiritual hunger gives me the extra ability to do so.

I've been tempted to quit when pastors who were touched powerfully in revival deserted me. I was tempted when one preacher told me that I needed to forget the call of God and go home and be a mother. When he gave me the three reasons that I needed to quit: (1) I was a woman, (2) Alaska was cold, and (3) I had no husband, I was tempted for about an hour. However, spiritual hunger overrode that discouragement.

When the man gave me these three reasons, I went to Noel and Edna DeVrie's home (the couple in my church who were my right hand). They said, "You take the phone off the hook and get ahold of God. We're not going to tell anyone where you are. The first time that you walked into our church, we looked at each other and said, 'There is anointing here. This lady is going all over the world, and we are going to help her. You hear from God and write down what He tells you, and don't you look back.'" I am so thankful for this couple. I did just what they suggested, and God spoke to me. He came upon me so powerfully that I knew that I was going to prophesy. I put a cassette tape in and began to prophesy to myself. I still have that tape, and most of it has already come to pass. I got up and never looked back. I heard from God. Little did I know that in just a few weeks, God would send another man of God to Anchorage, Alaska, to prophesy word for word what I already prophesied to myself.

The next few months were not easy, but oh, they were glorious. I was willing to work in a used clothing store while living with Noel and Edna. I saved up enough money to go out every few weeks to another village and preach the Gospel. I had pastors threaten to run me out of town, flew in two-seater planes through blizzards, slept on village floors with no running water or blankets to keep me warm, and ate strange food like moose-head soup and Eskimo ice cream. I had to use outhouses in the middle of the night and more. What kept me going? I was hungry, not only for an intimate relationship with God but also hungry to be used by Him to bring His precious Gospel to many tribes and nations.

Later, I faced Vietnamese communist interrogation, a rebel roadblock in Uganda, officials in nations waiting for me to bribe them to let me go, civil war in Burundi, and more. However, there was a burning fire shut up in my bones, and I couldn't stop if I wanted to. Whether friends, relatives, in-laws, or out-laws believed in me or not, I still had that fire shut up in my bones. When the going got tough, God toughened me to get going. He will do the same for you.

When Pastor Rodney came to Anchorage, Alaska, in November of 1992, I had a lot of reasons not to go to the meetings. I was pastoring and heading up a prison ministry. I also had a village missions trip planned for that week and had no gas in my car. I had to travel over icy roads, where moose frequented.

I also knew that we were already experiencing similar meetings in my church, the prison, and the villages of Alaska. I was having some ministry success. However, the deep hunger in me was calling out to the depths of God. I knew there was more, and I wanted all that God had for me. Hunger will bring about humility and destroy pride. It causes you to realize that you have not arrived and must continue to seek God until He takes you from faith to faith and glory to glory.

This kind of hunger will drive you past obstacles, financial setbacks, disappointments, and friends' comments. You won't care when they call you a fanatic. Just remember that they will call you that when you have more of Jesus than they do.

Before Pastor Rodney left Anchorage, Alaska, in November of 1992, he announced that he was going to have a summer camp meeting in Louisville, Kentucky. I knew the moment that he announced it that I would find a way to attend. I didn't have the finances, but I had two things that were better than finances. I had spiritual hunger and thirst that would enable me to find a way to go, and I also had a big God. I put the plane tickets, hotel rooms, and rental car for both my assistant and myself on a credit card. I didn't wait for the money. I felt this camp meeting was more important than buying a house or a car. Many people think nothing of buying a home or car on credit but will not spend the finances to have their lives changed forever. When you are hungry, nothing will stop you.

I don't think that it is a coincidence that I was called out and prophesied over in that meeting. I did not expect or even dream that Dr. Rodney would remember me from Alaska, let alone remember my name. I was wrong. He called me out of a crowd of several thousand people and not only prophesied over me but announced that if anyone wanted to have an on-fire evangelist in their church, I was the one they should have. I wondered if I was dreaming.

> When the Lord turned again the captivity of Zion, we were
>   like them that dream.
> Then was our mouth filled with laughter, and our tongue
>   with singing: then said they among the heathen, The
>   Lord hath done great things for them.
> The Lord hath done great things for us; whereof we are glad.
> Turn again our captivity, O Lord, as the streams in the south.

DESPERATE HUNGER GETS GOD'S ATTENTION

> They that sow in tears shall reap in joy.
> He that goeth forth and weepeth, bearing precious seed,
> > shall doubtless come again with rejoicing, bringing his sheaves with him.
>
> > PSALM 126:1-6

What singled me out of that crowd of thousands of people? Spiritual hunger. It singled out the woman with the issue of blood. It singled out Blind Bartimaeus, Elisha, and many others in the Bible.

While at the camp meeting, I couldn't help but think back on the last few months. I thought about the man telling me to go home. I refused to. Thank God that I canceled my busy schedule to attend Dr. Rodney's Anchorage meetings. This is where he first called me out and prophesied. He said, "The Lord has a Word for you. He says that although a man of God came to Alaska a short time ago and discouraged you and told you to forget the call of God, He has now sent me here to encourage you. Everything God told you as a child is about to come to pass. It shall be an international ministry comparable to the magnitude of… (He named several well-known ministers). Your husband could have been at your side, but He chose another way. However, that does not negate the call of God upon your life. God knows that you have no money, no reputation, no contacts, and no one to help you. He will raise you up out of obscurity, and He will receive all the glory. People will know that what He's done for you, He will do for them, for He is no respecter of persons, only a respecter of principles. What He has done for one, He must do for another. But that person must get hungry like someone else got hungry and must obey and yield as someone else did. Then he will receive the same results."

I seriously do not believe the prophetic word would have come to pass if I had not pressed in. One man of God told me to forget the call of God and go back to Nebraska. Another man of God told me it was not over but only just beginning, and God was about to use me powerfully. One man of God said yes, and one said no. What do I do now? Do I run to Las Vegas and take two out of three? No, we have the Holy Spirit living on the inside of us if we are born again. We are led by the Spirit. We don't have to go to a prophet to find our donkeys as they had to do in the Old Testament. We can hear from Heaven for ourselves. I had to get ahold of God myself and ask Him if I should continue in ministry or go home. Once I pressed in, prayed it through, and heard from Heaven, God was able to bring someone along to confirm the word that I received from Him for myself. Prophets should only confirm what we've already heard from God about. In tough times, you can't depend on someone else's word. You must receive it directly from Heaven so that it becomes your anchor when the winds of adversity try to blow away your calling and assignment.

I have learned, in many different circumstances, the importance of remaining hungry. In 1996, I had the privilege of carrying The Gospel to the nations of New Zealand and Australia. I spent two weeks in New Zealand and four weeks in Australia. We had a glorious revival in both nations; churches, a Bible college, and a women's conference in a large venue on the Gold Coast. Revival was spreading across Australia, and they asked me to stay and continue in more cities. I was tempted but knew that I would have to miss Dr. Rodney Howard-Browne's camp meeting in Tampa, Florida. I told several pastors that I had to leave to attend that camp meeting. They asked, "Won't Dr. Rodney understand if you miss one? After all, you have attended many of them over the years." I replied, "Yes, I believe that he would understand but for me to continue to flow in the anointing, I must continue to be filled with the anointing that has changed my life. What it takes to get, it takes to keep. I must stay hungry and continue to receive myself. I will be in those prayer lines with my hands up, preparing my heart to receive like it is the first and possibly the last time."

If we don't keep our hearts hungry, nothing else will matter. I don't care if you speak Hebrew and Greek, have ten doctorates in theology, and get all A's on your tests. If you do not stay hungry and thirsty for God, you will have nothing to give anyone else. I would rather have someone with a kindergarten education who is full of The Holy Ghost lay hands on me than someone with great head knowledge who lost their hunger for God.

I agree with Mr. Smith Wigglesworth, who said, "I'd rather have the Holy Ghost on me ten minutes than to own the whole world with a fence around it. There is nothing that can compare to the presence and impartation of The Holy Spirit."

Some of you may have to admit to yourself and to God that you are not as spiritually hungry as you need to be. Be honest. God knows your heart. There is no fooling Him. Just sincerely call out to Him. "God help me to become hungry and thirsty for you. Show me what to do to get myself hungry."

It takes more than going through the motions. Many people are sitting in the same chair in church, taking sermon notes, yet the spark that they once had in their eyes is missing. Everyone else can see it but them. The fire in their belly left a long time ago.

You must be consumed with revival until all you eat and breathe is revival.

True revival requires a supernatural encounter with the manifested presence of God. Let God become a holy obsession. Divine deposits are preceded by divine desire. They are birthed out of the heart of God.

Circumstances can either drive you from God or to God. It is not that God creates tough circumstances in our lives, but He'll use them. Whatever the enemy meant for harm, you and God together will turn around through hunger, thirst, and humility. Hunger will drive you to get desperate. That kind of desperation creates spiritual hunger.

> The Spirit of the Lord God is upon me; because the Lord
> > hath anointed me to preach good tidings unto the meek;
> > he hath sent me to bind up the brokenhearted, to
> > proclaim liberty to the captives, and the opening of the
> > prison to them that are bound;
> > To proclaim the acceptable year of the Lord, and the day of
> > > vengeance of our God; to comfort all that mourn;
> > To appoint unto them that mourn in Zion, to give unto them
> > > beauty for ashes, the oil of joy for mourning, the garment

> of praise for the spirit of heaviness; that they might be called trees of righteousness, the planting of the Lord, that he might be glorified.
> And they shall build the old wastes, they shall raise up the former desolations, and they shall repair the waste cities, the desolations of many generations.
>
> ISAIAH 61:1-4

God is good at giving beauty to ashes. Let Him do just that for you. Get so hungry and thirsty for Him that He transforms you into something so beautiful that you will astound people. For Him to do that, you must learn to protect your heart day and night.

> Keep thy heart with all diligence; for out of it are the issues of life.
>
> PROVERBS 4:23

There are many things that you can do to cultivate hunger. One is to live a holy life. John G. Lake knew Charles Parham's sister-in-law, Lillian Thistleweight. He said, "It was the divine holiness that came from her soul and was the living Spirit of God that came out of the woman's life." At that time, Lake was self-satisfied with all of his successes but said that when he listened to that woman telling of the Lord and His love and sanctifying grace and power, he realized that she knew what real holiness was. It wasn't her arguments or logic; it was she herself. It was the divine holiness that came from her soul. It was the living Spirit of God that came out of the woman's life.

His heart became so hungry that he fell on his knees, and those who were present said they had never heard anybody pray as Lake prayed. Bosworth said long afterward, "Lake, there is one instance that I shall always remember in your life; that was the night that you talked with Lillian Thistleweight and observed the one supreme thing in that woman's soul was the consciousness of holiness. She said, 'Brother, that is what we prayed for; that is what the baptism brought to us.'"

Some of the ways that you must cultivate your spiritual hunger is by yielding yourself to God and praying in The Holy Ghost. What does it mean to yield to The Spirit of God? The definition of yieldedness, according to Strong's concordance, is "to give or present yourself, to give up possession." Yielding is a big part of making Jesus Lord of your life, not just Savior. He is asking us to surrender all.

> Neither yield ye your members as instruments of unrighteousness unto sin: but yield yourselves unto God, as those that are alive from the dead, and your members as instruments of righteousness unto God.
>
> ROMANS 6:13

> Do not continue offering or yielding your bodily members [and faculties] to sin as instruments (tools) of wickedness. But offer and yield yourselves to God as though you have been raised from the dead to [perpetual] life, and your bodily members [and faculties] to God, presenting them as implements of righteousness.
>
> ROMANS 6:13 (AMPC)

> Know ye not, that to whom ye yield yourselves servants to obey, his servants ye are to whom ye obey; whether of sin unto death, or of obedience unto righteousness?
>
> ROMANS 6:16

> I speak after the manner of men because of the infirmity of your flesh: for as ye have yielded your members servants to uncleanness and to iniquity unto iniquity; even so now

> yield your members servants to righteousness unto holiness.
>
> ROMANS 6:19

When you see a *yield* sign on the interstate, what does that mean? You don't just take the foot off the gas, put the gear-shift in park, stop, and shut off the gas, or you will cause an accident (which is what many pastors and board members have done with the move of The Holy Ghost). You must keep the car in the drive position, keep your foot on the gas pedal, and continue to steer. You must be very attentive, look ahead, stay alert, and perceive what you must do to blend in. You might need to speed up and try to keep up with what the majority are doing. The traffic that is going through has the right-away.

> In the last day, that great day of the feast, Jesus stood and cried, saying, If any man thirst, let him come unto me, and drink.
> He that believeth on me, as the scripture hath said, out of his belly shall flow rivers of living water.
>
> JOHN 7:37-38

You have to actually drink, not just put the water to your mouth or come to where water is. Jesus didn't say, "Let him sit back and see what happens."

Learn what The Holy Spirit likes and do only what He asks you to do and say only what He asks you to say. Learn to flow with him. That will stimulate your hunger.

Another important thing in cultivating spiritual hunger is to pray and worship in The Spirit, in other tongues. People have said that tongues are the least of the gifts. Why, then, are so many theological wars fought over tongues? The Devil is scared of tongue-talkers. Tongues are supernatural and only seem mysterious because we live on this earthly side.

DESPERATE HUNGER GETS GOD'S ATTENTION

Many times, we hear the ridiculous saying, "Don't be so heavenly-minded that you are no earthly good." People repeat that as though it is the Bible, but it is only found in the book of "I-say-a-so." There is no such thing as being so heavenly-minded that you are no earthly good. There is such a thing as being so flaky-minded that you are no natural good. Heavenly-minded and spiritually-minded are not the same thing as flaky. A flaky person does not have good doctrine. The problem, most of the time, is that church people are so naturally minded that they are no heavenly good.

If speaking with tongues and praying with tongues is not for us today, that would mean this is one help of the Holy Spirit, which the body of Christ has been denied today. Some will try to tell us that tongues have been done away with, but they haven't. This gift of the Spirit is for the entire church age dispensation.

Without tongues, we'll never have much of the anointing or power of God.

> And, behold, I send the promise of my Father upon you: but tarry ye in the city of Jerusalem, until ye be endued with power from on high.
>
> LUKE 24:49

> And, being assembled together with them, commanded them that they should not depart from Jerusalem, but wait for the promise of the Father, which, saith he, ye have heard of me.
> For John truly baptized with water; but ye shall be baptized with the Holy Ghost not many days hence.
>
> ACTS 1:4-5

Jesus used some of His last words to tell His disciples to not do anything until they were endued with this power. These are people who had already been used mightily. Why do we think we can do it without Him today? We need this same power today to compete with the occult, new-age, gangs, drugs, and all kinds of sin. Without The Holy Spirit, we will only build more and more religion. God reveals everything to us by His Spirit.

> But ye shall receive power, after that the Holy Ghost is come upon you: and ye shall be witnesses unto me both in Jerusalem, and in all Judaea, and in Samaria, and unto the uttermost part of the earth.
>
> ACTS 1:8

These were all Jews, and they knew about the Spirit, but only upon prophet, priest, and king. However, they had a promise that it was about to change.

> I indeed baptize you with water unto repentance. but he that cometh after me is mightier than I, whose shoes I am not worthy to bear: he shall baptize you with the Holy Ghost, and with fire.
>
> MATTHEW 3:11

Jesus made big promises about what The Holy Spirit would do.

> And I will pray the Father, and he shall give you another Comforter, that he may abide with you for ever;
> Even the Spirit of truth; whom the world cannot receive, because it seeth him not, neither knoweth him: but ye know him; for he dwelleth with you, and shall be in you.
>
> JOHN 14:16-17

> Nevertheless I tell you the truth; It is expedient for you that I go away: for if I go not away, the Comforter will not come unto you; but if I depart, I will send him unto you.
>
> JOHN 16:7

Nobody had ever called the Holy Spirit the helper or comforter before.

> But the Comforter, which is the Holy Ghost, whom the Father will send in my name, he shall teach you all things, and bring all things to your remembrance, whatsoever I have said unto you.
>
> JOHN 14:26

> Howbeit when he, the Spirit of truth, is come, he will guide you into all truth: for he shall not speak of himself; but whatsoever he shall hear, that shall he speak: and he will shew you things to come.
> He shall glorify me: for he shall receive of mine, and shall shew it unto you.
>
> JOHN 16:13-14

When Christians walk around dumb as a post, it's a disgrace. There is a place in The Holy Spirit where you and I don't have to miss it anymore. He'll tell you of the things to come. None of us are as good at this as we can be and are going to be. I have looked back on decisions in my life that cost me greatly. I realize that if I would have been more sensitive to The Holy Spirit, I would have made other decisions. Sometimes, we get tired and allow our emotions to override His voice. However, all we can do at this point is to repent, learn from those mistakes, and ask Him to help us become more sensitive to that still voice on the inside.

When did all of this happen? It happened on the day of Pentecost, with the celebration of the harvest and the birth of the church. It was when they were baptized with The Holy Spirit. What was the evidence of that baptism? Tongues.

> And they were all filled with the Holy Ghost, and began to speak with other tongues, as the Spirit gave them utterance.
>
> ACTS 2:4

We are baptized into The Holy Spirit and fire. Baptism means to dip, and that word was first used in the "dyeing trade." They dipped the cloth into the dye, and the cloth accepted the characteristics, nature, and color of that dye when it came out! The cloth was in the dye, and the dye was in the cloth. Jesus baptizes you into a river of liquid fire, and when He pulls you out of that baptism, you will have the nature, character, and color of that glorious fire! We are people of the fire of God. We have been baptized into a fire of divine enablement.

You and I learned our language by human wisdom. It is the ultimate ego to think if all of God can be explained in the language we learned in the first grade, we have reduced God down to the human brain. That is like trying to put nuclear physics into baby talk. God says, "I was here first. Learn to speak my language."

If you don't do something in God that you don't understand, you'll never do anything. If you don't pray in tongues, you won't walk in much of the anointing or intense power of God. The mysteries of God come through tongues. If you can keep God in your hand, He's too small. The purpose of tongues is to get out of your mind and into your heart. God's not doing mystery anymore but trying to reveal it. We can't receive that by our heads.

The *key* to operating in The Spirit is to be praying in tongues. If you step into the spiritual arena with natural wisdom, the result is religion.

Churches that don't believe in tongues shut the door on the rest. Tongues are only the doorway into the supernatural realm.

> For he that speaketh in an unknown tongue speaketh not unto men, but unto God: for no man understandeth him; howbeit in the spirit he speaketh mysteries.
>
> 1 CORINTHIANS 14:2

We are not speaking unto men, but unto God, spirit to Spirit, supernaturally.

> For if I pray in an unknown tongue, my spirit prayeth, but my understanding is unfruitful.
>
> 1 CORINTHIANS 14:14

> Likewise the Spirit also helpeth our infirmities: for we know not what we should pray for as we ought: but the Spirit itself maketh intercession for us with groanings which cannot be uttered.
>
> ROMANS 8:26

> ...my spirit [by the Holy Spirit within me] prays...
>
> 1 CORINTHIANS 14:14 (AMPC)

Tongues provide a way for things to be prayed about that no one is even aware of. Sometimes, there is a need that needs to be prayed for, which we have no idea of, in the natural. The Holy Ghost knows everything, and He is our Helper in prayer.

Praying in the Spirit with other tongues serves multiple purposes. It is good for intercession. Intercession means one who takes the place of another.

Praying in The Spirit is one of the best ways to intercede for the lost or the backslider. Sometimes, as you step over in The Spirit, you may feel lost yourself. Kenneth E. Hagin told us many times that he cried out in prayer, "lost, lost." He felt that he was lost as he prayed for the unsaved. He also said that he prayed out many of his sermons before he preached them. Many times, he knew in prayer who would be in the audience and who would be healed. He saw himself praying for them ahead of time. He even knew at times who would come to The Lord. One reason more people aren't being saved is because God cannot find people to step over in this kind of prayer.

Praying in the Spirit helps you grow spiritually. You won't become an expert overnight. It takes some effort to press into the things of God.

Praying in the Holy Ghost will edify you. It is like charging up a battery.

> But ye, beloved, building up yourselves on your most holy faith, praying in the Holy Ghost.
>
> JUDE 1:20

Howard Carter, an English preacher, said, "It's a flowing stream that should never dry up, will enrich one's life spiritually."

Praying in The Holy Spirit eliminates the possibility of selfishness entering our prayer life. For example, God did not want Israel to have a king, but they wanted one, so God permitted it. A king was not His perfect will for them. If we pray a prayer out of our own minds and our own thinking, it may be unscriptural.

Romans 8:26 says, *"We know not what we should pray for as we ought."* Even if we know how to pray, it doesn't mean we know what to pray as we ought. P.C. Nelson (a great Greek Bible scholar of several years ago) said that this verse literally reads, "The Holy Ghost maketh intercession for us in groanings that cannot be uttered in articulate speech or regular speech." I Corinthians 14:14 says, *"For if I pray in an unknown tongue my spirit prayeth..."* The Amplified Classic Bible says, "*...my spirit (by the Holy Spirit*

DESPERATE HUNGER GETS GOD'S ATTENTION

within me) prays..." You do the talking, but the Holy Spirit gives the utterance. He helps us pray but doesn't do the praying for us.

Praying in The Holy Ghost helps us to trust Him better. It builds faith. Trusting God in one area helps us learn to trust Him in other areas. It's also a rest and a refreshing.

> For with stammering lips and another tongue will he speak
> to this people.
> To whom he said, This is the rest wherewith ye may cause
> the weary to rest; and this is the refreshing: yet they
> would not hear.
>
> ISAIAH 28:11-12

Praying in The Holy Ghost makes us continually aware of His indwelling presence. That will affect the way we live. It sharpens us spiritually. God seldom speaks to man through the physical senses. He does so only when people cannot receive from Him any other way. Satan is the god of this world. Don't ask God to manifest that way. You can get into satanic deception, like when people put out fleeces. Fleeces were used in the Old Testament before people had the indwelling of The Holy Spirit to depend upon. We have to exercise our spirits. God doesn't talk to your head because He doesn't live in your head. He comes into your heart, your spirit. You speak out of your spirit when in tongues, not your head. Your mind will tell you that praying in tongues is silly. Many don't even realize they are spirit beings. People are used to living their lives in a carnal way. You must train yourself to live in The Spirit.

> But ye, beloved, building up yourselves on your most holy
> faith, praying in the Holy Ghost.
>
> JUDE 1:20

Paul charged Timothy to stir up gifts.

> Wherefore I put thee in remembrance that thou stir up the gift of God, which is in thee by the putting on of my hands.
>
> 2 TIMOTHY 1:6

Paul commanded Timothy to stir up the gift within him. Praying in tongues stirs up gifts on the inside of you and stimulates those gifts. When you pray in the Holy Ghost, it energizes your human spirit, and you begin to hear The Holy Ghost. This is a way to get into Spirit. People don't realize how big a deal it is to speak in tongues.

John G Lake, the great healing revivalist who went to South Africa and had over 100,000 people healed in a five-year period, wore a hole out in a rug praying in tongues. God will use people who wear out the carpet praying in the Holy Ghost. God's going to use the church to show the Devil how smart He is, and He is going to do it through a supernatural, Spirit-led church. Churches that don't believe in tongues shut the door on the rest. It's a full-time job to keep a Pentecostal church, Pentecostal. Many who start out in the fire, end up in an iceberg.

We can speak in tongues to ourselves and to God in church. That means anywhere and anytime. Praying in tongues is not the only thing, but it is a big one. Wigglesworth said, "I'm a thousand times bigger on the inside, than I am on the outside. I used to have an argument but now I have an experience in the Bible and outside the realm of argument."

Being filled with The Holy Spirit gives us power and boldness to witness. When we have God for us and in us, there can be no defeat. It also assists us with the Worship of God. It is a way to give thanks to God.

> What is it then? I will pray with the spirit, and I will pray with the understanding also: I will sing with the spirit, and I will sing with the understanding also.
> Else when thou shalt bless with the spirit, how shall he that occupieth the room of the unlearned say Amen at thy

DESPERATE HUNGER GETS GOD'S ATTENTION

> giving of thanks, seeing he understandeth not what thou sayest?
> For thou verily givest thanks well, but the other is not edified.
>
> 1 CORINTHIANS 14:15-17

> And be not drunk with wine, wherein is excess; but be filled with the Spirit;
> Speaking to yourselves in psalms and hymns and spiritual songs, singing and making melody in your heart to the Lord;
> Giving thanks always for all things unto God and the Father in the name of our Lord Jesus Christ.
>
> EPHESIANS 5:18-20

It's a big step toward being fully able to yield all of your members to God.

> But the tongue can no man tame; it is an unruly evil, full of deadly poison.
>
> JAMES 3:8

You have a direct line to God, spirit to Spirit.

Tongues take us through the door of the natural into the door of the supernatural realm. This is not just about tongues but about an ongoing experience with The Holy Spirit. When we receive the Holy Spirit baptism, it is just the beginning.

We can't forget that speaking with tongues is not only an initial sign or evidence of the Holy Spirit's indwelling, but it's a continual experience. Many get so concerned about the initial experience that they miss the reality of the indwelling presence of the Holy Ghost. Make sure that you don't look back at some experience at the altar years ago as your only contact with the Divine Person. Because I grew up in Pentecost, I have seen this many times. People thought that when they were baptized in The Holy Spirit, it became their badge of honor. It gave them bragging rights. They would speak of it with pride as though they had arrived and had something that others did not.

Sometimes, who were baptized in The Holy Ghost in 1949 never spoke in tongues since. They may have leaked out before they got to the parking lot of the church. They spoke in tongues one moment and were yelling at their mate and acting like a jerk the next moment. We have a challenge before us to stay filled and sharp in The Holy Ghost. Let Him become more real every single day of your life.

There is a difference between being baptized in The Holy Ghost and being used in the gift of the spirit called the gift of tongues. Being baptized in The Holy Spirit is promised to every believer. The gift of tongues is *"as The Spirit wills."*

> But the manifestation of the Spirit is given to every man to profit withal.
> For to one is given by the Spirit the word of wisdom; to another the word of knowledge by the same Spirit;
> To another faith by the same Spirit; to another the gifts of healing by the same Spirit;
> To another the working of miracles; to another prophecy; to another discerning of spirits; to another divers kinds of tongues; to another the interpretation of tongues:
> But all these worketh that one and the selfsame Spirit, dividing to every man severally as he will.
>
> 1 CORINTHIANS 12:7-11

I had not planned to teach on the baptism of the Holy Ghost in this book, but I realized how key praying and worshipping in other tongues is to remain spiritually hungry. I find myself speaking in other tongues often throughout the day, especially when I am alone. I have even caught myself speaking in other tongues when I am in a public place, shopping, or in a bathroom. It is a continual habit. It is one of the main ways that I stay edified and can overcome what life throws at me personally, as well as in ministry.

I want to help you to receive this gift if you have not already received it.

First, you must realize that it is promised to you as a believer. That is your only qualification. You don't have to strive for it. You receive it by faith, just like you receive salvation by faith.

Many times, people teach that you must "tarry" for it because the Bible says in Luke 24:49, "...*tarry ye in the city of Jerusalem, until ye be endued with power.*" The word *tarry* means to wait. Yes, it is a good idea to wait on God, and we should have more prayer meetings where people do just that. However, that is not a qualification for being baptized in The Holy Spirit. If it were, we would have to do the rest of the verse. We would have to wait in Jerusalem. People do not know how to rightly divide the Word of God.

The reason they had to wait was because The Holy Spirit had not yet been given. He was given on the day of Pentecost. We are not waiting for another Pentecost. We are not waiting on God. He is waiting for us. Now, we simply believe His Word and receive all that He has promised us.

One of my teachers at Rhema told us the story of how he was baptized in The Holy Spirit. When he got hungry for more of God, he attended a revival meeting where they gave the invitation to those who wanted to be baptized in The Holy Spirit. He answered the call. A circle of people surrounded him and began to pray for him. They shouted and worked up a sweat. One said, "Hold on, Brother, hold on." Another shouted, "Turn loose, Brother, turn loose." He had no idea if he should hold on or turn loose. They shook him and moved his mouth, but still he didn't receive. After several nights of this, and he still had not received it, one of them suggested that the reason was because he needed to go home and shave his beard and mustache. Even though he had no idea what that would have to do with anything, he was hungry and desperate. So, he followed their instructions and came back without facial hair. He still didn't receive it.

The next night, someone suggested that he put on a long-sleeved shirt instead of a short-sleeved shirt. Once again, he had no idea why that would have anything to do with him receiving, but he complied. He came back the next night with long sleeves and went through the entire process of crying, shouting, shaking, hanging on, turning loose, and still did not receive.

This man's wife was raised Catholic and did not understand any of these things. She didn't even come up for prayer to receive. She was sitting back in the church pew, praying, "God, I don't know what my husband is wanting, but could You give it to him, please? He is miserable to live with." The man could hear her praying that. The next thing he heard was his wife praying in other tongues. He couldn't believe it! She didn't have to go through anything that he did to receive. He came to realize later that there is a spiritual principle at work. What you want for someone else, because you love them, often comes to you.

This man left those revival meetings blessed but not baptized in The Holy Ghost. Shortly after that, someone gave him a copy of Kenneth Hagin's book, *Seven Vital Steps to Receiving The Holy Spirit*. When he read those steps and realized that it was a simple process to receive by faith, he was shocked. It is not a matter of works or getting righteous enough. We are made the righteousness of God in Christ Jesus when we are born again. This man put the book down, believed that he received, and then opened his mouth and began to speak in other tongues. He said that he wasn't shaking (although some do), he wasn't shouting (you can if you want), no one was yelling at him to hold on or break loose, and yet he took by faith what God has promised in His Word. It is just that simple.

Sometimes, people are told to start praising God in their native tongue first. However, no one can speak two languages at the same time. At some point, they will have to leave off speaking with their natural language to speak in other tongues. So, it makes sense to expect to speak in other tongues to begin with. It is important to open your mouth. God is not a ventriloquist or a demon. He does not take over your body and your mouth. He expects us to yield in faith. You must use your own vocal cords, tongue, and lips.

The supernatural aspect is that The Holy Spirit will give you the unction on the inside. You will have a desire to speak words or syllables that you have never spoken before. The enemy will tell your head that this is silly and does not make sense. He will also tell you that it is not real tongues and that you are making it up. You have to silence the Devil's lies, open your mouth, and let it fly.

This is your own prayer language. It won't sound like anyone else's. You don't copy someone else. Also, it will develop. When a baby begins to talk and only has one word or a few syllables and says, Da-Da or Mama, you don't slap him and say, "That's not a real language. Why can't you speak fluently?" No, you realize that his language will continue to develop. So will your spiritual language. As you continue to make a practice of praying in tongues, worshipping in tongues, and thanking God in other tongues, it will continue to change and develop until you are speaking in many languages. Spiritually hungry people desire all that God has for them, including baptism in The Holy Spirit. When you pray in tongues, it increases that hunger.

THREE

PEOPLE IN THE BIBLE WHO HAD AN ENCOUNTER

When you read the Bible, it does not take long to notice that the people God used in both the Old and the New Testaments were people who were spiritually hungry and thirsty. Their hunger caused God to do things for them and through them that were extraordinary. We are going to look at several of their lives, beginning with the Old Testament.

I find Enoch to be a unique example of spiritual hunger.

> And Enoch walked with God: and he was not; for God took him.
>
> GENESIS 5:24

Enoch was seven generations down from Adam. He was in the bloodline of Seth. He was a man of humility, faith, and hunger. He was not the only man in Genesis to walk with God. Noah and Abraham followed suit. These godly men lived in communion with God and in accordance to God's ways. Later in Scripture, God often referred to the necessity of Israel to walk in His ways as the means of staying in right fellowship with Him. By faith, Enoch walked in the ways of God amid a crooked and perverse generation.

This leads us to Enoch's being "taken up." According to Genesis 5:24, Enoch did not taste death. He lived a life of faith in which he walked with God, and amid that walk, "God took him." What a marvelous statement. The text does not say that Enoch simply went to Heaven, but God took Enoch for Himself. He did not taste death but entered into eternity as one who lived by faith, walked with God, and then was miraculously taken up into the presence of God.

The reward for hungering and thirsting after God is God Himself. He grew up sitting on his great-great-great-great-great-grandfather's knee, hearing stories about how Adam and Eve walked with God in the cool of the day. He heard the stories of the intimate relationship that his grandparents had with God until sin came into the picture. He must have thought and asked, "Why can't I have a relationship with God like that? I love God and want to know Him in such a way." I believe that he got so hungry from listening to Adam's stories that he decided to know the glory of God in such a way that he pressed into God more every day until he stepped from glory to glory. One day, he took one more step until he was home.

If we have been born again, we have already begun to experience the joy of that communion with Christ. However, the fullness of our reward is something we must continue to seek until we enter Heaven. Our great calling is to seek the things of God. As we do, the things of this world must, as the old hymn goes, "grow strangely dim in the light of His glory and grace."

Another man who hungered for God was Jacob. I don't think spiritual hunger could be displayed in any greater way than to decide to wrestle with God. I find Jacob's name change significant. When God changed someone's name, it was often a change in their life's direction or calling. Abram (honored father) became Abraham (father of nations), and Sarai (leader) became Sarah (princess). Yet, there is probably no more significant name change than that of Jacob.

When Rebekah was giving birth to twins, she named him Jacob because he grabbed the heel of his brother. The Hebrew meaning of Jacob is "supplanter." It is derived from the word for "to seize the heel," but figuratively, it can mean "to trip up" or even "to deceive." Later, as Jacob and Esau were being blessed by their dying father Isaac, Jacob lived up to his name. Jacob pretended to be Esau to gain his father's blessing:

> And he said, "Your brother came deceitfully and has taken away your blessing." Then he said, "Is he not rightly named Jacob, for he has supplanted me these two times? He took away my birthright, and behold, now he has taken away my blessing."
>
> GENESIS 27:35-36 (NASB 1995)

As a result, Esau wanted to kill him. But with the help of Rebekah, Jacob quickly left town and headed east to find shelter with his relatives.

Many years later, Jacob returned to the land of his fathers with two large companies of his family and livestock. When Jacob was left alone, he wrestled with an angel until daybreak. The socket of Jacob's thigh was dislocated while he wrestled with him. Then he said, *"Let me go, for the dawn is breaking."* But he said, *"I will not let you go unless you bless me."* He said, *"Your name shall no longer be Jacob, but Israel; for you have striven with God and with men and have prevailed"* (Genesis 32:24-29).

Jacob knew it was God he wrestled with, and he refused to give up until God blessed him. He was willing to face whatever judgment or consequence was necessary to receive it.

In Genesis, it says a "man" wrestled him. Yet, in Hosea 12:4, it says he wrestled with an "angel." But then, this angel himself, as He changed Jacob's name, said that Jacob wrestled with God. Afterward, Jacob names the place Peniel because *"I have seen God face to face, yet my life has been preserved"* (Genesis 32:30).

When Hosea says Jacob wrestled an angel, he used a Hebrew word that means "to prevail" or "have power as a prince." God gave him a new name and character as one of prevailing power and influence with God.

Before Jacob was even born, God had prophesied that the blessing would be his and not his brother's (Genesis 25:23). But it was not until Jacob took it through a wrestling match with God that it became his. He laid hold of the promise of God as we do through hunger and thirst, faith, prayer, and obedience.

The blessing you are searching for is not going to come from more striving or deceiving. It comes by hungering for God Himself and submitting to Him. Jacob got a blessing that was greater than an earthly blessing: the restoration of the relationship. A relationship with God is better than any of his blessings. God changes you from a *Jacob* to an *Israel*. Spiritual hunger and thirst brings about the restoration of your relationship with God.

Next, we will look at the life of Moses. Moses was desperate for God and His glory. God revealed Himself to Moses in a burning bush on the backside of a desert. It was normal to see a bush on fire in the desert, but this bush kept burning without being consumed. Moses wondered, "How can a bush burn so long?" So, he drew near to investigate. When God is up to something, it is important to draw near to investigate. Then came a voice, "Take off your shoes; you are on holy ground." Moses went into the mist of the cloud for forty days and nights.

> Who only hath immortality, dwelling in the light which no man can approach unto; whom no man hath seen, nor can see: to whom be honour and power everlasting. Amen.
>
> 1 TIMOTHY 6:16

Fire is real and will show on whoever it is upon. We have a quality of fire that no Devil can match. Ever since Moses met the God of fire, he was a different man. You can't meet the God of fire and not be changed.

Moses had a fire burning in his soul when he arrived in Egypt to speak to Pharaoh. Pharaoh could feel the fire burning. He could still see the reflec-

DESPERATE HUNGER GETS GOD'S ATTENTION

tion of the burning bush in Moses' eyes. That fire brought about the deliverance of an entire nation from bondage into freedom. It still does.

Our God is riding a chariot of fire. In His temple, there was a blazing altar, not a refrigerator. You and I have been born in the fire, and we shall live, serve, and die in the fire. God is a God of fire. That fire is one of divine enablement. We must come with a burning enablement, and our generation will be saved.

Later, Moses had to see God's glory at any cost. His hunger caused him to continue to pursue God. He wanted more. He wanted to see His face. So, he met with God on top of Mt. Horeb.

> And they saw the God of Israel: and there was under his feet
> as it were a paved work of a sapphire stone, and as it
> were the body of heaven in his clearness.
>
> EXODUS 24:10

This describes how God came down on Mt. Horeb. God set his little toe upon Mt. Horeb and His weight came down on that mountain. The Hebrew word for glory has to do with weight. When God set his weight on the mountain, His weight caused it to turn different colors. Moses was there to witness it.

After spending this extended amount of time with God, Moses came down the mountain, and his face was shining with the glory of God (Exodus 34:29). His face was radiant. If you have fellowship with a hot God, who is dwelling in everlasting burnings, you will reflect that glory. The glory was so bright on Moses' face that he had to wear a veil to conceal it when he spoke to the people. Moses spent forty days and nights with God on the mountain, and during that time, he did not eat or drink (verse 28). The glory of God sustained him. When you are hungrier for God's presence than for natural food, that is spiritual hunger. We don't know exactly what Moses' face looked like, but it was frightening to his brother, Aaron, the high priest, and to all the rest of the people. Everyone was afraid to come near Moses (verse 31). He wore a veil over his face to shroud the glory (verses 33–35). We are not told how long this lasted, but the glory began to fade when Moses was no longer regularly going into the presence of God.

In 2 Corinthians 3, Paul contrasts the glories of the Old and New Covenants, and he concludes that the New Covenant is far more glorious. The Old Covenant was written on tablets of stone; the New Covenant is written on the heart (verse 3). The Old Covenant is the letter of the Law, while the New Covenant is of the Spirit. The letter kills, but the Spirit gives life (verse 6). The Old Covenant brings condemnation; the New Covenant brings righteousness (verse 9). The Old Covenant had a glory that faded; the New Covenant has a glory that remains and far surpasses it. The Old Covenant appears to have no glory by comparison (verses 10–11).

The glory in the Old Covenant was temporary; the shining of Moses' face was destined to fade. Paul goes on to say that just as Moses gave Israel the Law with a veil over his face, even today, when the Law is read, a veil descends over the hearts of unbelieving Israelites. Then and now, Israel's vision is obscured, and they are hard of heart. The "veil" prevents them from seeing the true glory of God. The veil is only taken away when they turn to Christ (2 Corinthians 3:14–16).

Paul ends this passage by making a comparison to Moses. Moses beheld the glory of God, and his face reflected God's glory, so New Testament believers behold the glory of God and are transformed into that glory (2 Corinthians 3:18). Just as Moses was not content spiritually, but always pressed in for more, so must we be hungry and thirsty and God will continue to reveal Himself to us.

Elijah was so hungry for God that he would not compromise and was a voice to turn the people back to God. I have noticed that spiritual hunger is identified with the God of fire on many of these occasions. We read a powerful story in 1 Kings 18:16-45. Elijah dares Ahab to a challenge. It was a challenge of his god, Baal, versus the God of Elijah at Mount Carmel. They were to offer sacrifices to their own deities and see which one could start a fire. Ahab's prophets prayed for hours to Baal, but nothing happened. Elijah soaked the altar with water to show his trust in God to start a fire despite the sacrificial area being wet. He also did it as an offering unto God. Water was an extremely precious commodity during the drought. After Elijah's victory over the prophets of Baal, when he called down fire from Heaven, the drought ended.

When a person is spiritually hungry for God, there is no room for compromise. Fire burns out the chaff, sin, jealousy, apathy, and lukewarmness. It draws a line in the sand. Elijah asked, "How long will you waver between two opinions? If the Lord is God, follow Him; but if Baal is God, follow him." Elijah repaired the altars of The Lord, tore down the altars of Baal, killed the false prophets, and restored righteousness to Israel.

Elisha is another man of God who pursued the anointing because he was hungry for God. Both he and Elijah were two of the most notable prophets who helped to restore Israel in a time of wicked rulers.

What we want to concentrate on here is his spiritual hunger. Elisha refused to be denied. He started his ministry by illustrating desperate hunger.

> So he departed thence, and found Elisha the son of Shaphat, who was plowing with twelve yoke of oxen before him, and he with the twelfth: and Elijah passed by him, and cast his mantle upon him.
> And he left the oxen, and ran after Elijah, and said, Let me, I pray thee, kiss my father and my mother, and then I will follow thee. And he said unto him, Go back again: for what have I done to thee?
> And he returned back from him, and took a yoke of oxen, and slew them, and boiled their flesh with the instruments of the oxen, and gave unto the people, and they did eat. Then he arose, and went after Elijah, and ministered unto him.
>
> 1 KINGS 19.19-21

Elisha knew that he would be leaving his father and mother and wanted to kiss them goodbye. Elijah let him know that if he wanted to go back and do that, he would not be anointed by him. Elisha did not go back and decided to slay everything that attached him to his present season of life. He was a farmer but killed the oxen and gave an offering unto the people. Then he left with Elijah.

The Bible tells us to love, honor, and respect our parents, but we have to prioritize relationships in proportion to our love for God.

> If any man come to me, and hate not his father, and mother,
> and wife, and children, and brethren, and sisters, yea,
> and his own life also, he cannot be my disciple.
> And whosoever doth not bear his cross, and come after me,
> cannot be my disciple.
>
> LUKE 14:26-27

Jesus said if we aren't willing to give up everything, we cannot be His disciples. The problem is we are bombarded with earthly distractions.

Elisha maintained that hunger for God all the way through his life. In 2 Kings 2, Elisha understood that Elijah would soon pass away and asked to be blessed with a double portion of his anointing. Elijah was then carried into Heaven by a whirlwind in a chariot of fire. Elisha picked up Elijah's mantle and used it to cross the Jordan on dry land. He received the double portion he asked for and did double the number of miracles that Elijah did.

Elisha knew where to find the anointing. We need to be in pursuit of the anointing. We must be able to discern the anointing. We must know where it's moving and who it's moving upon. The word pursue means to chase after. It does not mean to watch or look but involves forward movement. Elisha asked for a double portion of the anointing that was upon Elijah's life. We must ask for how much we want and go wherever we have to go to get it. However, you must make sure that you can carry the anointing that

DESPERATE HUNGER GETS GOD'S ATTENTION

you ask for. We don't have details as to why Elisha died sick. Maybe he asked for more than he was prepared to handle.

A spiritually hungry and thirsty person will not quit and will not draw back when the going gets tough. We have to have relentless pursuit. Relentless means to be oppressively constant, incessant. We must be that way at this hour. To pursue means to follow (someone or something) in order to catch them. You and I have to want the power, healings, and miracles more than we want to be liked or accepted.

Elisha was a man who demonstrated relentless pursuit. When Elijah told Elisha that he was to stay and not follow him, Elisha refused to stay. He knew that if he saw Elijah being taken to Heaven, he would have what he asked for. So, Elisha walked about thirty-five miles on foot to follow Elijah. That is over a day's journey of walking. At each step of the journey, Elijah said, "Stay here. I don't want you to go any further." He was testing Elisha to see how much Elisha wanted to follow him. Elisha passed the test. Elisha said in his own way, "There is no way that I am going to leave you. I am staying with you."

The first place they went to was Gilgal, the place of separation. Gilgal was the first place that the Israelites came to when they entered the Promised Land. They set up stones there as a monument and a reminder of what God had done for them. God always wants His people to remember His acts on behalf of His people. Just don't live there.

It was Gilgal where they were reminded that they had not been circumcised. After the whole nation was circumcised, they remained where they were in the camp until they were healed. The Lord said to Joshua, "Today I have rolled away the reproach of Egypt from you." So the place was called Gilgal, which means the "rolling or 'roll-away.'" God was saying, "I have rolled away the past. I have rolled away the reproach of Egypt." They were now a separated people unto a living God, which is what circumcision speaks of.

The next place that the two men walked to was Bethel, which means The House of God. Jacob had an awesome experience there with God's presence. Bethel was where the Ark of the Covenant was kept. The people went to Bethel to enquire of the Lord. It was known as the House of God. Bethel speaks of The Lord's presence.

Elijah and Elisha walked on together to Jericho. This is a place where you have to walk by faith. The presence of God was Elisha's desire in good times and in bad times. This was the place where Joshua asked, "How is Israel going to win this battle?" The Lord was going to fight and win it for them. They had to walk around the walls of that city in faith. God taught them the principle of fighting their battles by faith. Hunger will lead you to faith because you want to please God. After all, the Bible says:

> But without faith it is impossible to please him: for he that
> > cometh to God must believe that he is, and that he is a
> > rewarder of them that diligently seek him.

> > > HEBREWS 11:6

The next place they walked together was to Jordan. Jordan is a place that represents both death and resurrection. It speaks of baptism in death to resurrection.

Elisha knew this, and when the call of God came, he let go of his own life, hopes, and dreams, and followed the call of God to wherever that would lead him!

> But what things were gain to me, those I counted loss for
> > Christ.
>
> Yea doubtless, and I count all things but loss for the excel-
> > lency of the knowledge of Christ Jesus my Lord: for
> > whom I have suffered the loss of all things, and do count
> > them but dung, that I may win Christ.

> > > PHILIPPIANS 3:7-8

DESPERATE HUNGER GETS GOD'S ATTENTION

It was only after Elisha's hunger for God took him to the places of Gilgal, Bethel, Jericho, and Jordan that he saw God take Elijah to Heaven and he received the double portion.

> And he took the mantle of Elijah that fell from him, and smote the waters, and said, Where is the Lord God of Elijah? and when he also had smitten the waters, they parted hither and thither: and Elisha went over.
> And when the sons of the prophets which were to view at Jericho saw him, they said, The spirit of Elijah doth rest on Elisha. And they came to meet him, and bowed themselves to the ground before him.
>
> 2 KINGS 2:14-15

When your spiritual hunger takes you to the places where you pass the tests, you can have what others have upon them. God will do the same for you that He does for someone else. He is no respecter of persons. However, these things do not fall on you like ripe cherries off of a tree. They must be walked out.

King David is another good example of Old Testament spiritual hunger and thirst. Look at all the "oh's" in the Psalms. Here are a few.

> O taste and see that the Lord is good: blessed is the man that trusteth in him.
>
> PSALM 34:8

> O Lord my God, I cried unto thee, and thou hast healed me.
>
> PSALM 30:2

O Lord, thou hast brought up my soul from the grave: thou hast kept me alive, that I should not go down to the pit.

PSALM 30:3

Oh how great is thy goodness...

PSALM 31:19

O God, thou art my God; early will I seek thee: my soul thirsteth for thee, my flesh longeth for thee in a dry and thirsty land, where no water is.

PSALM 63:1

O Lord, how manifold are thy works! in wisdom hast thou made them all: the earth is full of thy riches.

PSALM 104:24

O give thanks unto the Lord, for he is good: for his mercy endureth for ever.

PSALM 107:1

O God, my heart is fixed; I will sing and give praise, even with my glory.

PSALM 108:1

Oh that thou wouldest rend the heavens, that thou wouldest come down, that the mountains might flow down at thy presence,
As when the melting fire burneth, the fire causeth the waters to boil, to make thy name known to thine

adversaries, that the nations may tremble at thy presence!

ISAIAH 64:1-2

King David showed this kind of passion more than any other man in the Old Testament. He passionately wrote about his love for the law of God in Psalm 119:97, *"Oh, how I love your law! I meditate on it all day long."* He was also passionate about his own obedience. In verse 5 of the same Psalm, the Bible says: *"Oh, that my ways were steadfast in obeying your decrees!"* You can hear his hunger connected to his obedience.

Why do so many of the Psalms begin with the word *oh*? It is because the exhortation is stated as an exclamation. Webster's dictionary says that it is used to express an emotion (such as surprise or desire) or in response to physical stimuli. Oh! is a word of strong emotion that flows from a heart of wonder. When I saw the Grand Canyon, the arches of Utah, the majestic Rocky Mountains, and Victoria Falls for the first time, I exclaimed, "Oh, there are no words for this beauty."

I believe that David was a man after God's own heart because he loved God and His presence passionately. He was never ashamed to display it. He was also one to repent when he missed the mark. He loved God too much to stay out of relationship with Him. That is why he said in Psalm 51:10-12 *"Create in me a clean heart, O God; and renew a right spirit within me. Cast me not away from thy presence, and take not thy holy spirit from me. Restore unto me the joy of thy salvation; and uphold me with thy free spirit."* That hunger brought him back from sin to great restoration.

God himself is passionate and speaks words of passion. One of the best examples of this is found in Deuteronomy 5:28-29 after the leaders of Israel had begged God to stop speaking to them with such awesome power from Mount Sinai. They begged Moses to be the intermediary between God and Israel. This was God's passionate reaction: *"I have heard what this people said to you. Everything they said was good. Oh, that their hearts would be inclined to fear me and keep all my commands always so that it might go well with them and their children forever!"* Why does God speak with so much emotion? It is because He longs for the obedience and blessing of His people. So, He says, "Oh!" to us. *"Oh, that you would follow my ways!"*

When Jesus saw a Gentile woman filled with faith in the Bible, we read in Matthew 15:28, *"Then Jesus answered and said to her, 'Oh woman, your faith is great; be it done for you as you wish."* He showed great emotion when He saw such relentless faith. It is contrasted to when He saw the lack of faith in His disciples. He said, in Luke 24:25, *"'Oh foolish men and slow of heart to believe in all that the prophets have spoken!"*

God is passionate, and we should be as well. We are made in His image. Our relationship with God should be one of passion. If there is no "Oh!" in your walk with God, could it be that you have become lukewarm? If so, all you have to do is to ask God to restore your hunger and passion for Him and His kingdom. Become passionate about seeing people come to a saving knowledge of Christ and become passionate about the powerful God you serve.

Let's now look at some of the New Testament characters. I find the story of Blind Bartimaeus in Mark 10:46-52 to be one of the best examples. His name means son of the unclean. He was born blind. He was a beggar with no future or hope. However, one day, he heard a commotion. He wanted to know what was going on but could not see. He had to find someone with eyes because he was determined not to miss his moment. If you don't have eyes to see, find someone who does. So, he did the only thing he could. He cried out. If he had listened to his friends, he would've missed his divine appointment. If he had listened to the disciples, who basically said, "Shh, we don't do it that way here. Calm down. God's not deaf. You don't have to get too excited," he would have missed his moment and his miracle. The enemy uses people to oppose you and to try to get you to quit. He will use the world, your church, family, and friends, whoever he thinks you will listen to.

A powerful woman of God by the name of Lillian B. Yoemans said this about Bartimaeus, "He used what he had to secure what he lacked. He didn't have eyes, but he did have a voice." What do you have? You have a

DESPERATE HUNGER GETS GOD'S ATTENTION

voice, and you have a measure of the God kind of faith. Jesus said your faith has made you whole.

One cry was not enough. If the first voice you hear after your hungry cry says, "Calm down," it probably won't be the voice of God. They were offended because cries are distracting. He would not be dissuaded. He let them know, "You're not the one who's blind. God's nearby, and I won't let Him pass me by." He was a desperate man with a date with destiny. He would never be the same. He had raw, unrestrained hunger and passion. He was not ashamed to show it with an open display of emotion.

Jesus doesn't stop for the proud, but He stops His plans for the hungry and the humble. He will bypass thousands for the one who can't get enough of Him. Once Bartimaeus knew that Jesus was headed his way, he took off the clothes that attached him to blindness, poverty, begging, doctrines of tradition, religion, demons, and hopelessness. He got ready for his miracle ahead of time. You must leave behind old garments of sin, defeat, poverty, sickness, disease, religious tradition, the doctrines of men, demons, fear, insecurity, dysfunction, and the words spoken over you in the past. Jesus has great things in store for you. You must let go of the past to receive the good things and blessings that God has in store for you.

> Brethren, I count not myself to have apprehended: but this
> one thing I do, forgetting those things which are behind,
> and reaching forth unto those things which are before,
> I press toward the mark for the prize of the high calling of
> God in Christ Jesus.
>
> PHILIPPIANS 3:13-14

Make a decision and say, "I'm pressing into Jesus." There are cities and nations to take. Every lie of the Devil has to be opposed. God's looking for water walkers, not dry boat sitters who criticize anyone else who is walking on the water. You must get to the place where you say, "I'm gonna die if I don't have You." Get so desperate that you no longer act like yourself. Get so hungry that it's written all over your face. Pray this prayer, "Set my heart on fire with passion."

Let's look at the story of the man with palsy.

> And it came to pass on a certain day, as he was teaching, that there were Pharisees and doctors of the law sitting by, which were come out of every town of Galilee, and Judaea, and Jerusalem: and the power of the Lord was present to heal them.
> And, behold, men brought in a bed a man which was taken with a palsy: and they sought means to bring him in, and to lay him before him.
> And when they could not find by what way they might bring him in because of the multitude, they went upon the housetop, and let him down through the tiling with his couch into the midst before Jesus.
> And when he saw their faith, he said unto him, Man, thy sins are forgiven thee.
> And the scribes and the Pharisees began to reason, saying, Who is this which speaketh blasphemies? Who can forgive sins, but God alone?
> But when Jesus perceived their thoughts, he answering said unto them, What reason ye in your hearts?
> Whether is easier, to say, Thy sins be forgiven thee; or to say, Rise up and walk?
> But that ye may know that the Son of man hath power upon earth to forgive sins, (he said unto the sick of the palsy,) I say unto thee, Arise, and take up thy couch, and go into thine house.
> And immediately he rose up before them, and took up that whereon he lay, and departed to his own house, glorifying God.
> And they were all amazed, and they glorified God, and were

> filled with fear, saying, We have seen strange things to day.

LUKE 5:17-26

This story says a lot about spiritual hunger. The friends of the man with palsy were hungry enough to press in for him. It is important that we not only get hungry for ourselves but hungry enough to help others. Some will only believe in God for their own needs to be met, but it is time to grow up and believe in God for big things. Let's not have the attitude, "I have enough for us four and no more." That is selfish. We must press in with hunger and faith to see the needs of others met. It is time that we get healed inside and outside and give our hospital beds to someone else who needs them.

In this story, a crowd was in the house. People were stuck everywhere: in the bathroom, spare bedroom, closets, and the pantry. Instead of giving up, this man's friends were determined to get him to the healing service. Their faith went beyond even thinking of the consequences of tearing up a roof. They had to consider the fact that they could be arrested. After all, tearing up a roof was against the law. Roofs are expensive, and someone was going to have to pay for that damage. Hungry and desperate people do the most unusual things. They get aggressive to receive from God.

> And from the days of John the Baptist until now the kingdom of heaven suffereth violence, and the violent take it by force.

MATTHEW 11:12

Everything in you will scream for an easier road. It's easier to give up, but nation shakers and water walkers can't give up. If it were an easy thing to obtain everything in God, everybody would be doing it. If it were an easy thing to finish the race, no one would backslide.

Notice that Jesus saw their faith. How can faith be seen? It is seen by what it does. Faith has action. Smith Wigglesworth said, "Fear looks but faith jumps."

James said:

> Even so faith, if it hath not works, is dead, being alone.
> Yea, a man may say, Thou hast faith, and I have works: shew me thy faith without thy works, and I will shew thee my faith by my works.
> Thou believest that there is one God; thou doest well: the devils also believe, and tremble.
> But wilt thou know, O vain man, that faith without works is dead?
> Was not Abraham our father justified by works, when he had offered Isaac his son upon the altar?
> Seest thou how faith wrought with his works, and by works was faith made perfect?
> And the scripture was fulfilled which saith, Abraham believed God, and it was imputed unto him for righteousness: and he was called the Friend of God.
> Ye see then how that by works a man is justified, and not by faith only.
>
> JAMES 2:17-24

The passage in Luke 5 tells us that the power of God was there to heal. They could have all been healed, but we have no record of anyone else being healed. Lack of hunger is dangerous and costly. It isn't enough to be sitting in the meeting. Your heart must be hungry enough to activate faith.

It is also interesting that there were scribes present who were reasoning with themselves. Jesus still knows the hearts of people, even as He did then. We cannot fool Him. We must quit lying to God and to ourselves. If we aren't hungry, let's be honest with Him and start from there.

There are still many scribes, Pharisees, Sadducees, Wouldn't-sees, and Couldn't-sees in our midst today. They refuse to see spiritual evidence right in front of them. They would rather say that miracles, signs, and wonders have ceased than pay the price to have them again. They could have all received their healing that day. They were present, Jesus was there, and God was willing, but we only have evidence that this man received because of his friends' faith.

Hunger will reach out and receive that which bypasses others. God is not moved by someone with needs when that person has no hunger or faith. The man was healed and his sins forgiven as a result of hunger, thirst, and faith.

We find another example of great spiritual hunger in a little man named Zacchaeus.

> And Jesus entered and passed through Jericho.
> And, behold, there was a man named Zacchaeus, which was the chief among the publicans, and he was rich.
> And he sought to see Jesus who he was; and could not for the press, because he was little of stature.
> And he ran before, and climbed up into a sycamore tree to see him: for he was to pass that way.
> And when Jesus came to the place, he looked up, and saw him, and said unto him, Zacchaeus, make haste, and come down; for to day I must abide at thy house.
> And he made haste, and came down, and received him joyfully.
> And when they saw it, they all murmured, saying, That he was gone to be guest with a man that is a sinner.
> And Zacchaeus stood, and said unto the Lord; Behold, Lord, the half of my goods I give to the poor; and if I have taken any thing from any man by false accusation, I restore him fourfold.
> And Jesus said unto him, This day is salvation come to this house, forsomuch as he also is a son of Abraham.

> For the Son of man is come to seek and to save that which was lost.
>
> LUKE 19:1-10

Zacchaeus was a publican, a despised tax collector. The word publican is an English translation of the Greek word telónés, which means "tax-farmer." A publican had the job of collecting taxes, and they were known for collecting additional fees above their extravagant salaries. They were Jews who worked for the hated Roman government. They were despised. The Roman government employed citizens to do its dirty work. They promised hefty bonuses to publicans and allowed them to extort as much money from the citizenry as they could. So, it is easy to understand why the publicans were despised as traitors to their nation. They had no friends or associations except fellow companions among other publicans or criminals. To associate with a publican brought on a bad reputation for that individual.

The first thing that comes to my attention in this story is the description of Zacchaeus. He was not just a publican but a chief one. Even though he was rich, it did not help him see Jesus. Often, we think that because someone is blessed in one way, they do not have needs. However, they do, and we need to be sensitive to those needs. Jesus was passing by, and Zacchaeus wanted to see him but could not because he was too short. He could hear the commotion, the excited shouts of people as Jesus passed by. He would not settle for others' descriptions. He wouldn't settle when he heard someone say, "I see Him." Many would have given up. He would not settle for the church as usual. He determined to find a way to see Jesus. It was Zacchaeus' hunger that started everything in motion. Jesus is present for everyone but does not stop for everyone. He only stops for the hungry and thirsty. Zacchaeus realized that where there is a will, there is a way. He got in a tree-climbing mood.

That tree had been planted many years before. It takes a long time for a tree to grow large enough for a man to climb it. Maybe God made sure that someone would plant that tree and that someone else would guard it. It

DESPERATE HUNGER GETS GOD'S ATTENTION

had to be protected for a long time in order to be large enough to climb. God knew that Jesus and Zacchaeus would have an opportunity to meet someday. God could not make Zacchaeus climb it. That would be up to him alone. Remember that old saying, "You can lead a horse to water, but you can't make him drink?" It applies here. We each have to act on what God has done in order to have what He has for us. It will not be automatic.

Zacchaeus had to humble himself to climb that tree. You may have to do something more than you're doing. You may have to take off a roof or climb a tree in your own way to have an encounter with Jesus. His humility and hunger together caused him to climb it. Most politicians are not going to do something that would cause people to point, laugh, and ask, "What in the world does he think he is doing?" Zacchaeus did not care. He only cared about seeing Jesus. He sensed his moment with destiny to have his life changed forever. He initiated the change through his hunger, and Jesus was about to answer that hunger with His love, grace, and power.

Jesus was a rabbi, and religious society would never even share the same road with such men. *"Why do you eat and drink with tax collectors and sinners?"* they asked Him (Luke 5:30). *Jesus answered, "It is not the healthy who need a doctor, but the sick. I have not come to call the righteous, but sinners to repentance"* (verses 31–32).

Tax collectors were assumed to be beyond hope and not worthy of forgiveness. But Jesus forgave Publicans like He did all sinners. People thought that Jesus was breaking protocol by entering a publican's house (Luke 19:7). But the result was a changed life: *"Zacchaeus stood up and said to the Lord, 'Look, Lord! Here and now I give half of my possessions to the poor, and if I have cheated anybody out of anything, I will pay back four times the amount.' Jesus said to him, 'Today salvation has come to this house, because this man, too, is a son of Abraham'"* (verses 8–9). Zacchaeus' faith in Christ resulted in a changed life. I find it very interesting that when he was converted, he became like his Father and couldn't wait to give.

Let's look at the Woman with the issue of blood in Luke, chapter 8. It appears in Matthew 9:20-22, Mark 5:25-34, and Luke 8:43-48. We will look at Luke's account, who was also a medical doctor.

> And a woman having an issue of blood twelve years, which had spent all her living upon physicians, neither could be healed of any,
> Came behind him, and touched the border of his garment: and immediately her issue of blood stanched.
> And Jesus said, Who touched me? When all denied, Peter and they that were with him said, Master, the multitude throng thee and press thee, and sayest thou, Who touched me?
> And Jesus said, Somebody hath touched me: for I perceive that virtue is gone out of me.
> And when the woman saw that she was not hid, she came trembling, and falling down before him, she declared unto him before all the people for what cause she had touched him, and how she was healed immediately.
> And he said unto her, Daughter, be of good comfort: thy faith hath made thee whole; go in peace.
>
> LUKE 8:43-48

This is an outstanding story of hunger, determination, and the refusal to give up. This woman lived a hopeless life. Her world was black. She had a terrible medical condition for twelve long years. The blood loss would have made her extremely weak. Blood flowing from your body for twelve years would rob you of your strength. Today, physicians would give her blood transfusions.

She found no relief from the physicians. According to Luke (a physician himself), she suffered a great deal at the hands of the doctors, and they made her worse, not better. She had tried everything this world had to offer to get better. She had spent all that she had and was worse.

It is bad enough today to undergo medical tests and procedures, but in Biblical days, the practicing physicians practiced in a very limited way. The treatments for a woman with a female issue were horrific. Sometimes, treatments can be worse than living with a disease. William Barclay says in his commentary that "the Talmud gives no fewer than eleven cures for such an illness." She had probably tried all of them. Some of the superstitions included carrying the ashes of an ostrich egg in a linen cloth. But when you're desperate for a cure, you will give it a try. The money had finally run out, and now she had to deal with financial strain on top of physical strain. We have all heard of people committing suicide just from financial pressure. Yet she had physical, financial, spiritual, and emotional pressure from all directions.

All chronic conditions cause emotional turmoil. This woman had strict procedures she had to follow that would also affect her emotionally. The woman's condition disqualified her from marriage as well as religious life in general (Leviticus 15:25–33).

I have read about people who were quarantined as a part of their cancer treatment. They couldn't leave the room or have direct contact with their husband or wife, kids, pets, or visitors. Everything they touched was contaminated. They had specific rules to follow for everything, including their personal hygiene (no one else could use their bathroom. They had to wipe down the toilet with bleach, take showers daily, and scrub/disinfect the shower after each use). They all said that having zero physical contact with their loved ones was the most difficult part of their illness. Yet, they were only separated for days, not twelve years!

So this woman had twelve years of no hugs, kisses, handshakes, pats on the back, or shared meals. She couldn't go out in public, couldn't get together with the other women to draw water from the well, and couldn't worship at the temple. Twelve years without human contact would take a toll on anyone's emotional state.

It affected the woman spiritually. She suffered for twelve years from being unclean, according to the law. She was unable to live a normal life and was, in a sense, dead to the people around her. According to the laws of ritual purity, she should have been at home during her flow of blood (Leviticus 15:19-31).

Under Mosaic laws, a woman with an issue of blood was considered unclean and was "put apart" for seven days. During this time, anything she lay on or sat on was considered "unclean." Anyone who touched one of those things would have to wash his clothes and bathe in water to become clean again. Also, during this time, if any man was sexually intimate with her, he was also unclean for seven days and must adhere to the same sort of "setting apart" as a woman. The Mosaic law also stated that if a woman had an issue of blood that lasted longer than seven days, all the days of her issue were considered unclean, and she must be treated as such (Leviticus 15:25). This means that this woman had been unclean for twelve years and that she had to live "put apart" from others for all that time. If she had been married, her husband probably would have divorced her. She would have been unable to care for her children without making them all unclean. She was probably unable to attend the temple or other worship services.

Because of how long she endured this disease, the purity laws had become a terrible burden for her. She could not go out, could not touch members of her family, and could not enjoy a normal life. Satan would have been messing with her mind with lies that left her feeling unworthy. She probably could not understand why she was not seeing her breakthrough.

She was an outcast and shunned. A common belief for the Jews was that if a person suffered in any way, it was an outward sign of inward (hidden) sin. Also, they intertwined old wives' tales and superstitions into their daily lives. She probably had many people suggest different methods "guaranteed" to gain healing. I can imagine the hopelessness, the looks, and the remarks she might have received year after year. We got a glimpse when we saw how people treated one another during COVID-19.

What drove this woman to leave her home and go out into the crowd to touch the hem of His garment? She had tenacious faith. The definition of tenacious is keeping a firm hold on something, clinging or adhering closely, determined. Persisting, not giving up easily. The Bible says that "when she had heard the reports concerning Jesus, and she came up behind Him in the throng and touched His garment, for she kept saying, If I only touch His garments, I shall be restored to health" (Mark 5:27-28).

How did she hear about Jesus? She probably heard that Jesus was healing everyone. How do we receive faith? By hearing the Word of God. This is why we must publish or herald the goodness of God and how powerful His anointing is. There had to be truth spoken to her heart that was so much more powerful than her years of hopelessness and bad reports. She must have heard about the anointing upon Jesus to such an extent that she was moved by that truth enough to get ahold of power. We need to tell others of His goodness and about the move of The Spirit in the earth today. People must hear enough to overshadow all the lies that are in the world today. We must say enough to move someone out of a hopeless situation into hope and faith.

The woman said to herself, "If the spirit's on Him, then all I have to do is get to Him and touch Him." Thank God that she didn't hear from present-day theologians who may have told her that God had a purpose for her being sick.

She decided to risk everything. She was desperate. She was hungry, thirsty, and tenacious. She pressed in. She did something to make the divine connection for her healing to be manifested. Hunger and desperation drove her to do the seemingly impossible. Hunger has to propel you past every excuse of not making the connection.

She came to the meeting when she didn't feel good and was weak. Today, we hear people say, "I couldn't come to the healing meeting because I wasn't feeling good," or "I couldn't come to the joy meeting because I was too depressed," or "I couldn't come to the financial breakthrough meeting because I didn't have any gas money for my car." She could barely walk. She probably fell and had to crawl part of the way to Jesus. She also believed in confession. The Bible says that she said within herself. Sometimes, you have to keep saying what God says.

By the time she gets to Jesus, He's busy and surrounded by a crowd of people. Jarius, the most important man in the community, asked Him to help his daughter. Jesus turned to go with him. The woman's window of opportunity was closing, and her hope was fading. But she must take a chance. Her very survival depended on it. She slipped in from behind and touched His robe. She was thinking to herself, "If I can put a finger on his robe, I can get well." It was a risky decision. To exercise faith means you must be willing to take some risks. To get to Jesus, she had to get past the roadblocks. She had to get past the possibility of rebuke and someone recognizing her. All she had was a belief that Jesus could help her. The Bible says that as soon as she touched the hem of His garment, *"straightway the fountain of her blood was dried up."*

With just one touch of Jesus' garment, her flow of blood immediately dried up. She knew that she was healed physically! What is not possible with men is possible with God. Her disease was long, but she was healed instantly.

As soon as the woman touched Christ's garment, He felt that *"virtue had gone out of Him"* and turned about and said, *"Who touched me?"* By touching Jesus during that sort of blood loss, she would have "ceremonially contaminated" Jesus. He immediately recognized that virtue or *dunamis* power went out of Him into her. Jesus looked around and said, "*Who did that? Who put a demand on my ability?*" He was asking, "Where did that ability go? Who placed a demand on my anointing?" He was looking around to see who had done this thing. We see that He's not operating as God, or He would know who did it. He was operating in the ministry as a man anointed by God. He was God but laid that power down to give us an example of a man anointed by The Holy Ghost.

The disciples rebuked Jesus by saying, *"Thou seest the multitude thronging thee, and sayest thou, Who touched me?"* Many touched Him, but He recognized the touch of faith. Can you imagine the fear this woman felt when Jesus drew attention to what happened? This woman hadn't touched or been touched in years. She was trying to hide. This was a very brave thing for this woman to do. She stepped forward in front of everyone, fell at the feet of Jesus, and confessed that she was a lawbreaker. Because of breaking Jewish Law, the people could have stoned her to death. She still had emotional wounds. She had feelings of shame, fear, and anxiety. While still shaking, she confessed. *"She told him all the truth."* She probably said, "I'm sorry, I should have asked permission, but I've been sick many years, and I heard You had an anointing on You that removes every sickness and destroys the yoke of infirmity. I could sit here and be sick and confused for the rest of my life, or I knew that I could come and touch the hem of Your garment and be made whole. So I pressed through the crowd, came behind You, and touched You and I was healed."

Jesus immediately responded. Instead of condemning her, He took time and acknowledged her. He called her daughter, publicly claiming her as His own. I love how the KJV puts this: He told her that *her faith made her whole*. She was commended for Her Faith. Jesus said, *"Daughter, be of good comfort; thy faith hath saved thee."* When He called her daughter, it must have brought emotion that she had not experienced in years. It meant that Jesus loved her and claimed her as one of His own.

Notice how many people were thronging Him, and yet we have no record of anyone else getting anything. He never gave the microphone to any of them. When someone catches hold of the virtue or anointing, it singles them out. The Bible does not talk about or list the multitude here. They're insignificant to what The Holy Spirit wanted to be recorded in His Word. It is not that God doesn't love them the same, but He responds to hunger and faith. He wants His goodness and will to be recorded in His Word. It's all about where the anointing moves and makes a difference. When we hunger for Him and His anointing, the anointing will touch us. We can be in the middle of millions of people, but when the anointing touches us, it sets us apart. When The Spirit of the Lord is upon you, God knows that there's somebody in the crowd who has something to say. He wanted what happened to this woman to be put in His Gospel. He's not going to give equal time to people who are not getting touched. We are not going to give the microphone to anyone who says, "I went to that campmeeting and got nothing."

Are you tenaciously going to the Lord's door and knocking? Are you staying close to God even when you don't feel like it? Do you go to meetings even if you are busy or don't feel like it?

Let's look at another hungry, thirsty, and desperate woman, the Syrophoenician woman.

> Then Jesus went thence, and departed into the coasts of Tyre and Sidon.
> And, behold, a woman of Canaan came out of the same coasts, and cried unto him, saying, Have mercy on me, O Lord, thou son of David; my daughter is grievously vexed with a devil.
> But he answered her not a word. And his disciples came and besought him, saying, Send her away; for she crieth after us.
> But he answered and said, I am not sent but unto the lost sheep of the house of Israel.
> Then came she and worshipped him, saying, Lord, help me.
> But he answered and said, It is not meet to take the children's bread, and to cast it to dogs.
> And she said, Truth, Lord: yet the dogs eat of the crumbs which fall from their masters' table.
> Then Jesus answered and said unto her, O woman, great is thy faith: be it unto thee even as thou wilt. And her daughter was made whole from that very hour.
>
> MATTHEW 15:21-28

It is the spiritual hunger that got her daughter healed and delivered. When you are hungry, it doesn't matter if you have setbacks, terrible circumstances, or if people tell you that you need to forget the promises of God. You must refuse to listen or give in to that. You must hang onto God's Word and His promises with the grip of a bulldog.

This lady is not a Jew or a Jewish proselyte. The Syrophoenician woman would be considered a sinner today, someone outside the covenant. She used the phrase *"Son of David,"* which would mean nothing to her. She was saying, "You're the Messiah who will restore the Kingdom." She was using a borrowed phrase (like Charismatics do!). Someone may come into a church and want to fit in so much that they use phrases they have heard but do not know the meaning of. It may be "Amen" or "Halleluia," but they have no concept of what it means. It just sounds good. This is what she was doing.

She may have heard the two blind men of Matthew 9 use it. She's not coming to receive Jehovah as God or to become a proselyte. She's only after healing for her daughter. She is acting like many people today who come after the healing and not the healer. These people will get only as close as is necessary to get healed and then go back to their old lifestyle.

The Lord wants us to want Him, not just for what He has. How would we feel if someone acted like that with us? It doesn't bless us when someone just wants our favor for what we can do for them. Her words sound right, but there was no evidence of a deeper love for the Lord. Jesus doesn't even respond to her. He knew that she was in no position to receive.

A lot of the time, we're in the same position. We can't receive until we listen to God, humble ourselves, and change. Then we can receive what He has for us. If we are not willing to do that, we will get offended and stay in the same condition.

Jesus ignored her. The Bible says that *He answered her not a word.* That must have taken courage on His part. I can only imagine what people would do today. As an evangelist, I frequently have healing prayer lines. What if someone spoke out, "Debbie, please help me," and you watched me walk on without even glancing their way? I think most people would find it appalling. They probably would not even come back to my meeting. However, what if I was being led by The Holy Spirit to ignore that person until their heart was softened and he or she was able to receive? People need to learn to trust that those of us in charge of a meeting are listening to The Holy Spirit and following His direction.

In this story, Jesus is following the leading of the Holy Spirit. But others see Him as a man who is being hard and uncaring. Today, traveling preachers and crusade teams get the same reaction. We, too, must only do what we see The Father do and say what we hear The Father say. Yet, others have no idea why we do some of the things we do. If people are not in a position to receive, the most loving thing we can do is to instruct them as to what they need to change to get into a position to receive.

This woman could have gotten offended. She had the opportunity. Some of us probably would have. Today, church people might say, "How dare he! He's supposed to be a minister of the Gospel and I asked him nice, and his crusade team wants to send me away! We, Syrophoenicians are as good as anybody!" She probably would have accused Him of racism, sexism, or being female-phobic.

The root of offense is pride. To be offended is pride. Sometimes, we need to face the fact that some things from our family heritage aren't good, and we need to get away from them. Pride could have caused her daughter to stay sick.

The blessings of God belong to those who receive Jesus today. Under the Old Covenant, they belonged only to the Jews. The day was coming in the future for the Gentiles, but it was not yet. Healing is for the children of God today, not necessarily for those who don't belong to Him or call Him Lord. Sometimes, God is gracious and heals even atheists through a gift of healing or with the healing anointing. It has nothing to do with the person's own faith.

There was a day when Avon ladies went door to door selling their Avon products. I can remember one of those ladies giving my mother free products, perhaps a small moisturizer or a perfume sample. She also handed my mother her business card with it. It had her name and phone number. She knew that if my mother liked the free samples, she would come back for more of the product that was attached to the lady's name. God is certainly smarter than an Avon lady, and He chooses to give out free *samples* of His good gifts from time to time. They are attached to His Bible and the name of Jesus. He says, "I am good all the time. If you like that

DESPERATE HUNGER GETS GOD'S ATTENTION

healing, come back for salvation, the baptism of The Holy Spirit, and more." However, He expects His children to take Him at His Word and operate in faith. This woman was outside of the covenant.

Thank God that she humbled herself and said, *"Even the dogs get the crumbs, don't they?"* The Master recognized her humility and knew that her heart made the adjustment. I have said more than once in this book that hunger and humility go together. You cannot have one without the other. It doesn't necessarily take months or years for this to be accomplished in your life. You can make the adjustments immediately. She worshipped Him and said, "Please, help me." In response, Jesus told her that her faith was great.

Jesus refers to this healing and deliverance as the children's bread.

> But he answered and said, It is not meet to take the children's bread, and to cast it to dogs.
>
> MATTHEW 15:26

> Or what man is there of you, whom if his son ask bread, will he give him a stone?
>
> MATTHEW 7:9

> Give us this day our daily bread.
>
> MATTHEW 6:11

> I have been young, and now am old; yet have I not seen the righteous forsaken, nor his seed begging bread.
>
> PSALM 37:25

We should be glad He didn't say that healing is the children's pie or cake, which would be an extra or a dessert. No, He used the word bread. Bread was a staple in Bible times. It was a necessity that was essential to maintaining a reasonable standard of living. He was letting us know that He considers healing to be a necessity to maintain a reasonable standard of living. We can't do much for the kingdom if we are sick.

He also associates the bread of healing with His Word.

> He sent his word, and healed them, and delivered them from their destructions.
>
> PSALM 107:20

> My son, attend to my words; incline thine ear unto my sayings.
> Let them not depart from thine eyes; keep them in the midst of thine heart.
> For they are life unto those that find them, and health to all their flesh.
>
> PROVERBS 4:20-22

> But he answered and said, It is written, Man shall not live by bread alone, but by every word that proceedeth out of the mouth of God.
>
> MATTHEW 4:4

> It is the spirit that quickeneth; the flesh profiteth nothing: the words that I speak unto you, they are spirit, and they are life.
>
> JOHN 6:63

> Neither have I gone back from the commandment of his lips;

> I have esteemed the words of his mouth more than my necessary food.
>
> JOB 23:12

> Thy words were found, and I did eat them; and thy word was unto me the joy and rejoicing of mine heart: for I am called by thy name, O Lord God of hosts.
>
> JEREMIAH 15:16

He is saying that if you eat God's Word, you'll have life in you.

> Thou preparest a table before me in the presence of mine enemies: thou anointest my head with oil; my cup runneth over.
>
> PSALM 23:5

What's on this table? Bread! The Lord prepares a table, has a table spread, and then He calls, "Come and Dine!" This is spiritual provision and bread. The Lord knows how to put on a spread. It's full of delicacies, including bread. He's not talking about Heaven here because it's in the presence of our enemies (symptoms, circumstances). I can sit and partake of the children's bread even while the enemies are growling around my feet. I can say, "Please, pass the bread!" People think they have to wait until the symptoms are gone and all the bills are paid. Let the demons howl on. I say, "Give me a cake of peace (instead of a piece of cake) and a cup of new wine. I'll feast on a supper of holy bread!"

> For I have received of the Lord that which also I delivered unto you, that the Lord Jesus the same night in which he was betrayed took bread:
> And when he had given thanks, he brake it, and said, Take,

> eat: this is my body, which is broken for you: this do in remembrance of me.
> After the same manner also he took the cup, when he had supped, saying, this cup is the new testament in my blood: this do ye, as oft as ye drink it, in remembrance of me.
> For as often as ye eat this bread, and drink this cup, ye do shew the Lord's death till he come.
>
> 1 CORINTHIANS 11:23-26

The Lord's Supper specifies that the bread is the body of the Lord, the Word, which we consume and which becomes our wholeness.

You have had a teaching on healing that should help bring about your healing. However, I have not changed subjects. What caused her to change so that she could receive healing for her daughter? She hungered to see her daughter healed. She then hungered to change. She went from putting on a meaningless pretense to humbling herself to worship The Lord and have a relationship with Him.

Now, let's look at The Apostle Peter. We can learn much from not only his mistakes but from His victory over those mistakes. Peter loved Jesus so much that tradition tells us that when he was being crucified, he wanted to be crucified upside down. He felt that he was not worthy to be crucified in the same position that his Lord was crucified in. That tells me that he underwent a major change from denying The Lord to martyrdom.

Peter's story is a story of restoration and revival. His heart was definitely set ablaze after he was restored to his faith and baptized in The Holy Ghost on the day of Pentecost. Revival is about starting over and being restored to your first love. It's about true repentance. Many of these spiritually hungry Bible characters sinned and failed miserably. Some even worked at covering their sin for a while, like David. They blew it in a big way. Even when we sin big, God wants to forgive us and help us get back on track. As long as we keep a defiant attitude, we can never get right with God.

Hunger requires us to stop hiding behind proud hearts and confess our sins to God.

True spiritual hunger will bring about a change in our thoughts, attitudes, and actions. We like to take credit for our accomplishments, but we often blame our failures on extenuating circumstances. How many times have you heard someone say something like this? "I'm sorry that I lost my temper. It's because I'm so tired, or I'm under pressure, or you were getting on my nerves." Our natural tendency is to blame someone or something else whenever we fail.

It's not always easy to accept responsibility for our failures, but we have to do so if we want to get our lives back on track and please God.

We have to change our minds about who is in control of our lives. We have to stop blaming others and accept responsibility for our actions. We cannot blame our sin on anyone else. We cannot blame our sin on the Devil. It does no good to say, "I am a victim of my environment, circumstances, genealogy, or bad luck." True Godly hunger requires a change of heart.

Psalm 51:4 says, *"Against you only have I sinned..."* David was saying, "I am responsible for my actions. I can't blame anyone but myself." If you are spiritually hungry, it will eventually cause a change of direction. We can mess things up on our own without anyone's help, but it takes an act of God to get us back on track. We must depend on Him to cleanse us, wash us, and forgive us. Many times, we are guilty of trying to clean ourselves up and make ourselves "good" so that we will be acceptable to God. There is only one way that I can come to God—"Just As I Am." Then, *He is faithful and just to forgive us and cleanse us from all unrighteousness* (1 John 1:9). We must stop going our own way and start going His way. It means that we must spend time alone with God on a consistent basis.

David said, *"Do not cast me from your presence. Do not take your Holy Spirit from me"* (Psalm 51:11). He recognized that we need the Holy Spirit's power in our lives to overcome the power of sin. In the next verse, he also said, *"Restore to me the joy of your salvation,"* because he knew that a relationship with God is supposed to make you happy, not miserable.

Some people think that repentance is feeling guilty, but feeling guilty isn't enough. There's more to repentance than just feeling bad. If you feel guilty too long, you haven't repented. Repentance removes guilt and results in joy.

Ask God to help you change your heart, mind, and direction.

Peter had a breaking point in his life.

> And when they had sung an hymn, they went out into the mount of Olives.
> And Jesus saith unto them, All ye shall be offended because of me this night: for it is written, I will smite the shepherd, and the sheep shall be scattered.
> But after that I am risen, I will go before you into Galilee.
> But Peter said unto him, Although all shall be offended, yet will not I.
> And Jesus saith unto him, Verily I say unto thee, That this day, even in this night, before the cock crow twice, thou shalt deny me thrice.
> But he spake the more vehemently, If I should die with thee, I will not deny thee in any wise. Likewise also said they all.
>
> MARK 14:26-31

> Then took they him, and led him, and brought him into the high priest's house. And Peter followed afar off.
> And when they had kindled a fire in the midst of the hall, and were set down together, Peter sat down among them.
> But a certain maid beheld him as he sat by the fire, and earnestly looked upon him, and said, This man was also with him.
> And he denied him, saying, Woman, I know him not.
> And after a little while another saw him, and said, Thou art also of them. And Peter said, Man, I am not.

> And about the space of one hour after another confidently affirmed, saying, Of a truth this fellow also was with him: for he is a Galilaean.
>
> And Peter said, Man, I know not what thou sayest. And immediately, while he yet spake, the cock crew.
>
> And the Lord turned, and looked upon Peter. And Peter remembered the word of the Lord, how he had said unto him, Before the cock crow, thou shalt deny me thrice.
>
> And Peter went out, and wept bitterly.
>
> LUKE 22:54-62

I heard Bishop T.D. Jakes give a sermon called "He's the God of the Second Chance." It was powerful, and I took good notes, which I am now sharing with you.

John McCain told that after years of pressure, he found out, as a prisoner of war in Vietnam, that he could be broken enough to say whatever the enemy wanted him to say. His training and discipline held out for only so long. He later regretted it, but he had a breaking point. Many times, people find out that they too have one. We don't want to admit it, but after years of pressure, some have broken.

T.D. Jakes's mother was an educator. She said that all of the kids played with yardsticks. The children found it fascinating to watch how far they could bend the yardstick before it broke. They could bend it a long way, but if one of them kept applying pressure at the right point, it would break. The point differs depending on the material, but at some time, it will break if enough pressure is applied. Do you know where your breaking point is?

Romans 6:1 says, "*What shall we say then? Shall we continue in sin, that grace may abound?*" The implication is that you can go a long way in sin and grace may abound, but at a certain point, God will forbid grace from continuing. We don't know at what point God gets tired of winking at our sins and putting up with our excuses. Only God knows where the limit is and when you've gone too far. Most of us don't know our own limitations and aren't prepared for the battle.

We have an enemy. There is opposition. It's a war out there. We deal with issues in our lives that are almost overwhelming, and life becomes torturous at times. Sooner or later, something will press you until you feel like you're going to snap.

Jesus understood that when He finished the communion and said *one of you is going to be offended.* He said, *"One of you is the devil."* And they said, *"Lord is it I?"* During that supper, Peter announced, "Somebody may be offended, but it won't be me." Jesus said, *"One will be offended and deny Me before the night is over."* It was a very long night. Have you ever gone through a long night? The Bible says tha*t weeping endures for a night but joy comes in the morning*! A night can last six months sometimes or years before you see the breaking of day. It seems as though, before things get better, they get worse. Just when you thought you were going to come out of it, you get more bad news!

Peter says strongly, "It won't be me!" and then says more strongly, *"If I should die with You, I won't deny You in any way."* The problem with Peter is this—he didn't know himself. Most people don't know themselves and their limitations, so they make rash statements about how strong they are. Then they become critical of other people and say, "How did you let that happen to you? If you were really a Christian or read your Bible as you should, you should never be depressed."

Many times, they have never been tested and never had the pressure applied. We need to be careful about thinking we know what we would do if we were in someone else's shoes.

Many times, people have a breaking point when it comes to their children. There is a point where you reach the end of your rope and say, "If you get arrested one more time, Momma won't be there." Others say, "If my boss does that one more time, I quit." Maybe someone else says to their mate, "I'm on the edge right now, and if you go past this point, I won't make it back." Yet, someone else says, "If you knock this chip off my shoulder one

DESPERATE HUNGER GETS GOD'S ATTENTION

more time." Even that quiet little person who never raises their voice may have a breaking point if you push them hard enough. Have you ever seen a person flip out that you never expected to do so?

Most of the people in the Bible had a breaking point. For some, it was so severe that they wanted to quit, throw up their hands, and say, "I'm through. I've had enough." For instance, Moses was misunderstood in his mission and tried to fight the battle with his own strength. He ended up having to flee from Pharaoh's house. The Bible says he feared and fled and sat down by a well. He told God that the people wouldn't believe him or listen to him. Then he told God that he was slow of speech and of a slow tongue. He had to spend forty years on the backside of the desert before he cried out in his own way, "I'm out of it. I quit. I don't want to be bothered anymore."

Elijah, who called fire down from Heaven, faced 450 prophets of Baal and found himself under a juniper tree, saying, "It's enough. Let me die with my fathers."

1 Kings 19:4. He had a breaking point.

Job talked real tough about how he trusted God when he said, *"The Lord giveth and the Lord taketh away, blessed be the name of the Lord. Naked came I into the world and naked shall I return."* However, as the battle got worse, he said *"Cursed is the day I was born and the breasts that gave me suck."*

> Then Job broke the silence. He spoke up and cursed his fate:
> "Obliterate the day I was born.
> Blank out the night I was conceived!
> Let it be a black hole in space.
> May God above forget it ever happened.
> Erase it from the books!
> May the day of my birth be buried in deep darkness,
> shrouded by the fog,
> swallowed by the night.
> And the night of my conception—the devil take it!

DR. DEBBIE RICH

Rip the date off the calendar,
delete it from the almanac.
Oh, turn that night into pure nothingness—
no sounds of pleasure from that night, ever!
May those who are good at cursing curse that day.
Unleash the sea beast, Leviathan, on it.
May its morning stars turn to black cinders,
waiting for a daylight that never comes,
never once seeing the first light of dawn.
And why? Because it released me from my mother's womb
into a life with so much trouble.
"Why didn't I die at birth,
my first breath out of the womb my last?
Why were there arms to rock me,
and breasts for me to drink from?
I could be resting in peace right now,
asleep forever, feeling no pain,
In the company of kings and statesmen
in their royal ruins,
Or with princes resplendent
in their gold and silver tombs.
Why wasn't I stillborn and buried
with all the babies who never saw light,
Where the wicked no longer trouble anyone
and bone-weary people get a long-deserved rest?
Prisoners sleep undisturbed,
never again to wake up to the bark of the guards.
The small and the great are equals in that place,
and slaves are free from their masters.
"Why does God bother giving light to the miserable,
why bother keeping bitter people alive,
Those who want in the worst way to die, and can't,
who can't imagine anything better than death,
Who count the day of their death and burial
the happiest day of their life?

DESPERATE HUNGER GETS GOD'S ATTENTION

> What's the point of life when it doesn't make sense,
> when God blocks all the roads to meaning?
> "Instead of bread I get groans for my supper,
> then leave the table and vomit my anguish.
> The worst of my fears has come true,
> what I've dreaded most has happened.
> My repose is shattered, my peace destroyed.
> No rest for me, ever—death has invaded life."
>
> JOB 3:1-26 (MSG)

He said all of this because he had a breaking point.

The Apostle Paul said, *"I was crushed above measure and beyond strength so much that I despaired life itself. I got to the point I wanted to give up and die."*

> For we do not want you to be uninformed, brethren, about the affliction and oppressing distress which befell us in [the province of] Asia, how we were so utterly and unbearably weighed down and crushed that we despaired even of life [itself].
>
> 2 CORINTHIANS 1:8 (AMPC)

Jacob received so much bad news after he had stood up for God and had a massive change in his life that he shook his head in depression and said, *"All these things are against me."*

> And Jacob their father said unto them, Me have ye bereaved of my children: Joseph is not, and Simeon is not, and ye will take Benjamin away: all these things are against me. And Reuben spake unto his father, saying, Slay my two sons, if I bring him not to thee: deliver him into my hand, and I will bring him to thee again.
>
> GENESIS 42:36-37

Read the Psalms and realize David had a breaking point and, at times, was depressed because of his sin, his sickness, etc. There is a breaking point in your life, and it's part of the process. It helps to develop your faith, not to destroy it. It's only when you come face to face with human limitations that you begin to understand the magnitude of God's grace and power. As long as life hands you stuff you can handle, you will always worship yourself because you think you're a strong person. But after you've been broken down and lost all hope of standing in your own strength, finally you come to the point where you depend on God. God can't use anyone effectively who's not experienced a breaking point in his or her life.

People who have not been there tend to be judgmental, critical, gossipers, and busybodies who stick their noses in others' affairs because they haven't been to a breaking point yet. But if you've ever been there, it's a humbling experience. It changes your attitude and your disposition.

Breaking means coming unglued, falling apart, breaking your own promises, and disappointing yourself. This is a place where tears are leaping down your face and you're uncertain of anything and everybody. You are not even sure of yourself. Sometimes, you aren't sure of your friends or your environment. If you are honest, at that moment, you are not even of the Lord.

Peter thought he knew what he'd never do. He had said, "I'm telling You Lord, no matter what the night brings, I won't deny You." However, the Bible shows us what happened to Peter as the night progressed and the pressure mounted. You begin to see the decline in the relationship between Peter and Jesus. It's not that he didn't love Him or wasn't with Him. The Bible says subtle things that give us hints as to what is happening. It says as the pressure mounted, Peter began to lapse backward. The Bible says he followed Jesus afar off. He was still following Him, but...still coming to church, but he's following afar off. This is the danger of not walking close to Jesus. God doesn't like it when we follow Him at a distance, and it is very dangerous for us. He said, *"If you draw nigh unto me, I'll draw nigh unto you."* It is not following a long way off in the distance.

This is a person who comes to church but follows the Lord afar off and would call themselves a secret Christian. They are neutral and lukewarm. When the pressure is on, they could go either way. They don't make commitments to anything. They are not too committed to the Lord or church. They come in late and leave early. They don't want anyone to know they're Christians. They don't pray over their food. They don't want to be too closely associated with that wild, radical, revival crowd.

When you take a stand for God, you'll run into pressure, opposition, and controversy. Not everyone's going to like you. If you start doing something for God, I can guarantee that you will face some pressure. It won't just be from the outside but inside. When that happens, people, in an attempt to save themselves, begin to follow afar off. When it's convenient to say your name, or it opens a door, they will use your name. But when it brings controversy, they say that they never knew you.

Peter was radical and loved The Lord. He wasn't a wimp, nor mediocre in his commitment. He was a businessman who had multiple ships. He gave up everything to follow Jesus. He said, "You can use my boat, my resources." We are talking about someone who was sold out. Peter stood head and shoulders above the other disciples. He was bold when all of the other disciples weren't sure or wouldn't take a stand as to who Jesus was. He stood up when the other eleven were silent and said, *"Thou art the Christ, the Son of the living God."* When talking about Peter, we're not talking about an upstart but somebody so radical for Jesus that he took out his sword and cut off the ear of the soldier who came to arrest Jesus. He wasn't someone timid or passive. He was willing to fight. He was the man who woke up Jesus when the whole ship was going down and said, "Lord, don't you care that we perish?" His boldness saved the day! When he saw Jesus walking on the water, he said, "Lord, bid me to come." He walked on water and did things that other men had never done.

Radical people will go where no one else has gone. We are talking about mighty men and women of valor, faith, and tenacity. These are people who'll step off the boat in the middle of the storm and are willing to take the blows of criticism while others stay in the safety zone. They'll take the risk and go where others haven't gone before. It costs you something to be radical, a trendsetter, a giant killer—one who will step out of the boat and walk on water.

Peter had success after success after success. When you have a lot of success, you begin to think you're invincible. Out of his background of successes, he made a bold, fervent statement, "I will not deny You." It's clear he had no desire to deny the Lord, or he wouldn't have cut off that soldier's ear, walked on the water, or taken a stand for God at any time. But Peter had not experienced the breaking point yet.

Pressure is something you can't even see. It starts to break down a man who was willing to fight things he could see before. He fought the storm, the boat, and the soldier whose ear he cut off. But the breaking point is not brought about by the enemies you can see but by the unseen, relentless pressure that continues to be executed in your life until, little by little, you begin to decline your commitment, and nobody even notices that you aren't following as close as you were before, you're not praying like you used to pray, and you don't even pick up your Bible until it's time to go to church. You wear your Bible like a watch. You don't use it like a soldier's weapon. It is only decoration for Sunday. Nobody notices that when the worship is going on, you are really thinking about something else. If the preacher preaches too long, it used to excite you. But now, it gets on your nerves. You find yourself thinking that the lines are too long, the parking is too far away and they don't have enough of it, and you didn't get the seat you wanted. You have an attitude. Nobody's noticing that your priorities are so out of line that anything inconvenient will drag you away. Yes, you're a Christian, and yes, you follow Jesus, but afar off. How close are you?

You're under a lot of pressure and stress. It seems like everything is closing in on you, and you feel like you're going to break if anything else happens. You are now saying, "If you knock this chip off my shoulder, if you do one more thing, I quit."

Peter followed Jesus afar off, and he sat down with the enemy at the fire of the world, the secular. He was one with the world, one in fellowship with the Jesus haters. He sat down close enough to see Jesus but not close enough to be associated with Him. He has fellowship with the world and fellowship with the church. He was warmed at the fire of the enemy's camp. You cannot warm yourself at the enemy's fire and still be God's man or woman. You have to make up your mind. *"Choose you this day whom you will serve.* Will it be God, or will it be man?" You've got to make up your mind. Are you going to care about winning people or winning God? Where do you stand?

Be careful where you draw your strength from, who you let comfort you, or who you let be there for you. The enemy wants to neutralize you until you're ineffective. He will do one of two things: either dilute you until you don't have the strength that you need or pollute you with foreign matter. Don't let life dilute you or break down your message, what you used to think, what you believe, and where you stand. Don't let him pollute you. You've got to be careful who you allow to talk to you. Don't listen to people who bring you bad news and pollute your spirit.

A little girl looked at Peter and said he's one of them. When you belong to God, you can go to the club, and they will still know you. When you really belong to God, they'll still look at you and say that you belong to God. There's something about having really been touched by God that leaves an indelible impression on you, and it won't come off. You can be a backslider in the hog pen, and it won't come off. If you ever knew Him, that will be the case. It could have been twenty years ago, but if you've ever tasted of His goodness, you can't get so high or drunk that people can't tell you've been with the Lord. You might not be with Him right now, but you've been with Him, and they can look at you and know. You don't even dance right. Once you've experienced Him, you can't wash it out.

Many times, it's your grandma's prayers that have brought you through the storm, and people can tell you've been with the Lord. I once heard a story about two drunks trying to witness each other in a bar. Eventually, they both realized that they had known the Lord.

When she pointed at Peter, he said: "No, I never knew Him." You say, "I would never do that." It wasn't the specificity of the words that mattered.

He compromised his own principles. He didn't want to deny Jesus. But before the night was over, he was doing what he didn't want to do. Have you ever done anything that you didn't want to do? Have you been anywhere that you didn't want to be? Have you ever gotten into something that you said you wouldn't ever get into? Have you said *yes* to something you always said that you'd say *no* to? Have you ever shocked yourself with the bad decisions you made when you were under pressure? Have you ever done what you liked but didn't like what you did?

Peter was tortured by the conflict that exists in the life of a person who's at the breaking point. Because when you're near the breaking point, you deny your own principles, laws, and things that you said you wouldn't do. You've broken your own law. The question becomes how then does an officer arrest himself? Peter survives by lying and saying, *"I knew Him not."* A man walked up and said, "Yes, I now remember you. I remember how you used to praise God and how you used to get up in the morning, rushing to go to church. You couldn't wait for Sunday night's service and Bible study on Wednesday evening. Now, you still follow, but you follow afar off because you're too busy. There is too much to do. The world is demanding all of these things of you. Meanwhile, you're getting closer and closer to the breaking point."

It's a terrible thing to be close to the breaking point but not close enough to God to get the help you need. The enemy always causes the pressure to mount as the distance increases between you and The Lord. Peter denies Him three times, and on the third time, when asked if he knew him, he replied, "I know Him not." The agonizing thing is that when he said it the third time, the cock crowed twice. Separation sounds in the ears of covenant people. The Bible says that Jesus, while in the midst of His persecution, turned and looked at Peter. Peter remembered what the Lord told him when He said that before the cock crows two times, you will have denied Me three times. He wept bitterly because Peter never knew what was in him. He never knew he could be tortured and pressured by life to the point where he could deny his own principles and do things he never thought he would.

DESPERATE HUNGER GETS GOD'S ATTENTION

How well do you know yourself? Won't life show you what's really in you?

If you just keep living, you'll get ready to say something about someone else and remember something you went through—sickness, whether to have chemo or not, bankruptcy, a kid who went crazy on you, or a spouse who left you for someone else.

We see little difference between Peter and Judas. Maybe Jesus should have said at the Last Supper that the two of you are devils. Both of them were concerned about public opinion, both betrayed the Lord under pressure, both denied public commitment to the Gospel of Jesus Christ, both regretted their decision, both got caught in their own trap, and both wept sorely. How little difference is there between Peter and Judas? Now, we see why the Lord tells us not to try to separate the wheat and tares, and we are to let Him do it. If we try to do it, we might save Judas and destroy Peter if we look at the outward appearance.

Peter could have walked away, saying, "Maybe it was me who was the Devil. Maybe I didn't really know Him." Have you ever just thought, "Maybe I don't know Him, or maybe He doesn't know me? Maybe I shouldn't have gone into the ministry. Maybe I wasn't sincere. Maybe my enemies were right. Maybe He didn't call me to preach the Gospel, maybe I shouldn't have joined the church, maybe I shouldn't have married this man, taken the job, adopted the child. Maybe I shouldn't have moved or taken the position. Maybe I'm not a good husband or a good wife after all. Maybe I shouldn't have had kids." Under the breaking point, you start reevaluating everything. Is there anybody who didn't ever have to live with a maybe? When pressure comes, you begin to reevaluate everything. At the breaking point, you sit up in bed at night and ask yourself about twenty maybes. At the breaking point, you aren't sure of anything or anybody, including yourself.

I am talking to people who've been to Hell and back. People who've looked out the window and couldn't see anything except the blackness of night. You were trying to figure out, "Who am I, and what am I? Have I wasted my life? Did I make a mistake?" I want to talk to people who don't have it all together, haven't arrived yet, people who are thinking, "Maybe I did make a mistake."

No matter how tough you are, how strong you are, or how sure of yourself you are, if you keep living, you're going to question your own decisions. This is what makes you feel lonely. How do you pick up the phone and tell people, "I don't know if I should have done this or not." You wish you could talk to someone about the breaking point in your life but feel that you can't.

Some may not have a clue of what I am talking about and what this is all about. You're still so sure of yourself because you haven't gotten to the breaking point yet. You're still at the shouting point, the dancing point, still cutting off the ears of people. But someday, you're going to run into something where you don't do so well, and you might say, "This costs too much, it's too tough, it's too hard to be in the race, or to be in the ministry." Maybe if you keep on living, you're going to run into something you can't handle.

They beat Jesus to a pulp, and Peter was the guy who said he'd always be there. He wasn't there when Jesus needed him most. The guy who cut off another man's ear in Christ's time of need wasn't there this time. Our sin took Jesus to the cross. They hung Him high and stretched Him wide, and Peter was not there. The sun refused to shine, and the ground began to tremble. The veil in the temple was ripped from top to bottom, and Peter wasn't there. They brought His cold, dead body off the tree, wrapped Him in linen, and prepared Him for burial, and Peter was not there. The reason for that is you can't count on people when they're at the breaking point. They buried Him in a borrowed tomb, rolled the stone over it, and it looked like it was over. Yet, Peter, who was there for everything else wasn't connected like he should have been. It was the moment of Jesus' greatest struggle, and He couldn't depend on Peter.

What a shame it is when life catches you out of place, and you're not there because you're distracted by a crisis of your own. This message is about two words: "And Peter." When Jesus rose from the dead and three women came to the tomb looking for Him, the angel spoke and said: *"Go tell the disciples – And Peter – to meet me in Galilee."* Can you imagine how Peter must have felt at that moment after he messed up and blew everything? He was embarrassed, had disgraced his ministry, and had fallen short of his convictions. Peter must have said, "Oh no, He doesn't want me. He saw me deny Him. He saw me mess up and go back. He saw me blow it." "No Peter, you're wrong. He wants you. He didn't ask for Bartholomew by name, He didn't ask for Matthew by name, but He specifically said And Peter. The Lord still wants you!"

Jesus died thinking about Peter, and when He rose again on the third day, He rose up thinking about Peter. You can't sink so low that God forgets the promise that He made with your life. As soon as He got up out of the grave, He told the angel, "Go tell Peter to meet me in Galilee." Is there anyone reading this book who's been like Peter? You've been through hellish trials. When The Lord got done giving instructions, He ascended on a cloud back into the Heavens. But before He left, at some point, there had to be a discussion because there was going to be a revival ten days later in Jerusalem. It was the first meeting of the New Testament church, and they had to decide who was going to preach in the meeting. It wasn't Matthew, Luke, or John, but none other than Peter. The Lord said, "I want you to preach My message."

God can't use people who haven't been broken. That's what earned Peter the right to preach with power on the day of Pentecost when the church was birthed.

It was not all the things he had done before the breaking, but it's something about the breaking itself that gives you the power to stand up and preach. He not only preached a bold message, but he preached it to the same people that he had denied Jesus. He went back with the power of Pentecost, filled with the Spirit, and said, "Let the House of Israel know assuredly that the same Jesus, whom you have crucified, has been made Lord and Christ."

Some of you can live your safe little lives, or you can go through hellfire and come out and get a handwritten invitation from God Himself because you withstood the breaking point. The Lord had me write this to encourage several people who are at their breaking point and who've not lived up to their ideals and principles. You think it's all over, but the Lord said to tell the disciples, and Peter.

Bishop Jakes thought several times over the last thirty-some years of preaching the Gospel that he would die or wouldn't make it. He failed, got tired, got frustrated, got mad, quit, and resigned. It's hard to resign though, when you really love Him, even if you're not hanging close but find yourself hanging back. He came back from the grave to preach! You can survive the breaking point.

Sometimes, he broke because they didn't have food to eat, sometimes they didn't have anyone to preach to, and sometimes because he thought they were going to lose everything they had. The lights and water were turned off, and people were threatening to take the church. Sometimes, he broke because he trusted people who betrayed him or because he betrayed himself, disappointed himself, and broke his own promises. Sometimes, he broke because he thought God should've picked someone else.

But the angel said, "Go tell the disciples and Peter." I'm calling people who've quit, messed up so bad that you thought it was over, you thought that nobody would want you now, and God nor anyone will ever use you now. Maybe you messed up your marriage, messed up your children, or your job. I want to call Jonah out of the belly of the fish and the prodigal son out of the hog pen. I want to be the angel who tells Peter that God still wants you. Maybe you've verbally denied the Lord, but deep down in your heart, you're homesick for Him. You don't feel qualified, but you know that He's called you. It is time for you to come home. Get so hungry for God that you call out for Him to restore you.

It is possible for people to initially sound hungry for God, but they aren't hungry enough to repent and obey Him. I am not talking about hungry talk. I am talking about actual spiritual hunger and thirst until you are filled and changed.

In the Bible, we have the story of the rich young ruler.

DESPERATE HUNGER GETS GOD'S ATTENTION

> And a certain ruler asked him, saying, Good Master, what shall I do to inherit eternal life?
> And Jesus said unto him, Why callest thou me good? none is good, save one, that is, God.
> Thou knowest the commandments, Do not commit adultery, Do not kill, Do not steal, Do not bear false witness, Honour thy father and thy mother.
> And he said, All these have I kept from my youth up.
> Now when Jesus heard these things, he said unto him, Yet lackest thou one thing: sell all that thou hast, and distribute unto the poor, and thou shalt have treasure in heaven: and come, follow me.
> And when he heard this, he was very sorrowful: for he was very rich.
> And when Jesus saw that he was very sorrowful, he said, How hardly shall they that have riches enter into the kingdom of God!
> For it is easier for a camel to go through a needle's eye, than for a rich man to enter into the kingdom of God.
>
> LUKE 18:18-25

This story starts out promising. It was an evangelist's dream to have someone approach him or her, asking what they must do to have eternal life. Most would say, "You don't have to do anything. God loves you just the way you are." Yes, He does, but He also loves you too much to leave you like you are. He sounded hungry and made a few inquiries. But he was not hungry. True hunger is followed by action. It is always displayed.

Jesus looked into his heart, and by Word of knowledge, He knew that the man would not commit. He could see what was blocking it. In his case, it was his love of money.

> For the love of money is the root of all evil: which while some coveted after, they have erred from the faith, and pierced themselves through with many sorrows.
>
> 1 TIMOTHY 6:10

Money is not the problem, but the love of it is. God will have no other gods or idols before him. Many people's wallets and purses are their gods. How I wish we could get people to see that when you fall in love with Jesus and put Him first, He will withhold no good thing from you. He wants to bless us and prosper us. He will get it to us if He can get it through us. He is not after our money; He is after our hearts. But, many times, money is wrapped around hearts, and hearts are wrapped around money. We will never know what God had in store for this man because the man refused to surrender.

Jesus asked the man to sell everything, give to the poor, and come follow Him. The Bible says that He was very sorrowful, for He was rich. His riches kept him from receiving eternal life. His riches kept him out of Heaven. His riches caused him to reject Christ. They also kept him from knowing how much God would have blessed him if only he had been obedient.

The Bible says he walked away sad. There was no reason for that. It was his own decision that caused him to go into depression. We read earlier that Zacchaeus received Jesus with joy and couldn't wait to give. It was his own idea to give. I find it interesting that they both were rich, they both seemed hungry at first, they both inquired of Jesus, and yet their responses and decisions were opposite of each other.

Hunger has to take you past surface curiosity. God demands our total commitment. Little hunger seems to have the same results as no hunger. It doesn't count at all and will cause you to lose out on everything with God, including eternity. Revelation says it another way.

> I know thy works, that thou art neither cold nor hot: I would thou wert cold or hot.
> So then because thou art lukewarm, and neither cold nor hot, I will spue thee out of my mouth.
> Because thou sayest, I am rich, and increased with goods, and have need of nothing; and knowest not that thou art wretched, and miserable, and poor, and blind, and naked:
> I counsel thee to buy of me gold tried in the fire, that thou mayest be rich; and white raiment, that thou mayest be clothed, and that the shame of thy nakedness do not appear; and anoint thine eyes with eyesalve, that thou mayest see.
> As many as I love, I rebuke and chasten: be zealous therefore, and repent.
>
> REVELATION 3:15-19

Being neither cold nor hot makes a person lukewarm, and God says He will spew us out of His mouth. That sounds like we will be vomited out of His mouth. I don't want to be close to any condition that gives God the flu. I find it interesting that this passage has also to do with money. We should never make money our god, nor be smug and think that because we are doing well financially, we don't have to be dependent on God. He is the one who blesses, and it could all blow away when you are not serving Him. You cannot only be hungry in pretense or words. Your hunger must be followed by action.

FOUR

HUNGER THROUGHOUT CHURCH HISTORY

A revivalist is a person who has been touched and changed by revival, he or she carries revival, and then is able to transmit revival. A revivalist knows that the presence of God is what transforms lives and cultures. The people who carried revival in the last few centuries all had very different preaching styles and backgrounds, and some were from different countries. Yet, all of the great revivalists had one common denominator: they were spiritually hungry and thirsty.

Revivals bring about a renewing and empowering work of the Holy Spirit that results in a deeper awareness of who God is. He becomes very personal to people, and they have a more intimate relationship with Him. Revivalists conduct revival meetings where the presence of God is manifested in a powerful way. The revival can last for days, weeks, months, or even years on some occasions.

John Wesley is one of my favorite revivalists. He was a traveling preacher and founder of the Methodist Church. Before his conversion in 1735, he traveled from England to the United States. A terrible storm rose up, and Wesley feared for his life. He noticed that the group of German Moravians were not afraid at all. Later, he asked the Moravian leader about his peace. The Moravian asked Wesley if he had faith in Christ.

Wesley began to do some soul-searching and became hungry to find answers. His father was an Anglican priest, and his mother, Susanna, taught the Bible to her nineteen children. He attended Oxford and was ordained into the Anglican ministry. At Oxford, he joined a society (founded by his brother Charles) whose members took vows to lead holy lives, take Communion once a week, pray daily, and visit prisons regularly. They also spent three hours every afternoon studying the Bible.

Yet, after speaking with another Moravian, Wesley realized that he lacked saving faith. On May 24, 1738, he was born again. That experience changed everything. "I trusted in Christ alone for salvation, and an assurance was given me that He had taken away my sins." His hunger increased for the things of God.

After his conversion, his primary focus was on the doctrine of salvation and the relationship between grace, faith, and holiness. Wesley had a great hunger for God and His holiness and did not believe that you could separate the two. He was right! We need that revelation to come back into the church today. He saw in the Bible that "without holiness no one can see the Lord" (Hebrews 12:14).

Wesley was so hungry for God that he developed nine distinct points while in pursuit of holiness: We don't necessarily have to do these things religiously, but you can see his hunger here.

1. an intention to yield one's life to God completely, for God's glory, and become like Jesus Christ
2. rising at 4 or 5 a.m. to pray
3. fasting two days a week until 3 p.m.
4. meeting regularly to discuss Scripture and other Christian texts
5. accountability at those regular meetings
6. weekly reception of the Eucharist
7. reading and meditating on Scripture daily
8. acting in compassion for the poor, prisoners, and the elderly
9. pursuing simple living.

DESPERATE HUNGER GETS GOD'S ATTENTION

John Wesley was radical. Spiritually hungry people are radical about the things of God. That characteristic accompanies spiritual hunger. When we get as spiritually hungry as John Wesley, we will make adjustments in our lives that will change our priorities. Paul writes:

> I beseech you therefore, brethren, by the mercies of God,
>   that ye present your bodies a living sacrifice, holy, acceptable unto God, which is your reasonable service.
> And be not conformed to this world: but be ye transformed
>   by the renewing of your mind, that ye may prove what is that good, and acceptable, and perfect, will of God.
>
> ROMANS 12:1-2

Next, I want you to see the hunger of Jonathan Edwards. He was born in 1703, a little over seventy years after the first Puritan settlement of New England. He is considered to be the greatest theologian of British American Puritanism. He started the Great Awakening in 1734. He conducted a great revival in Northampton and along the Connecticut River Valley. Those revivals continued to bring our country together.

Edwards grew up in a Puritan household and was ordained to the ministry in 1727. He studied thirteen hours a day. He entered Yale College at the age of thirteen. He experienced a spiritual crisis that led to what he later described as "religious joy." Notice that this was many years before this present-day move of The Holy Spirit. Spiritual joy is a God-thing and a Bible thing. Jonathan Edwards believed that such an intense spiritual experience was a part of salvation. It was his spiritual hunger that caused him to be unsatisfied with religion. He pressed in until he had an experience with God.

Edwards said that during the Great Awakening, "It was a very frequent thing to see a house full of outcries, faintings, convulsions, and such like, both with distress and also with admiration and joy." Because God became real to him, he was able to make God real to the people.

Edwards would not allow people who did not profess Christ as Savior to participate in the communion. Because of that, the congregation voted Edwards out of his pastorate, which he had held for twenty-two years. He was a man who refused to compromise.

He was a man hungry after God. That hunger resulted in multitudes being born again in The Great Awakening. It also resulted in thirteen disjointed colonies coming together to unite and become The United States of America. Do not disdain spiritual hunger. God will use it to bring about a nation-shaking revival.

The next revivalist whom I want to talk about is another one who was used in the Great Awakening. George Whitefield was an Anglican evangelist and one of the greatest preachers in the history of Christianity.

In 1740, Whitefield traveled to North America from England, where he preached a series of revivals that became part of the "Great Awakening." His methods were controversial (as the methods of many evangelists are today).

Whitefield preached at least 18,000 times to perhaps 10 million listeners in Great Britain and the American colonies. He was gifted to keep the attention of his listeners. His preaching brought about a strong emotion in his people.

Before his conversion, he tried good works to be saved. He was so spiritually hungry that the need for salvation pressed upon him. He spent entire nights groaning and praying to be saved. He gave up anything that he thought could be preventing salvation. However, the revelation finally came to him that he was to trust in Jesus alone for the forgiveness of his sins. When he did, he was born again in an instant. He had a total transformation as he was saturated with the presence of The Holy Spirit. George was saved, and he knew that he was saved. He was ecstatic with joy.

We keep seeing joy with the revivalists of yesterday as well as the present. Later, Whitefield wrote: "I know the place... Whenever I go to Oxford I cannot help running to that place where Jesus Christ first revealed Himself to me and gave me the new birth."

DESPERATE HUNGER GETS GOD'S ATTENTION

The Church of England did not assign him a church, but spiritually hungry people will find a place to preach. He began preaching in parks and fields in England, reaching out to people who normally did not attend church. In 1738, he went to the American colonies, specifically Savannah, Georgia. He put up no posters, had no speakers or microphones, and no organization behind him. There were no ushers, counselors, musicians, or singers, and there was no platform. He simply showed up one day with a friend and went around to some of the houses, inviting people to come and hear the Gospel. Taking his stand on a hill, he raised his booming voice as he declared, *"Blessed are the poor in spirit, for they shall see the kingdom of God."* He immediately caught the attention of anyone standing nearby. Whitefield's voice and preaching pulled people in. Around two hundred gathered to hear the twenty-four-year-old preach to them about Jesus and the new birth.

Whitefield preached about man's sin, God's love, Heaven, Hell, and Christ's redeeming sacrifice. Many cried. By the time he returned, word had spread about the amazing young preacher. Instead of 200, he now preached to 2,000. Rough and tough coal miners received Christ as their Savior.

He began preaching outdoors and eventually went to London and preached to huge crowds there. The crowds increased, and before long, he was preaching to audiences of tens of thousands. With only his natural voice, everyone could hear him.

Benjamin Franklin heard of Whitefield preaching to enormous crowds in England and became curious to hear him. When Whitefield preached in Philadelphia, Franklin was determined to discover if it was even possible for Whitefield to be heard by such large numbers of people. Franklin started at the front and continued to walk as he measured his steps. He wanted to see how far he could go before he could no longer hear. At the end of his walk and measurements, Franklin determined that Whitefield could be heard and understood by at least thirty thousand people!

Whitefield preached day after day, sometimes as much as three or four sermons a day. That eventually took a huge physical toll on him. Often, he would throw up blood after preaching. Nevertheless, a hungry person won't quit, even when facing physical symptoms. Multitudes came to Jesus, churches were strengthened, and communities were transformed.

Whitefield returned to America. The "Colonies" were a series of towns and villages running up and down the East Coast. Whitefield didn't live to see America declare its independence from England, but he helped bring it to pass.

He went to the major cities, small towns, and villages. He became a celebrity in the colonies. In Philadelphia, almost the entire city came to hear him preach. He preached to a crowd of nearly twenty thousand people, the largest gathering of people America had ever seen up to that time.

There were nearly always tears in his meetings. People weren't used to that. A spiritually hungry person is passionate about the things of God, and their passion ignites others. That passion stirs emotion in the people who are listening. That is not manipulation. It is produced through a person who hungers for God. Whitefield was a highly anointed and yet tender man. He almost never was able to get through a sermon without breaking into tears because of his love for Christ and for man. When Whitefield cried, the audience followed him. His enemies mocked him for his tears, but Whitefield replied, "Since you will not weep for your own souls, I must weep for you." He was hungry for God.

Many thousands of people were born again, and hundreds became ministers of the Gospel. He knew how to welcome the presence of the Holy Spirit. The fires of revival that sprang up during his ministry continued after he graduated to Heaven.

George Whitefield played a large part in this country becoming one nation under God and maintaining Christian principles for many years. We owe him a great debt. George Whitefield's preaching brought about a Great Awakening that united our colonies and helped birth the United States of America. Hunger will shake nations.

DESPERATE HUNGER GETS GOD'S ATTENTION

Whitefield preached in homes, churches, and the outdoors. During his prime, he was preaching between forty and sixty hours a week. He had no hobbies. Hunger causes a person's focus to narrow. From morning until night, he was working in ministry.

Throughout his life, he faced enemies, as do all revivalists. His hunger for God caused him to rise above their criticism. Often, his enemies were other preachers who fought him with words, pamphlets, and sermons. While he preached, people threw things at him: sometimes tomatoes, dead cats, feces, or rocks.

By his mid-forties, Whitfield wore himself out. His constant travel, the thousands of sermons preached at the top of his voice, and a heart condition he had since his twenties caused him to age prematurely. By the time he was in his fifties, he looked like an old man. He was often so weak that he was forced to stop all activity and lie in bed. Yet after a few days or a few weeks, he would feel better and resume his preaching and traveling schedule until the next episode brought him close to death.

Jonathan Edwards died at the premature age of fifty-five. He was in America doing what he loved: preaching the Gospel. John Pollock describes his last sermon:

> "The words came hoarse and sluggish at first, the sentences disjointed as if his brain refused to focus. His mind suddenly kindled and his voice rose and he thundered in tones that reached the edge of the immense crowd: 'Works? Works? A man get to Heaven by works? I would as soon think of climbing to the moon on a rope of sand!' After that, any weakness seemed engulfed in a mighty power that swept him into an unforgettable sermon in which he proclaimed, once again the glories of Christ.
> "He went on preaching for two hours, and some who had heard him several times declared it was his best sermon ever. Toward the end, Whitefield declared, 'I go to a rest prepared. My sun has arisen and by the aid of Heaven has given light to many. It is now about to

set.' Whitefield was dying and he knew it, but he had preached as well as he ever had.

"At the end of the sermon, the weakness returned and he had to be helped off the platform. At 6:00 a.m. on Sunday morning George Whitefield saw His Lord. He died on September 30, 1770. This was just six years before America gained her independence."

Due to the spiritual hunger of this passionate preacher, our colonies were united and thousands saved. Hunger pays off.

Whitefield loved Jesus Christ and could not get enough of Him. He never tired of proclaiming the Gospel. He realized that his calling was a noble one and that he enjoyed the privilege of inviting men, women, and children to come to Jesus and receive the gift of eternal life. I, too, am thankful for that awesome privilege. I am also thankful that hungry and anointed men of God have paved the way for many of us.

On one of my revival campaigns in Norway, a good friend asked me if I had ever heard of a Norwegian evangelist by the name of Hans Nielsen Hauge. I had not, but I decided to look up my own information about him. This man was born in 1771 and died in 1824. He and his followers led the country of Norway to independence from Denmark. His speaking and writing influenced the whole country.

Hauge had very humble beginnings, as did most revivalists. He was a farmer's son from southern Norway. On April 5, 1796, at the age of twenty-five, he experienced his spiritual breakthrough while he was out plowing on his father's farm when Heaven's glory came down. He considered himself to be a Christian, had been baptized and confirmed, and read the Bible daily. One day, while working under the open sky, he was singing a hymn when God met him there. This experience became the anchor for Hauge's calling and faith. He grieved over sin, had compassion for people to be saved, and exhorted them to repent. God told him, "You shall confess My name before the people, to turn from the darkness into the Light." He was given a divine commission to show people to Jesus. When he came home from the fields that April evening, his countenance was changed.

He said, "The first people I spoke to were my siblings. All seven of them received what I had." During the first three weeks after his call, he had no desire to eat or drink, and he barely slept. He spent his time reading the Bible. That is an example of spiritual hunger and thirst. He was hungrier for God than for his natural food. He was compelled to bring all people to a living experience of Jesus Christ. In the course of two months, a revival was underway.

He put his message into print. In the next four years, Hauge produced several books, one after another. He became Norway's most-read author. It is estimated that at least 100,000 people read his books. In the famine year of 1809, he produced seventeen books and was the country's most well-read author. He founded Norway's oldest publishing firm, which I have had the privilege of visiting.

In the course of eight years, he traveled throughout most of Norway. Hauge often held four meetings a day. During the eight years that he preached, he covered about 10,000 miles, mostly on foot, and became the first great spokesman to arise from the common people.

God gave Hauge great wisdom when it came to industry and innovative ways to help Norway prosper. These were days long before we heard of "prosperity preachers." Yet, it is obvious that God wanted to prosper His people. Hauge walked up and down the country, knowing where a spinning mill should be. He started a series of businesses, including corn shipping, a paper factory, brickworks, a printer shop, a newspaper mill, salt works, and spinning factories. I can see that he realized the need for Kingdom businessmen before we heard the term today.

Norway had been in an economic depression until he came on the scene. He was led by God to start businesses, and the economy of Norway flourished. The revival was not only spiritual but also in the economic, social, and political arenas. True revival will affect all of these areas. The Haugians became the first people's movement in Norway. They later led Norway to her independence from Denmark.

However, it was against the law at that time for anyone to preach who was not an ordained Lutheran priest. Hauge was imprisoned time and again, and then Norway slumped back into depression. The authorities of the land recognized that he was needed for prosperity and pulled him out of prison temporarily to bring the country out of economic depression.

Spiritual hunger enabled him to withstand persecution. Some people tried to convince him to return to what they deemed "normal" life. He said, "Most of them mocked me." He experienced strong resistance. He was arrested many times and underwent many trials and struggles in prison.

One of the most interesting stories about Hauge's experiences in prison and his uncompromising stand for God is one about a notorious prostitute. She was brought into the prison to tempt him. He looked her in the eyes and spoke a few words to her, at which she burst into tears over her sins. She was seen and heard running out of his cell with tears running down her face, shouting, "I've just met the Savior. My sins are forgiven."

Another time, the jailor sent a group of youths into the jailhouse with a fiddler so they all could dance. The sheriff's wife took Hauge by the hand and asked him to dance. He replied, "Yes, he would dance." Then he began to lead the singing of a hymn. He said that the sheriff's wife let go of his hand and the dance stopped.

From the day of his vision, he spent more days in prison than he did free.

He was arrested eleven times. His last imprisonment lasted ten years.

His writings were confiscated and banned, he was sent to the cellar reserved for drunks, and he was put in solitary confinement. He described it to be a terrible room with a dirt floor. It had so much water seepage that prisoners had drowned there. This was the limit of his world for many years. That last prison sentence broke his health.

Just before Hauge died, he became weak and bedridden. However, when other spiritually hungry and thirsty people came to visit, he would rally, get out of bed, go out to the living room, and preach with a strong voice. What enabled him to do that? Spiritual hunger. As soon as he finished, his voice would become weak again, and he returned to bed. He died at almost fifty-three years of age.

Another example of spiritual hunger bringing about revival is the Hebrides Islands Revival of 1949-1952. The revival was an answer to the prayers of several hungry people. God used Evangelist Duncan Campbell, who came to conduct a two-week evangelistic campaign and ended up staying for two years.

Two elderly women, Peggy and Christine Smith, lived in a small cottage in the village of Barvas. They were both in their eighties. Peggy was blind, and her sister was crippled with arthritis. Because they were unable to attend church, their cottage became the place where they met with God. They became burdened when they heard of the lack of spiritual hunger in the church they used to attend, so they decided to pray twice a week. They prayed from ten in the evening until four in the morning.

Peggy had a vision of the church crowded with young people. They persuaded their minister to call "a session." Seven men covenanted "not to give rest nor peace to the Almighty until He made their Jerusalem a praise in the earth." They met on Tuesday and Friday nights for several months because they were hungry for God.

One night, as they waited upon God, a deacon read part of the twenty-fourth Psalm: *"Who shall ascend into the hill of the Lord? Or who shall stand in His holy place? He that hath clean hands and a pure heart; who hath not lifted up his soul unto vanity, nor sworn deceitfully. He shall receive the blessing from the Lord."* The deacon lifted his hands toward Heaven and cried: "Oh God, are my hands clean? Is my heart pure?" He got no further but fell prostrate on the floor.

Spiritually hungry people do not put on pretenses, but they allow God to burn pride out of them. As they humble themselves before God, confess sin, and repent, God moves. Many times, it is not just the praying that ignites revival, but the repentance that follows the praying. The glory of

God filled the barn. God promised them: "I will pour water upon him that is thirsty and floods upon the dry ground," so they reminded God of His promise day and night in prayer.

Peggy asked Duncan Campbell to come to their small village to hold a meeting. The people of this village did not favor the revival and had already made it clear. Duncan explained to Peggy that he didn't think he should come. "I have no leadings to go to that place." She said, "Mr. Campbell, if you were living as near to God as you ought to be, He would reveal His secrets to you also." Her intimacy with The Holy Spirit brought about great boldness.

Duncan accepted the rebuke as from the Lord and asked if he could pray with them. She agreed, and they prayed together. Peggy prayed: "Lord, You remember what You told me this morning, that in this village, You are going to save seven men who will become pillars in the church of my fathers. Lord, I have given Your message to Mr. Campbell, and it seems he is not prepared to receive it. Oh Lord, give him wisdom because he badly needs it!"

"All right, Peggy, I'll go to the village," said Duncan. When they arrived, they found a large crowd, with many assembled outside. When Duncan finished preaching, a number of people were mourning over their sins, including the seven men God promised would be saved.

On December 13, 1949, at the end of the meeting, all had left except Campbell and one other. The deacon said, "Don't be discouraged. God is hovering over us, and He'll break through any moment. I can already hear the rumbling of Heaven's chariot wheels." He began to pray before falling to the ground in a trance.

Later, the house shook as wave after wave of divine power swept through the building. Duncan's mind, however, was in the fourth chapter of Acts, where the early Christians were gathered in prayer and we read: *"When they had prayed the place was shaken where they were assembled together; and they were all filled with the Holy Ghost."* These things still happen today.

DESPERATE HUNGER GETS GOD'S ATTENTION

Rev. Duncan was assisting at a Communion service; the atmosphere was heavy and with the Spirit of God. The church resembled a battlefield. On one side, many were prostrated over the seats weeping and sighing. God had come!

Sometime later, six or seven hundred people gathered around the church at 11:00 p.m. They'd been moved by a power they could not explain. A hunger and thirst gripped them, and the meeting continued until four in the morning. Strong men trembled in God's presence. Nearby, a dance was in progress, but the young people ran from it and ran to the church.

Others who had gone to bed were woken by the Holy Spirit, got dressed, and ran to the church. There had been no publicity except for an announcement from the pulpit on Sunday that a man would be conducting a series of meetings in the parish for ten days. Today, we seem to rely on social media, but when God moves mightily, they will come.

Over the next few nights, hundreds gathered in different places such as churches, barns, fields, and homes. There was a prayer meeting every day at noon, and those converted the night before were expected to attend. All work stopped for two hours as people gathered for prayer. An awareness of God gripped the whole community. Little work was done as men and women only thought about eternal things, and God seemed to be everywhere.

The revival continued for several years and spread to many of the islands. People who had never been near a meeting before were suddenly arrested by the Spirit of God. They stopped work and began to seek God. Men were found walking the roads at night in distress of soul. Social evil and crime ended. Districts were completely changed. The entire place was filled with the presence of God.

We see these things happening in Tampa, Florida. I am part of The River at Tampa Bay Church with Pastors Rodney and Adonica Howard-Browne. The crime rate has been reduced drastically in the city, and the sheriff of the county has testified to that fact. The Howard-Brownes have been given awards from the city council for their great service to the community. Revival affects the entire area.

When people get hungry for God, they will pray. Once the revival started, people prayed everywhere and all the time. However, it does not stop there. They get up and obey God.

When people get hungry, they have an awareness of the presence of God.

Some men were walking home from a meeting in the early hours of the morning. They stopped and looked back, and without saying a word, they removed their caps and stood in the darkness while one of them said softly, "Brothers, God is everywhere."

When people get hungry, God comes on the scene with an Intensity. There was an awareness of the holiness of God that was overwhelming. There was also a prevalent conviction of sin. People were broken over their sins. Some were under such conviction that they writhed in agony.

When people get hungry, God leads them into the Word of God. It becomes a primary emphasis. Without it, people do not stay strong and faithful. With spiritual hunger and true revival, there is a return to anointed preaching. Duncan Campbell preached with tremendous authority and boldness. His preaching was personal, passionate, and powerful.

Where there is great hunger, there is also great joy. Everywhere, people rejoiced at what God had done for them. Young people sang on their way home, on the road. Many new hymns were written. When people finally get hungry, it brings about love and unity with no age gap. There were no children's meetings. Young and elderly people came to the Lord. It was as if the old became young.

Once people get hungry, there is timelessness. There will be no time in Heaven. The Spirit took away tiredness. People arrived home from meetings at 3, 4, or 5 a.m. and had to get up at 7 to go to work. They testified that they were not tired. Sometimes, they would have no sleep at all but would feel no after-effects. The sense of time seemed to vanish. I have noticed that when revival is really burning, people today lose the sense of time, as well. Time has become a god to people of the Western world. When we lose our sense of time and wait on Him, He shows up.

When people get hungry, and there is a revival that follows, we see the faithfulness of converts. After two and a half years, there was little backsliding. When people get hungry for God, manifestations of The Holy Spirit follow, such as people falling into a trance. In the Hebrides Revival, a house shook as if in an earthquake. At times, people reported hearing heavenly music.

Where there is hunger and revival, we will find opposition. No one gets a free ride. Much of the opposition to this revival was from the leaders. It was the same in Jesus' day, and it still is today. Hungry people learn to rise above the opposition.

If we get hungry enough, we will not be dependent on outside things to promote the revival. When revival came to The Hebrides in 1949, the churches had no choirs, organs, musical instruments, or padded seats. There were no meetings for children and young people and no power points. But God performed miracles and brought thousands to Himself. There was hunger and prayer. Then came anointed preaching. That was it. God did the rest.

The price for Heaven-sent revival has never changed. People have to get hungry enough to pray, to allow God to have His mighty way with them, and then for a preacher to get enough fire to transmit that fire and anointing and transform the region.

Charles Finney (1792–1875) was an American Presbyterian minister and leader in the Second Great Awakening in the United States. He was a twenty-nine-year-old lawyer who decided that he must settle the question of his soul's salvation. In those days, in the United States, The Bible was used as a textbook in law schools. He read enough for The Bible to bring conviction of sin to his heart. On October 10, 1821, he headed out into the woods near his Adams, New York, home to find God. "I will give my heart to God, or I never will come down from there," he said. That is spiritual hunger in demonstration. He experienced such emotion that he questioned those who could not testify to a similar encounter. "The Holy Spirit ... seemed to go through me, body and soul. I could feel the impression, like a wave of electricity, going through and through me. Indeed, it seemed to come in waves of liquid love."

Charles G. Finney was one of the greatest evangelists and theologians since the days of the apostles. It is estimated that five hundred thousand persons professed conversion to Christ in his meetings.

Over eighty-five percent of people professing Christ in Finney's meetings remained true to God. Finney had the ability to help people understand the necessity of holy living in such a way that they had lasting results. At Gouverneur, New York, not a dance or theatrical play could be held in the place for six years after Finney held meetings there. No one was interested anymore.

In one meeting, Finney urged all who were willing to accept Christ to rise to their feet and all who were willing to reject him to remain in their seats. This was very unusual in those days and made the people so angry that they were almost ready to mob him. The next day, he spent the day in fasting and prayer, and that evening he preached with such unction and power that a great conviction of sin swept over the people. All night long, they were sending for him to come and pray with them. Even hardened atheists were brought to Christ.

He continued to preach the Gospel with increasing power. Sometimes, the power of God was so manifested in his meetings that almost the entire audience fell on their knees in prayer. Sinners were often brought under conviction of sin as soon as they entered the city where he was preaching.

People were often brought under conviction just by looking at him. In Utica, New York, he visited a large factory to look at the machinery. As Finney walked into the Cotton Mill, a young lady employee, who had been opposed to his meetings, saw him. Looking at her co-employee, she began to laugh. Charles Finney simply looked at this young lady without saying a word. As he kept looking at her, the lady stopped working. The Spirit of God mightily convicted her of her sin, and she began to weep. Soon, her

DESPERATE HUNGER GETS GOD'S ATTENTION

companions were convicted and began to weep. Hundreds began to be overcome. The factory boss said, "Stop the mill and let the people attend to religion, for it is far more important that our souls be saved than the factory run." Finney said, "...a more powerful meeting I scarcely ever attended." Within a few days, nearly every employee was saved.

At a country place named Sodom in the state of New York, Finney gave one address in which he described the condition of Sodom before God destroyed it. "I had not spoken more than a quarter of an hour," says he, "when an awful solemnity seemed to settle upon them; the congregation began to fall from their seats in every direction, and cried for mercy. If I had had a sword in each hand, I could not have cut them down as fast as they fell. Nearly the whole congregation were neither on their knees or prostrate, I should think, in less than two minutes from the first shock that fell upon them. Everyone prayed who was able to speak at all." In Finney's meetings, people thought they were in Hell. Similar scenes were witnessed in many other places.

In Rochester, New York, in 1830, over ten thousand people were converted, and the bars were closed! Before he arrived, wickedness was everywhere, and dance halls flourished.

Finney believed, as do I, that revival was something that would come anywhere where certain conditions were met. He would say: "A revival can be expected when Christians have a spirit of prayer for revival. Revival can be secured from Heaven when heroic souls enter the conflict determined to win or die—or if need be—win and die! Revival is a renewed conviction of sin and repentance, followed by an intense desire to live in obedience to God. It is giving up one's will to God in deep humility." Spiritual hunger brings that about.

This revival was characterized by unusual signs and wonders. Horses bucked people off in front of the church. Most bars closed down during the revival, but the ones that stayed open witnessed some interesting things. The elbows of big men locked on the bar counter when they tried to bring their mugs to their mouths. They ended up pouring the alcohol behind them instead of being able to drink it.

That great revival started from one man's hunger and desperation. He pressed in through prayer, surrendered to The Lord, and flowed in The Holy Ghost. What can God do through you? The same Holy Spirit power in the life of Charles Finney is available to you and me.

Another powerful revivalist, John Alexander Dowie (1847–1907), was a Scottish-Australian minister known as an evangelist of faith who operated in a great healing ministry. He was born again at the age of seven. He experienced healing for himself. This led to his faith in healing and to the foundation of his International Divine Healing Association.

His family emigrated to Australia when he was thirteen; there he attended seminary. He began his career as a minister in Australia. He served as a pastor of a Congregational Church outside of Sydney, Australia. A plague swept through the land, and he buried nearly forty members of his church in just a few weeks. He asked, "Where, oh where was He who used to heal His suffering children?" This was the prayer of a pastor who was crushed by the suffering of his flock. He said, "There I sat (after visiting the sick) with sorrow-bowed head for my people until the bitter tears came to relieve my burning heart." This caused Dowie to seek God. Then, Acts 10:38 came to his mind by the Holy Spirit. *"How God anointed Jesus of Nazareth with the Holy Ghost and with power: who went about doing good, and healing all that were oppressed of the devil; for God was with him."* God gave him a revelation of this verse. The rest is history. He never buried another congregation member from the plague, and his healing ministry was born.

Dowie emigrated with his family to the United States in 1888. He moved to Chicago and bought land north of the city, and founded Zion, Illinois. Many other great healing ministries were birthed out of his ministry.

Notice that Dowie had to get hungry enough to obtain answers from God. He refused to quit or get discouraged. He pressed in until the plague was stayed from his congregation and thousands healed.

I want to include one of the greatest women pioneers in ministry, Mariah Woodsworth-Etter (1844–1924). In an hour when women couldn't even vote, she preached and started many churches. She also endured much heartache in her lifetime. However, she never felt sorry for herself, and she never quit. She was too hungry for God to allow the word "quit" to come into her vocabulary.

She was called the "Mother of Pentecost" because of her dynamic Holy Ghost ministry, yet she pre-dated the Pentecostal outpouring by twenty years.

Soon after her call to preach, she began to see many people born again and signs and wonders following her ministry. Those signs and wonders continued over fifty years.

Maria's early life was plagued with tragedies. Her dad was an alcoholic who often abandoned his family to binge drink, leaving them with no money for food or clothing. When Maria was eleven, her father died of severe sunstroke. There were eight children. Her widowed mother had no way of providing for her children, so the eldest daughters (including Maria) were sent out to work. Maria longed for an education, and now that dream was made impossible.

She continued to study and read at home whenever she could, but in her adult years, her education certainly was not as complete as that of the typical preacher during her day. However, she did not allow that to stop her.

She married at sixteen but fought a continual battle with ill-health and endured a terrible marriage. She lost five of her six children to death, one after the other. Mariah promised God that if He would heal her, she would serve Him completely. She asked God for the same apostolic power He gave the disciples and was baptized in the Holy Spirit. She said, "It felt like liquid fire, and there were angels all around."

Her first husband openly harassed, abused, betrayed, and persecuted her. He publicly humiliated her at her meetings. She finally could take no more and divorced him. She said that her second husband was the greatest love of her life and a gift from God. However, she buried him before she died.

Mariah traveled from American coast to coast, blazing a trail for women in ministry. Her hunger for God caused her to overcome everything. Despite her personal struggles with hostile attitudes toward female preachers, she continued in ministry with great success. Her ministry brought dead churches back to life, salvation to thousands, and encouraged believers to seek a deeper walk with God.

Many of her converts saw visions of Heaven and Hell, and some collapsed on the floor as if they'd been shot or had died. Thousands were healed, and many received the baptism of the Holy Spirit.

In 1889, she purchased an 8,000-seat tent and set it up in Oakland, California. Mariah said about the meeting, "The Holy Ghost would fall on the people while we were preaching. Men and women fell all over the tent like trees in a storm; some would have visions of God. Most all of them came out shouting the praises of God."

She declared that "if nineteenth-century believers would meet God's conditions, as the one hundred twenty did on the Day of Pentecost, they would have the same results. A mighty revival would break out that would shake the world, and thousands of souls would be saved. Instead of looking back to Pentecost, let us always be expecting it to come, especially in these days." I agree with Mariah, and that is one of the reasons that you are reading this book. I am convinced that if we get hungry and desperate for God, we will see the greatest revival that has ever taken place in these last days.

Her books were read across the world. In 1918, she built the Etter Tabernacle as her home church base. In her closing years, she still ministered with a powerful anointing despite struggling with health issues. On occasion, she had to be carried to the podium and yet preached with extraordinary power. When she was finished, she had to be carried home. She died on September 16, 1924.

Mariah's revival meetings were characterized by people dancing, laughing with joy, crying, and shouting with ecstasy. Some, including Mariah herself, fell into trances that sometimes lasted several days.

DESPERATE HUNGER GETS GOD'S ATTENTION

Mariah loved to minister to the common people. She didn't concern herself with the opinions of her male colleagues. She concentrated on her own ministry because she hungered for more of God.

How could she have overcome losing children, divorce, another husband's death, preachers opposing her, and religious people criticizing her in a day when women couldn't even vote? The answer is once again the fact that she was hungrier for God and to fulfill His assignment on her life than feeling sorry for herself. We must have that kind of spiritual hunger once again today.

The Welsh Revival of 1904 will never be forgotten. The Spirit of God swept across the land like a mighty tornado. Churches were crowded, and meetings went on day and night. Hundreds came to Christ.

The revival emptied saloons, theaters, and dance halls. Everyone went to church instead. Almost every home felt the impact of the power of God. Newspapers carried the news of it. Conviction of sin gripped the people, and crime disappeared in many cities. Saloons and theaters were closed while stores were sold out of Bibles. Members of Parliament, busy attending Revival services, postponed their political meetings.

Revival is an answer to the spiritual hunger of men and women. It brings conviction, demonstrates God's glory and power, and closes down places of sin. It changes people's priorities and values.

This revival was led by the Welsh evangelist Evan Roberts. He was spiritually hungry even as a child. He attended church regularly and memorized Scripture. Roberts was known as a young man who spent many hours praying each week both personally and at group prayer meetings.

Meetings lasted many hours, and there was a sense of conviction of sin. Lifestyles were affected. The pubs went from full to empty. Prayer meetings gathered huge crowds. One of the stories told is of the pit ponies not understanding the miners' commands as their language was cleaned up.

Evan asked his roommate (and later brother-in-law) if he believed that God could then "give us 100,000 souls." Within a few months of 1904, this was the case.

Earlier, Evan heard another preacher talk about the *Baptism of the Spirit* and believed the message. In October of that year, he began speaking at a series of small meetings. He was soon attracting congregations numbering thousands. Within two weeks, the Welsh revival was national news, and Roberts, his brother Dan, and his friend Sidney Evans, began traveling the country conducting revival meetings.

It started with only seventeen people gathered at Moriah Chapel on October 31, 1904, when Evan Roberts preached. All present gave their lives to Christ. When these seventeen people came to Christ, Roberts knew that the revival he had been praying his whole life for had come. In less than six months, over 100,000 people were saved, and the entire nation was radically transformed. This later became known as the Welsh Revival and preceded the Azusa Street Revival. The revival was again the result of a young man's spiritual hunger.

Charles Fox Parham (1873–1929) was another Pentecostal American preacher and evangelist. Together with William J. Seymour, Parham was one of the two central figures in the early spread of Pentecostalism. Parham saw what the Bible said about The Baptism in The Holy Spirit and assigned his students at his Bible school to study the subject. He asked them to give the scriptural proof of what the evidence of being baptized in The Holy Spirit was.

Parham's mother died, and his father remarried the daughter of a Methodist circuit rider. She loved The Lord, and the Parhams opened their home for services. Parham developed a greater spiritual hunger at that time.

He began conducting his first church services at the age of fifteen. He joined the Methodists but later left the Methodist church. He complained that Methodist preachers "were not left to preach by direct inspiration."

Rejecting denominations, he established his own itinerant evangelistic ministry, which preached the ideas of the Holiness movement.

Sometime after the birth of his son, Claude, in September 1897, both Parham and Claude fell ill. After being healed, Parham renounced all medical help and committed to preaching divine healing. In 1898, Parham moved his headquarters to Topeka, Kansas. He established the Bethel Healing Home and published the Apostolic Faith magazine.

Parham took a sabbatical from his work at Topeka in 1900 and visited various movements. When he returned, those left in charge of his healing home had taken over, and rather than fighting for control, Parham started Bethel Bible College at Topeka. He invited "all ministers and Christians who were willing to forsake all, sell what they had, give it away, and enter the school for study and prayer." About forty people responded. The only textbook was the Bible, and the teacher was the Holy Spirit (with Parham as mouthpiece).

Prior to starting his Bible school, Parham heard of at least one individual who spoke in tongues and had reprinted the incident in his paper. By the end of 1900, Parham led his students at Bethel Bible School to searching for the Biblical evidence of the baptism of The Holy Spirit.

When classes were finished at the end of December, he asked his students to study the Bible to determine what evidence was present when the early church received the Holy Spirit. The students had several days of prayer and worship and held a New Year's Eve watch-night service at Bethel (December 31, 1900). The next evening (January 1, 1901), Agnes Ozman felt asked to be prayed for to receive the baptism in the Holy Spirit. Immediately after being prayed for, she began to speak in tongues.

The local press ridiculed Parham's Bible school, calling it "the Tower of Babel." Several African Americans were influenced by Parham's ministry in Houston, Texas, where he started another Bible school. One man was William J. Seymour. Both Parham and Seymour preached to Houston's African Americans, and Parham had planned to send Seymour out to preach to the black communities throughout Texas. For about a year, he had a following of several hundred people. The evangelist John G. Lake was influenced by him and followed him.

Seymour initially considered his work in Los Angeles under Parham's authority. However, Seymour soon broke with Parham over his harsh criticism of the emotional worship at Asuza Street and the intermingling of whites and blacks in the services.

His most important theological contributions were his beliefs about the baptism of The Holy Spirit. There were Christian groups speaking in tongues and teaching an experience of Spirit baptism before 1901. However, Parham was the first to identify tongues as the *Bible evidence* of Spirit baptism. It is not clear when he began to preach the need for such an experience, but it is clear that he did by 1900.

Parham taught the doctrine of initial evidence—that the baptism of the Holy Spirit is evidenced by speaking in tongues. It was this doctrine that made Pentecostalism distinct from other holiness Christian groups that spoke in tongues or believed in an experience subsequent to salvation and sanctification. In a move criticized by Parham, his Apostolic Faith Movement merged with other Pentecostal groups in 1914 to form the General Council of the Assemblies of God in the United States of America.

One man's hunger not only saw many come to Christ, receive the baptism in the Holy Spirit, and get healed. Who is waiting for you to get hungry?

William Joseph Seymour (1870–1922) was an African-American holiness preacher. He was one of the most influential men of God in revival and the Pentecostal movement. He is considered "the father of Pentecost and the leader of the famous Azusa Street Revival." Seymour was a very humble man. Whenever you find a hungry and humble person, you will find someone whom God will use greatly.

William Seymour was a waiter in a restaurant while he preached to a black church. He was a student of Charles Parham, and believed, like Parham, that speaking in tongues was the sign of receiving the baptism in the Holy Spirit. In 1906, Seymour moved to Los Angeles, California, where he preached the Pentecostal message and sparked the Azusa Street Revival. He published *The Apostolic Faith* newspaper. Seymour broke with Parham

DESPERATE HUNGER GETS GOD'S ATTENTION

in 1906 over theological differences as well as Parham's unhappiness with interracial revival meetings.

Seymour had to overcome many obstacles, as most of the revival leaders in church history had to do. He had only one eye because of smallpox. He lived in a day of segregation and great racial prejudice. His mother and father were freed slaves, and he grew up in terrible poverty. However, his hunger for God was greater than his circumstances.

Seymour went on a quest to find great men of God to study under. He moved several times in that quest. When hunger becomes greater than the need for temporary security, you will find what you are looking for. That hunger led him to Parham's Bible school in Houston, Texas. He was not allowed to come inside the classroom because of his color. Most would have become offended and would have given up on God, but he again humbled himself. He asked if they could leave the door ajar so that he could sit in the hall and still hear. What he heard stirred him greatly.

He knew God as Savior and the power of God to heal, but as he listened to Charles Parham, he became convinced of a bigger thing: the baptism of the Holy Ghost. He went on to Los Angeles without receiving it but said he was determined to preach all he knew of God. He said, "Before I met Parham, I had such a hunger to have more of God that I prayed for five hours a day for two and one-half years."

He said, "I went to Los Angeles, and when I got there, the hunger was not less but more." He prayed, "God, what can I do?" The Holy Spirit said, "Pray more." He said, "God, I am praying five hours a day now," but increased it to seven. He prayed for a year and one half for God to give him what Parham preached; fire with tongues, love, and the power of God like the apostles had.

When Seymour looked for a building to hold meetings in, all he could find was a livery stable. He and his congregation worked for weeks, cleaning up after many animals had resided there. It did not look promising, but God was about to reward him.

It is said that William Seymour would put his head in a chicken crate and wait for God to move because he didn't want to be seen. He only wanted God to be seen. God was seen in a great way on Azusa Street in Los Angeles, California. The miracles were beyond imagination. People who were missing body parts and limbs had parts grow out before the people's eyes.

Multitudes were born again and baptized in The Holy Ghost, with the evidence of speaking in other tongues. News reporters came to witness this. They said that it was just a bunch of people babbling and that they predicted it would be over in a couple of weeks. They were partially correct. It was all over the world in two weeks. One man's spiritual hunger sparked a worldwide revival that began many Pentecostal denominations. What can your spiritual hunger spark in this hour?

The evangelist John G. Lake said, "I do not believe that any other man in modern times had a more wonderful deluge of God in his life than God gave to that man." When he preached, men shook, trembled, and cried out to God. Seymour continued to pastor the Apostolic Faith Mission that he founded until his death.

The story of John G. Lake is one of incredible displays of God's power through a man who wanted more of God. God used him in signs and wonders which confirm the words of Jesus in John 14:12, *"Truly, truly, I say to you, whoever believes in me will also do the works that I do; and greater works than these will he do, because I am going to the Father."*

We should all long to experience such things. I know that I do. They are not just reserved for special men and women of God. They are reserved for hungry, thirsty, and obedient people.

John G. Lake was an ordinary man who obeyed the voice of The Lord in radical ways. He was born in Ontario, Canada, in 1870. He was a smart businessman. He had a love for the Lord and was known by his friends as a man who dedicated himself to intimacy with The Lord. He couldn't get enough of God and His presence.

Lake built a very successful business career. By 1905, he was making $50,000 per year. That amount would be about 1.3 million dollars annually

DESPERATE HUNGER GETS GOD'S ATTENTION

today. Unfortunately, John grew up in a family that was plagued with sickness and death. His earliest memories were of sickness, death, and funerals. He had sixteen siblings, eight of whom tragically died of various diseases. He was tormented from a young age by death and disease. The enemy will often oppose destinies with radical circumstances of the very thing that we are called to walk in.

Lake saw dramatic healings when he visited John Alexander Dowie's ministry and was instantly healed of rheumatism. Just two short years into their marriage, Jennie Lake was diagnosed with tuberculosis and heart disease. Her condition worsened, and the doctors said that she would die. John allowed this situation to provoke him into faith.

As Jennie was on her deathbed, Lake was overcome with anger over sickness and threw his Bible against the fireplace mantle! When he went to pick up his Bible, it was opened to Acts 10:38, which says: *"How God anointed Jesus of Nazareth with the Holy Ghost and with power: who went about doing good, and healing all that were oppressed of the devil; for God was with him."* Lake had a surge of faith in that moment and sent a telegram to Dowie asking him to pray. Within an hour of Dowie praying, she was fully healed!

Not long after Jennie was healed, God called them to South Africa to begin their ministry. The Lakes gave away everything that they had. John gave up his mega-salary, and they left.

The Lakes experienced great financial miracles and provision while in South Africa. They also saw a great revival. Multitudes were saved, healed, and delivered throughout their five-year ministry tour in South Africa.

My favorite story from this season of revival takes place shortly after the Lake family and their team arrived in South Africa. A mighty plague was sweeping through the nation, and the death count was climbing. There were dead victims from the plague and no one to bury the dead; if someone were to come in contact with a dead body, they became infected and died. John G. Lake volunteered to bury the dead without any protective clothing. Physicians were in a panic and approached John and rebuked him for coming in contact with the dead. John boldly responded, "When the disease comes in contact with my skin, you can watch it die." The doctors thought he was insane, so he challenged them to put a drop of the plague on his skin and watch it under a microscope. When they did so, they saw that the plague cells burned up the second they came in contact with his skin! They died in his Holy Ghost hand.

God is raising up a generation of men and women who will radically obey God no matter the cost, as John G. Lake did. He is looking for men and women who will have the audacity to believe the Lord for dramatic moves of the spirit as Lake did when he challenged the laws of science, demanding that the physicians put the plague cells on his hand so they could watch the fire of God burn them up. The revival that is coming will come through vessels who are faithful in the small things so that the power and presence of God will remain pure and sustained. John G. Lake hungered for God, His healing anointing, revelation, and to be used by God. I think you can see that one man or one woman can plunder Hell and populate Heaven, set nations on fire, rebuke sin and death, and see Heaven come to earth. That man or woman has to be desperately hungry for God.

Smith Wigglesworth (1859–1947) was a British evangelist known as "The Apostle of Faith." He was one the leading figures of the Pentecostal revival movement at the beginning half of the twentieth century. He had childlike faith in Jesus. That faith resulted in miracles and a fresh outpouring of the Holy Spirit in the Church. That great English preacher saw over twenty people raised from the dead. He is one of my favorites.

Wigglesworth said, "The more I have of God, the better." He also said, "The only thing that I'm satisfied with, is my dissatisfaction." We should also never be satisfied and continue to press into God for more. He was so very hungry for God, and out of that hunger came great intimacy and great yieldedness. No wonder that he saw limbs grow out and many raised from the dead.

God spoke to Wigglesworth by that still small voice of The Holy Spirit, and said, "I'm going to burn you up until there's no Wigglesworth left, only Jesus will be seen." Wigglesworth's hunger allowed God to do just that.

Smith believed in the power of the name of Jesus. He prayed and fasted frequently. The sick were healed, and the demon-possessed were set free. Smith Wigglesworth was often criticized by other preachers due to his unyielding faith in God alone. The criticism never fazed him, and he believed it was important to depend completely on God. Thousands came to faith in Christ at his meetings. Many testified to being healed of serious diseases and illnesses.

We see great evidence of his spiritual hunger and thirst. As a young Christian, he longed for God and often sought him in prayer throughout his day. He frequently shared his faith with others and converted his mother to Christianity at age nine. By age thirteen, he preached at a meeting and spoke with a strong desire for people to know Christ. At age sixteen, he started ministering with the Salvation Army.

Wigglesworth said that the Bible was the only book he ever read and that he banned newspapers from his home, saying his family didn't need to read anything but the Bible. We know that this was not necessary, but his conviction displayed his spiritual hunger.

Aimmee Semple-McPherson, (1890–1944), was also known as Sister Aimmee. She was a Canadian Pentecostal evangelist and media celebrity in the 1920s and 1930s. She became famous for founding the Foursquare Church.

Before she became successful, she, too, endured much. Only her hunger for God, faith in His Word, and total dependence upon Him pulled her through. She was born in Ontario, Canada. She had early exposure to the things of God through her mother, who worked with the poor in Salvation Army soup kitchens. As a child, she would play "Salvation Army" with classmates and preach sermons to dolls. That is very similar to my childhood. I, too, preached to my dolls, friends, and even the ants in my parent's yard.

While attending a revival meeting in 1907, Aimmee met Robert James Semple, a Pentecostal missionary from Ireland. She was converted to Pentecostalism. They were married in 1908. After going on the mission field to China, both came down with malaria. Aimmee's husband died from it. She was pregnant and came home alone to give birth to their daughter, Roberta Star Semple. After her recuperation in the United States, McPherson joined her mother, Mildred, working with the Salvation Army. While in New York City, she met accountant Harold Stewart McPherson. They were married in 1912 and had a son whom they named Rolf.

During this time, McPherson felt as though she denied her "calling" to go preach. She suffered great emotional distress, and she prayed. In 1914, she fell seriously ill with appendicitis. McPherson later stated that after a failed operation, she heard a voice asking her to go preach. After accepting the voice's challenge, she said, she was able to turn over in bed without pain.

She did not have a good marriage and was divorced in 1921. Aimee Semple McPherson married her third husband, David L. Hutton, an actor and musician, in 1932. After she fell and fractured her skull, she visited Europe to recover. While there, she learned that Hutton was billing himself as "Aimee's man" in his singing act and was frequently photographed with women wearing very suggestive clothing. His scandals were damaging the reputation of the Foursquare Church, as well as Aimmee's reputation. They divorced in 1934. McPherson later publicly repented for marrying him, and sometime later, she rejected Gospel singer Homer Rodeheaver when he proposed marriage in 1935.

Aimmee pioneered the use of broadcast mass media. Media in the church had not been used like that before. She was a pioneer in many ways. She incorporated stage techniques into her weekly sermons at Angelus Temple. Hollywood actors and producers came to her meetings to get ideas. She was that creative. No one was ever bored with her services. She used humor to deliver her messages. Animals were frequently incorporated. McPherson gave up to twenty-two sermons a week. Many times, police were needed to help route the traffic through because of the great crowds.

The appeal of McPherson's revival events surpassed any event of theater or politics in American history. She broke attendance records. One reason she grew such crowds was because God showed up, and people were healed.

DESPERATE HUNGER GETS GOD'S ATTENTION

In her time, she was the most publicized evangelist. She conducted public healing meetings, where tens of thousands of people were healed. National news coverage focused on events surrounding her family and church members, including accusations that she fabricated her reported kidnapping.

In spite of losing her husband in China while pregnant, marrying men who were not what they seemed, constant media pressure, and possible kidnapping, this lady built a 5,300-seat auditorium in Los Angeles, California, that was debt-free. She founded The Foursquare denomination, took care of the poor, ministered to thousands, saw the sick healed, and preached The Gospel of The Lord Jesus Christ.

McPherson was a human being and not perfect. We will never know until Heaven if some of the rumors about her were true or not. However, I can see that she was always hungry for God. If she messed up, she repented. She was determined to not let any circumstances or problems defeat her. That is what spiritual hunger does.

Another great lady evangelist was Kathryn Kuhlman. She was born on May 9, 1907, in Concordia, Missouri. She had a close relationship with her father. She often said that her relationship with the Father God was extremely real because of her relationship with her own father.

Kathryn was born again when she was fourteen, at an evangelistic meeting held in a small Methodist church. When she was sixteen, she graduated from high school, which only went to tenth grade in their town. Her older sister, Myrtle, married an itinerant evangelist, Everett B. Parrott. They spent their time traveling and asked Kathryn to join them for the summer. Her parents agreed, and she went to Oregon to help out. She worked with them and often gave her testimony. When the summer was over, she wanted to stay, and the couple agreed. She ended up working with them for five years.

Denver was a great success for Kathryn. In 1935, they moved to an abandoned truck garage they named the Denver Revival Tabernacle. The church grew to about 2,000 members. She began a radio show called

Smiling Through and invited speakers from all over the country. In 1935, she invited an evangelist named Burroughs Waltrip.

He was a charismatic, handsome man, several years older than she was. There was an immediate attraction, but he was married and had two children. He was invited back to Denver to take the pulpit for two months. Shortly after, he divorced his wife and abandoned his two sons. He moved to Mason City, Iowa, and started a new ministry. He built a ministry building called Radio Chapel. There was an ongoing relationship between Kuhlman and Waltrip, and they married in September 1938.

The marriage was a disaster. She told her church that she and Waltrip were married, and most of the people in her congregation left. She gave up her church in Denver, lost some of her closest associates, and moved to Mason City. By October 1938, Waltrip could not meet his debts. Radio Chapel went into bankruptcy. The next few years were very hard. They went on the road as traveling evangelists, primarily staying in the Midwest. They were not accepted in many places due to their marriage history. In 1944, Kuhlman went on an evangelistic tour on the East Coast without Waltrip. Kuhlman never returned to Waltrip, and they eventually divorced in 1947. She left her marriage behind, and from then on, acted as if it never existed in the first place.

Kuhlman began preaching on radio broadcasts in Oil City, Pennsylvania. These became popular, and she was preaching throughout the area. She preached about the healing power of God. In 1947, a woman was healed of a tumor while listening to Kuhlman preach. Several Sundays later, a man was also healed while she was teaching on the Holy Spirit.

The Healing Revival began in 1947 and lasted for the next ten years. What was happening in Kuhlman's meetings was breaking out across the United States. It was at this time frame that the Voice of Healing Ministry was established and men like William Branham, Oral Roberts, A. A. Allen, and many others were preaching.

In 1948, Kuhlman held a series of meetings at Carnegie Hall in Pittsburgh. She eventually moved to Pittsburgh in 1950 and continued to hold meetings at Carnegie Hall until 1971. She was used by God to bring the charismatic message to many denominational churches. These were her best-known years. Her style was flamboyant. Her miracle services filled auditoriums. She was on radio and television shows. Hundreds of people were healed in her meetings, and many were healed while listening to her on the radio or television. People she prayed for would often be hit with the power of God and be "slain in the Spirit." She always pointed people to Jesus as their healer.

Kuhlman had been diagnosed with a heart problem in 1955. She kept a very busy schedule and overworked herself. She traveled back and forth from Pittsburgh to Los Angeles frequently, as well as taking trips around the world. Her heart was enlarged, and Kuhlman died on February 20, 1976, in Tulsa, following open-heart surgery.

Kathryn Kuhlman shook the foundation of twentieth-century Christianity. She was one of the major ministers after World War II who reintroduced the Holy Spirit and its gifts to the body of Christ.

Behind this ministry was a woman with many trials, tribulations, scandals, controversies, heartbreaks, and pain. All people see is the glamour—the white dress, the healing, and the miracles. They don't see the hours of prayer, the heartache, and the tears. They don't see the spiritual hunger. They only see the results of that hunger. Yet, most will never be willing to pay the price. It was her hunger for God and her intimate relationship with The Holy Spirit that defined her.

She described the day that she was born again and how real The Holy Spirit was to her. On a Sunday morning, she was standing beside her mama at exactly 11:55 a.m. when something happened to her. It was an indescribable and overwhelming presence that filled the sanctuary. She could feel an invisible force enveloping her, a force that seemed to emanate directly from the divine realm.

This encounter with the Holy Spirit set the course for her extraordinary life. She wanted nothing more than to be close to Him. The idea of a young woman, without formal theological training, becoming a preacher was met with resistance. But Kathryn Kuhlman was undeterred. Her determination was to follow her divine calling.

Kathryn's story is one of resilience, determination, and unwavering faith. She symbolizes what can be achieved when we follow our calling, regardless of the criticism. Her life and ministry continue to inspire believers around the world, reminding them of the possibilities that can be achieved through faith, devotion, and hunger for God.

She said on several occasions, "It costs everything. If you really want to know the price, it will cost you everything. Kathryn Kuhlman died a long time ago. I know the day; I know the hour. I can go to the spot where Kathryn Kuhlman died." This is all about her spiritual hunger. It enabled her to pay the price to carry the anointing. She wanted God more than she wanted her next breath.

I decided to only briefly mention a few great healing evangelists who were used powerfully during the great healing revival that swept the nation in the 1940s and 1950s. A. A. Allen was the son of alcoholics. Jack Coe's father gambled the house away. His mother walked him to an orphanage and left him there. These men had much to overcome in their early lives. Yet, they both became so hungry for God that they pursued Him in big ways. They wouldn't let go of God, like Jacob as he wrestled with God.

Oral Roberts (1918–2009) was the founder and president of the Oral Roberts Evangelistic Association and co-founder, president, and chancellor of Oral Roberts University. He was one of the most recognized preachers in the United States.

Oral Roberts was one of the first men of God who was brave enough to preach that God wants to prosper us. He emphasized seed faith. His ministry reached millions of followers worldwide, spanning a period of over six decades. His healing ministry became well known.

Roberts began life in poverty, as did so many of these evangelists. He nearly died of tuberculosis when he was seventeen but was healed by the power of God. When he was twenty-nine, Roberts said he picked up his Bible, and it fell open to 3 John 2, *"I wish above all things that thou mayest prosper and be in health, even as thy soul prospereth.*" He received a revelation of God wanting to bless His children in order to make them a blessing. He knew that he was to pray for the sick and expect God to heal them. He conducted evangelistic and faith-healing meetings across the United States and around the world.

In November 1947, he started *Healing Waters*, a monthly magazine. Thousands of sick people waited in line to stand before Oral Roberts so he could pray for them. Through the years, he conducted more than 300 crusades on six continents and personally laid hands for prayer on more than 2 million people.

In 1963, he founded Oral Roberts University (ORU) in Tulsa, Oklahoma. Roberts was one of the first evangelists to do television on a regular basis.

He had a vision from Jesus, who told him to build the City of Faith Medical and Research Center. It opened in 1981. At the time, it was among the largest health facilities of its kind in the world. It merged prayer and medicine.

What would enable one to do these things? His love and hunger for God. That is also what helped him overcome great persecution from the press, the church, and the world.

I was at Rhema Bible Training Center when Oral Roberts prophesied over Dr. Rodney Howard-Browne. It was one of the most powerful and memorable moments of my life. Oral Roberts spoke of knowing that a young man was coming on the scene to lead the world into revival. Then he turned toward Dr. Rodney and pointed and declared, "Thou art the man." I have always known that but to hear a great general like Oral Roberts declare it was an unforgettable time.

Kenneth E. Hagin was one of the great generals of the faith in my time. I had the privilege of attending his Bible school (Rhema Bible Training Center) in Broken Arrow, Oklahoma from 1987–1989. I also worked for Kenneth Hagin Ministries after graduation until I left to become a missionary to Alaska in October of 1990. Kenneth Hagin taught on a daily basis during my time as a student. I am very blessed to say that I have not just read his books but sat in class as he taught daily for two years.

As he shared many "inside stories" with our class, it was easy to see that he overcame much in his life. Once again, it was because of spiritual hunger.

He was born August 20, 1917, in McKinney, Texas, with a deformed heart and an incurable blood disease. He was not expected to live long, and at age fifteen, he became paralyzed and bedridden. In April 1933, he was born again. He died three times in ten minutes, each time seeing Hell and then returning to life. He was paralyzed because of his condition. He could only move his fingers. On August 8, 1934, he was raised from his deathbed by a revelation of "faith in God's Word" after reading Mark 11:23-24. He was completely healed.

Mark 11:23-24 defined his ministry and was his most frequently quoted verse:

> For verily I say unto you, That whosoever shall say unto this mountain, Be thou removed, and be thou cast into the sea; and shall not doubt in his heart, but shall believe that those things which he saith shall come to pass; he shall have whatsoever he saith.
> Therefore I say unto you, What things soever ye desire, when ye pray, believe that ye receive them, and ye shall have them.
>
> MARK 11:23-24

We had a joke at Rhema that the Bible verse was called Hagin 11:23.

Kenneth Hagin began an itinerant ministry as a Bible teacher and evangelist in 1949 after an appearance by Jesus. He joined the Voice of Healing Revival in the U.S. with Oral Roberts, Gordon Lindsay, and T. L. Osborn. On January 23, 1963, he formed the Kenneth E. Hagin Evangelistic Association (now Kenneth Hagin Ministries) in Garland, Texas, but later moved

DESPERATE HUNGER GETS GOD'S ATTENTION

his ministry offices to Tulsa, Oklahoma. He eventually went on the radio and published many books.

At a camp meeting in 1973, Hagin announced the creation of a Bible training center and opened RHEMA Bible Training College, in Broken Arrow, Oklahoma, in 1974. In 1979, he founded the Prayer and Healing Center to provide a place for the sick to come and "have the opportunity to build their faith."

There was no one hungrier for the things of God than Kenneth E. Hagin. When his family and preachers gave him up to die, he was hungry to read God's Word and find out about the truth of healing for himself and others.

Kenneth Hagin told the students many stories of what he called "Believers Meetings." He talked of people getting so hungry for God that they came together in unity, and God did great things in their midst. He spoke of the glory of God coming in like a cloud. Everyone who was sick, was healed. The gifts of The Spirit were in operation in a great way.

As he spoke of these things, I became hungrier for God than ever before. I had never heard anyone speak of the glory of God being manifested in such a powerful way, and I longed to see that. I asked The Lord if I could see such a thing just once in my life. I now realize that I asked small because I was not yet in a place of seeing how big God wanted to be in my life and ministry. I have now seen the glory of God manifested in such a way a few times. If God's people will get hungry for His presence and learn how to yield to His presence, He will show up in a big way.

Kenneth E. Hagin is considered the pioneer of "The Word of Faith Movement." He was criticized by many leading Pentecostal denominations for his teaching on faith and healing. He was labeled by many as a heretic. It is so interesting to look through church history and see patterns repeated over and over. At the time of the formation of our Pentecostal denominations, they all stated in their doctrinal creeds that they believed in divine healing. They all believed that faith was an important element. The Bible says that *"Without faith it is impossible to please God,"* and that *"the just shall live by faith"* (Hebrews 11:6 and Romans 1:17). Over time, as denominations water down the Word of God to match their experience, instead of lifting their experience up to match the Word of God, their doctrine becomes skewed. Then, God has to raise up a pioneer again who believes His Word, is hungry for Him, has a radical experience with Him, and will not compromise the move of His Spirit. When that happens, the previous moves and denominations call him or her a heretic.

When I was going to church in Nebraska, a lady who loved Kenneth Hagin's ministry came to our church. She took a trip to Tulsa, Oklahoma, and visited many churches and listened to several people. Some had solid doctrine, and some did not. She put all of their stories together and came back with some wild reports. I heard those stories. One was of a lady who went to the car wash every day, washed her car, dried it, and waxed it with the appropriate solutions and cloth. However, when she got to the end of the story, we were told that it was the lady's "faith car." She did not have a physical car there. She went through the motions of washing, drying, and waxing an invisible car.

As I heard these ridiculous stories, I thought they were things that Kenneth Hagin taught, and I talked to my pastor about them. I wanted to make sure that no one in our church would believe such nonsense. I decided to read Kenneth Hagin's books to find out how he justified such heresy. As I read the first book, I saw nothing but the pure Word of God being taught. I thought to myself, "He must have gotten into heresy later in his life. I will find where he got off." I proceeded to read his books, one after the other, until I came to the conclusion that he was not preaching heresy. He was only preaching the pure Word of God. I then wondered why the body of Christ, in general, had quit preaching The Word in such a bold, plain, uncompromising way. That is when the desire to attend Rhema Bible Training Center came into my heart. I have found that most people do not even know what true *Word of Faith* teaching is and have only gained an opinion by listening to people who have listened to other people, and none of them have actually heard what the man teaches. Thank God for this mighty general of The Faith.

DESPERATE HUNGER GETS GOD'S ATTENTION

Lester Sumrall (1913–1996) was a Pentecostal pastor, evangelist, teacher, and missionary. He founded the Lester Sumrall Evangelistic Association (LeSEA) and its humanitarian arm, LeSEA Global Feed the Hungry, World Harvest Radio International, and World Harvest Bible College.

Sumrall began preaching at the age of seventeen, after a recovery from tuberculosis. At the age of nineteen, he founded a church in Arkansas and was ordained by the Assemblies of God.

In 1934, Sumrall began traveling abroad. He preached in Tahiti and New Zealand and established a church in Brisbane, Australia. He traveled with Howard Carter, another great Pentecostal pioneer, throughout eastern Asia and Europe.

Sumrall and his family spent many years in the Philippines during the 1950s. In 1953, he learned about the demonic possession of a woman in the Philippines and was directed by The Lord to pray for her and see her delivered. He did, and his ministry exploded. He established the Cathedral of Praise in Manila. With over 24,000 members, it is the largest congregation in the Philippines. I had the opportunity to minister there for a week several years ago.

In 1963, Sumrall moved to South Bend, Indiana, to pastor the Christian Center Cathedral of Praise (now Christian Center Church). In 1968, Sumrall began World Harvest Missionary Evangelism (WHME-FM). Sumrall has been called the "father of Christian television." From 1972 to 1997, he acquired television stations throughout the United States as part of World Harvest Television.

Sumrall wrote many books during his lifetime. There is a definite thread running through those books. He was a man who couldn't get enough of God. That caused him to press through any challenge, whether financial, physical, or spiritual. He wrote in his book, *Pioneers of Faith*, "Don't think if you're a healing preacher and you quit going to those kinds of meetings for awhile, that you can pick up where you left off. I make sure I keep going to like meetings of like anointings."

He went on to say, "The sad thing is that many of those praying for revival would not accept revival when it came, because it did not please them. It was not like the moves of God they had experienced before. They did not understand that what came before, was a foundation, or 'roots' for the next move of God. I have personally experienced every move of the Holy Spirit in the 20th century, and I have known many of the pioneers of each revival. The move of the Spirit will increase until Jesus comes. This is the latter rain, and I am glad that I am a part of it. It has amazed me to see over the years how God has found people in remote corners of the earth, brought them to the center of what He was doing in order to lay a new foundation in their lives, and then sent them back to take the move into farther and farther places. To be like them, and to be used like them, it is necessary to know what God is doing in every move of the Spirit.

"Many good Christians have rejected God's new moves and consequently, have become stagnant and missed His blessings. The Devil never wants us to get smart in spiritual things. If God sends a new breath of His power, Satan does not want us to know where it is. Or he wants us to think it must be wrong, because we did not get it that way. As far as I know, in all of history, no denomination ever made a radical change. People can make a change, but denominations rarely do. One of the reasons is because the leaders of a denomination would be embarrassed if people found out they did not know everything about God already.

"Jesus was despised because He brought change, a return to the Word of God in certain areas where they had moved into tradition. When Jesus showed up the religious leaders with new power they had a fit! They did not know what to do with Him, except to say 'Kill Him.' I am not afraid of wildfire. I know how to put a cover over it, but I am afraid of icebergs. I believe the greatest spiritual revolution in the history of the world is about to take place. I am not sure all Christians will be in on it, because it might be too radical. Preachers may not look dignified. The gifts of the Spirit will function mightily, moving governments and frightening political leaders. God's church will come alive just before Jesus comes. There will be some mainline denominational people who cannot bridge the gap anymore than they did in the past. There will be some Pentecostals and charismatics who cannot bridge the gap.

"People will say 'That's too far for me to jump from where I am; I'm going to stick it out right here. I'm comfortable where I am.' That is the reason people in other moves of God did not go with the flow of the Holy Spirit. They stayed where they were comfortable. I have asked God many times, 'Please do not do anything while I am alive unless you let me be a part of it.' I believe we are on the verge of a spontaneous move of God. The only one who can eliminate you from the blessings of God is yourself. Many of you reading this book will be here when Jesus comes, so you will want to be in the last blaze of glory! Do not expect your denomination or even your church to come with you. Just move with God yourself.

"I have been constantly in God's blessings every day of my life. You cannot retire from a blessing. If you are a healing preacher, and you stop going to healing meetings for about ten years then think you're going to jump back in and do the same thing, forget it! You will be as a tinkling cymbal, an empty drum. If you want God's blessings, you have to follow Him constantly. The more fanatical we are, the greater impact we are going to make on this generation. When people see that we are sincere to the core and not playing with religion, they will believe with us. I believe the great athletic coliseums are not for football and baseball. They are for the last big breath of God! With the great breath of God that is coming, no one is going to get tired. We are going to flow in the supernatural. You will find from studying the history of Israel and Judah that God blesses by generation. We need a new generation today, and I can see it beginning. I am convinced that I will at least see this last great revival."

Lester Sumrall invited Dr. Rodney Howard-Browne to his church in the 1990s. He told Pastor Rodney that he knew that the revival flowing through his ministry was the one that Smith Wigglesworth prophesied to him about many years earlier. He stated that when he saw the beginning of it, he knew that he could go home to be with The Lord. Dr. Rodney told him that he didn't want to come for a while then because the body of Christ needed Lester to stay around longer. The day finally came when Dr.

Rodney knew that it was time to go to Lester Sumrall's church. As he preached and signs and wonders were following the preaching of The Word, Sumrall was sitting on the front row, smiling. He told Dr. Rodney later that he was satisfied that he had witnessed the beginning of the revival that Wigglesworth had prophesied about.

Dr. Rodney Howard-Browne grew up in a wonderful Pentecostal home in South Africa. He was born again at the age of five and knew that he was called of God at a very young age. He used to play preacher with his stuffed bears. He preached to them and even baptized them in water. Of course, that caused their ears and nose to fall off so that made it necessary to have a healing service. He crawled out of his bedroom window and asked his younger brother to take over the service for him because he had to go to America to preach. Then he would crawl back through the window and announce that he was back to take over his service again.

We can see that he had great hunger, even as a child. He tells how God impressed the horrors of Hell upon him, and he knew that his job was to tell as many people about Jesus and the plan of salvation as he could. He also made a vow to The Lord after his older brother died that the Devil would pay for that, and people would laugh at the Devil all over the world. He had no idea at the time that "joy unspeakable and full of glory" would break out in his meetings all over the world. He only knew that he was hungry for God and would do anything God asked him to do.

The day came when Dr. Rodney knew that he had to have more of God than he had ever had before. He began to cry out, "God, either You come down and touch me with Your fire or take me home to be with You, but I have to have more." He cried out loud to God like that for over twenty minutes. He became hoarse in his voice but was desperate. Some would say that you don't have to do that. "God is not deaf, you know." No, He is not. But He loves our desperation and the fact that we are not embarrassed to express that desperation. After several minutes, the fire of God began to envelop and saturate him. The power of God was so strong that he almost felt that he could not contain it. He thought that God had heard his prayer and was going to take him home. He eventually had to ask God to let up a little on that power so that he could function. That is the fire and anointing of God that operates through him today to change lives. I am one of those whose life was turned upside down through his ministry. I have received of that fire.

I do not know how to adequately describe what this ministry has meant to me. I could write a book just on this subject. However, I will try to stick to the subject of this man's hunger. I have been associated with Pastors Rodney and Adonica Howard-Browne's ministry for over thirty years now. I have observed them in many different situations, both as evangelists and now as my pastors, for many years. I was with them in the beginning days when finances were tight, persecution was great, and when they lost their daughter, Kelly, who graduated to Heaven on Christmas morning 2002. I was with them when God spoke to him through a dream that he was to go to Madison Square Garden in New York City in 1999 to hold the largest soul-winning crusade since Billy Graham in the 1950s. He didn't have the finances, but he had faith and a hunger to see God do what He said that He would do. Almost fifty thousand souls were born again in that crusade.

I have watched them give over and over when it looked impossible, and God increased them each time. Since the beginning days, they have raised up a church in Tampa, Florida, that now has a membership of several thousand people. They have a Bible School called River University that has graduated multiple thousands who have started churches in many nations of the world. They have rented large stadiums all over the world for soul-winning crusades. I had the privilege of witnessing their soul-winning crusade in Cape Town, South Africa, where they just rented Athlone Stadium for three nights, and we saw 35,542 souls saved and 88,445 people in attendance. No wonder God tells us in His Word to "despise not the day of small beginnings."

My pastors give away cars on Sunday mornings in their services. I believe they have given over fifty cars away, at present. They give millions to other ministries every year. They have taken the Gospel into almost one hundred nations.

I have heard my Pastor Rodney say, "I am nothing special. I believe God is using me because I know that I am nothing without Him. He will use anyone who will yield themselves to Him completely. I am hungry for Him and will only do what He wants me to do."

That hunger is what caused the fire of The Living God to come to him and now run through him for a lost and dying world. It is that fire that has touched countless lives throughout the world. Because of one man's hunger, millions of souls have come into the kingdom, hundreds of thousands have been healed and baptized in The Holy Ghost, and thousands have been called into the ministry. Hunger seems to be the common denominator for people seeing great things accomplished.

FIVE

THINGS THAT KILL HUNGER

How do people backslide or pull out of revival? It is never sudden, like the touch of God is. It is gradual. People slowly cool off. They sit back in church a little further and give a little less. They don't witness the way they used to, attend revival services infrequently, and get too busy for prayer and Bible reading.

When people are not in revival the way they once were, they give lots of excuses: hurt, disappointments, becoming weary, not enough time, busy schedules, etc. But the real reason is that they quit being hungry for God. You have to cultivate hunger. You must protect your heart above all things. It's up to you to keep it hungry, day and night.

> Keep thy heart with all diligence; for out of it are the issues of life.
>
> PROVERBS 4:23

Your first love is easy to lose. We hear of married couples "falling out of love." The reason for that is they forget that what it takes to get, it takes to keep. They are willing to spend time with one another, court one another, communicate, and show affection in the beginning. Then, they start to take one another for granted. It doesn't work in natural relationships, and it doesn't work with God either.

> Nevertheless I have somewhat against thee, because thou hast left thy first love.
> Remember therefore from whence thou art fallen, and repent, and do the first works; or else I will come unto thee quickly, and will remove thy candlestick out of his place, except thou repent.
>
> REVELATION 2:4-5

The sad thing is that most don't even know when they lost their first love for God. Others can see it. You may be sitting in the same seat in church, taking notes as before. However, others can see that you don't have the same spark in your eyes, you don't have the same excitement in your voice, and you don't have the desire to reach others for Christ.

One reason people lose hunger is that they become content to live on revival memories. They become set in their ways and want to camp beside the last place the water came out of the rock. They refuse to move with the cloud. They refuse to move on with God.

> "Do not remember the former things,
> Nor consider the things of old.
> Behold, I will do a new thing,
> Now it shall spring forth;
> Shall you not know it?
> I will even make a road in the wilderness
> And rivers in the desert."
>
> ISAIAH 43:18-19 (NKJV)

He asks, "Do you not perceive it?" This tells us that God could be doing a new thing, but His people do not see it. It is so important that we remain spiritually sensitive and sharp in The Holy Ghost. Many times, Jesus mentioned that we need eyes to see and ears to hear. He told that to people who already had physical eyes and ears. He was talking about having spiritual eyes to see and spiritual ears to hear. That is something we must determine by our hunger for God.

God is sending fresh oil and a fresh wave of His Spirit to a new generation of believers who'll rise up and take hold of our destiny and settle for nothing less. It will come to those who are spiritually hungry and thirsty and to those who have refused to settle for less.

Another reason that people backslide and cool off is because their hunger was birthed out of their own fleshly desires, not God's. It is important that our hunger is birthed out of the right motives. There are different kinds of fires that come from various sources. It is vitally important that our fire is birthed from the fire off the altar of God. It cannot be from our own fire or natural desire.

People in the world have accomplished great things from a fire that beats within their chest. It can be a fire of hard work ethics. The person is success-driven and cannot relax no matter how much they accomplish. It may be from the need to prove to their hometown relatives, who told them they would never amount to anything, that they are successful. It may be a fire birthed out of insecurity. It could also be from competition. Some will do anything to come in first. They have a need to know that they are better than the rest. These are not motives birthed out of the holy fire of God's altar.

It's not uncommon to hear of an ambitious person who is hungry to accomplish things. Many times, people will speak of hunger pushing someone to do more than anyone thought possible. They use that term for athletes who want to make it to the professional leagues, actors who want to attain stardom, and business persons who want to become a CEO or president of a major corporation. These are people who drive themselves to work harder than others. They practice discipline and go without sleep.

They study harder than others. They will do anything to gain the attention of their superiors or fan club. They are self-promoters and can accomplish much on their own. They are ambitious, and that ambition sometimes knows no limits. It may even cost them their health, their family, or their lives.

Some are only hungry to have big ministries. Some accomplish great things out of their own willpower. They do it through hard work, ethics, self-promotion, and advertisement. There are things that I want to get better at, such as learning to utilize technology. It has been given to us on this earth for our use and to promote God's kingdom. However, some go after these things for the wrong reasons. The reason must be that it is birthed out of God's hunger to see the world saved and His church blessed.

There is a huge difference between hungering and thirsting for God and hungering to have a big ministry and fame. We can't want people to be healed to promote our ministry and make us famous. It must be because we love God, and we love His people. We are moved with compassion for them as Jesus was when He walked this earth.

You must have the fire burning from off the altar of Heaven. It must burn in the middle of you, in your spirit. You must be set ablaze like Jeremiah, who said that it was "just like fire shut up in his bones."

When you burn with holy fire, people will look at you and say, "I've never seen such tenacity." However, tenacity has nothing to do with it. When you have been touched with the fire of God, when Heaven has become real to you, and the hand of The Master has left His branding mark on you, you have no choice. He's touched you, and He's changed you. His thoughts and desires have become yours, and you feel about people what He feels about people. You couldn't stop telling people about Jesus if you wanted to because His love and mercy are just like fire shut up in your bones.

Why am I still traveling the world in my late sixties when I could be baking cookies and sitting in a rocking chair on my lanai in the Florida sun? It comes back to one thing: the fire of The Holy Ghost that consumes me.

DESPERATE HUNGER GETS GOD'S ATTENTION

I have learned to recognize revival killers. I guard against that. I have met too many others who once had that fire burning brightly, but they somehow ended up in a glacier. We can't even find a little spark now. How did that happen? There is a lesson to be learned in that. Don't let it happen to you! You must recognize that there is a thief who comes to steal, kill, and destroy. Learn how to head him off at the pass early on.

One of the things that the enemy uses to cause that fire to dissipate is hanging out with the wrong people. You must be very careful who you associate with. You must make sure they have same fire you do. It is important that they are not religious or flaky. They must know how to flow. It is important that they love revival and are revival carriers. I didn't say that they must be in the five-fold ministry but that they are revival carriers.

Another thing that kills hunger is condemnation and its twin, self-pity. You can make mistakes in life and may say, "Lord, you've picked the wrong person. Surely you can find someone better qualified." The Devil loves to remind you of your past. He brings it up more than once, especially when you are about to be used mightily by God. I'm sure that he brought up the Apostle Paul's past to him many times. He probably said, "You killer of the church. You should have known better. After all, you were a Pharisee who knew the Word. You should have recognized who the Messiah was. You even held the coat of Stephen as he was being murdered. You could have stopped it. His blood is on your hands." He probably even said, "Do you think the church is going to believe that you are even born again? Even if you are, no one will believe it. You would be better off to quit now."

However, when you are tempted to give into that, right in the middle of the pity party, you have to allow that hunger to churn again and become larger than the condemnation. Remind the Devil and yourself of what the Word of God says.

> There is therefore now no condemnation to them which are in Christ Jesus, who walk not after the flesh, but after the Spirit.
>
> ROMANS 8:1

Then, remind yourself that this is exactly what the blood of Jesus is for. God will never bring up your past again. Tell yourself, "I can't quit now. God has brought me too far. I'm too hungry for God to quit. I'm too hungry to see souls saved, people filled with The Holy Spirit, and to see people healed and delivered. I am hungrier than I am feeling guilty about my past. It's done, over and under the blood! If God doesn't remember it, neither do I. So, shut up Devil, or I will remind you of your future. A big angel is going to take you by the shoulders, bind you, and throw you into the lake of fire where you will be tormented forever."

One of the big things that I have witnessed that causes people to quit being hungry and then eventually backslide is the root of bitterness. That is dangerous.

> See to it that no one fails to obtain the grace of God; that no "root of bitterness" springs up and causes trouble, and by it many become defiled;
>
> HEBREWS 12:15 (ESV)

> Let all bitterness and wrath and anger and clamor and slander be put away from you, along with all malice.
>
> EPHESIANS 4:31 (ESV)

> A merry heart doeth good like a medicine: but a broken spirit drieth the bones.
>
> PROVERBS 17:22

Several physicians have said that they believe that there is a connection between many chronic diseases, bitterness, and unforgiveness. Many things can cause bitterness: seeing others with impure motives, feeling like God let you down, the politics of the church, you are not where you thought you would be in life by now, what others have done to you or what you perceive that they have done to you, persistent physical symptoms, or you haven't had the financial breakthrough that you think you should have by now, etc. The minute that you stop being hungry for God, you will take offense over anything. Offense is a sign that you are losing your hunger.

No matter which cause may be plaguing you, you have to decide to let God burn it out by His fire. When the voice says, "Quit, everyone is a phony. No one is real," you have to keep your eyes on Jesus and go beyond everything that you see.

There will be church politics, impure motives, and people in the flesh anywhere you go. You may see someone vibrating on the floor under the power of The Holy Ghost to the extent that they are carried out of the meeting. Then you see that they don't live according to The Word of God and continue to live in sin. Does that mean it wasn't the Holy Ghost all over them in the meeting? No, it means that they didn't fully cooperate with Him. They settled for the touch and resisted the change that He wanted to make on the inside. That is not a reason to think that the move of God is not real or that all people who you see being touched are phony. God wants to do spiritual surgery on the inside of all of us. However, we have to decide how much we will allow Him to do. We are not robots and have free choice. You must make up your mind to fully cooperate and leave others to Him. You must get so hungry for revival and God that nothing is going to stop you. You will keep your eyes on Jesus and not become distracted. You must make up your mind that nothing will stop you.

We're gonna be different: we are nation-shakers and water-walkers. We are revivalists on earth for such a time as this. We have to let God clean us out so people can see and hear Jesus in us. You must tell yourself, "There are a whole lot of people on their way to Hell, and God needs me to do what He has called me to do." My business is to let God do whatever He wants to do. I will pay the price, even if everybody else backs out of revival.

Unforgiveness is one of the things that causes bitterness and offense. It will cause spiritual hunger to dissipate. Unforgiveness and offense are closely related.

> (Love) does not behave rudely, does not seek its own, is not provoked, thinks no evil.
>
> 1 CORINTHIANS 13:5 (NKJV)

> Good sense makes one slow to anger,
> and it is his glory to overlook an offense.
>
> PROVERBS 19:11 (ESV)

I will not use the excuse that others have hurt me. An excuse is trying to justify a fault. That would mean that I am not spiritually hungry enough to keep going when things get a little rough. What He's done for me is worth anything that I go through.

Another thing that causes people to lose their hunger is worldliness. They begin to dabble in the things they were once delivered of. Worldliness consists of the desire to be a friend of the world.

> Ye adulterers and adulteresses, know ye not that the friendship of the world is enmity with God? whosoever therefore will be a friend of the world is the enemy of God.
>
> JAMES 4:4

> Love not the world, neither the things that are in the world. If any man love the world, the love of the Father is not in him.
> For all that is in the world, the lust of the flesh, and the lust of the eyes, and the pride of life, is not of the Father, but is of the world.
>
> 1 JOHN 2:15-16

> Now we have received, not the spirit of the world, but the spirit which is of God; that we might know the things that are freely given to us of God.
>
> 1 CORINTHIANS 2:12

> Wherefore come out from among them, and be ye separate, saith the Lord, and touch not the unclean thing; and I will receive you.
>
> 2 CORINTHIANS 6:17

It is not possible to love two things at the same time.

> No servant can serve two masters: for either he will hate the one, and love the other; or else he will hold to the one, and despise the other. Ye cannot serve God and mammon.
>
> LUKE 16:13

The more that you hunger for the world and give in to its temptations, the less you will love God and His holiness.

Another thing that causes hunger to decrease is pressure. It is easy to praise when you're sitting in revival and easy to sing, *"The world behind me and the cross before me."* However, just let a little pressure come into your life, and it can be a different story. That pressure can come in the form of finances, persecution, loved ones thinking you are making a mistake in giving your life for Christ, and other things. We must learn to cast our care over on The Lord.

> Casting all your cares [all your anxieties, all your worries, and all your concerns, once and for all] on Him, for He

cares about you [with deepest affection, and watches over you very carefully].

1 PETER 5:7 (AMP)

God wants us to roll our burdens upon Him. Direct those burdens on God Himself. We are to trust completely in Him.

> Cast your burden on the Lord,
> And He shall sustain you;
> He shall never permit the righteous to be moved.

PSALM 55:22 (NKJV)

My late husband was so good at this. He refused to worry about anything or carry anything. He said that The Lord taught him a long time ago how not to carry the burden. I heard him walk around the house saying, "I refuse to carry this burden. I cast it over on You, Lord." This takes practice. I've found that confessing these Bible verses out loud is a big step toward casting the burden onto The Lord.

It is important to not get caught up in the news of the day. We are living in the last days, and the Bible tells us how things will be. We are not preachers of the current news. We are preachers and proclaimers of how it can all be changed by the anointing of The Holy Spirit. We are not to dwell on the problems and make them big but dwell on a big God who will change them.

To stay on fire for God, you must rearrange priorities. Hunger has to propel you past every excuse of not making the spiritual connection that you need to make. No wonder Jesus said:

> If any man come to me, and hate not his father, and mother, and wife, and children, and brethren, and sisters, yea, and his own life also, he cannot be my disciple.

> And whosoever doth not bear his cross, and come after me, cannot be my disciple.
>
> LUKE 14:26-27

God doesn't expect us to hate our parents. He was talking about how our love for God must remain our highest priority. God has to be first in comparison with your love for any relative, friend, or anything.

You have to stay in the fire of God to stay hungry. Yet, you must remain hungry to stay in the fire of God. They run together simultaneously. You must say, like the old African-American preacher, "Lord, dip me in the kerosene of Your Spirit and set me ablaze." You must also say, "Lord, I'll do my part and trust You to do Your part. I will stay hungry for You all the days of my life."

Many fall out of love with Jesus because they cannot take any persecution. Revival comes with persecution. Any man or woman of God who has been used mightily has faced some amount of persecution. We read about Smith Wigglesworth, who had great miracles manifested through him but died a lonely man. Most people would not even have him in their churches. Many libraries are full of his books today, but most of the men and women who own the books would not have him in their churches today. They think they would, but they will not allow ministers in their churches who operate like Wigglesworth. He was known for not only his faith but what many called "gruffness." Most thought that he was crazy. They looked at him like he was an eccentric weirdo. Do you realize the opposition he had? People love him today, but that didn't help him at the time. If God allows him to look over the banister of Heaven in that cloud of witnesses, he is probably saying today, "Oh, they like me after all."

Lester Sumrall told the story about being a young man sitting at the feet of Wigglesworth. Smith Wigglesworth told Lester Sumrall how lonely he was. Sumrall hated to tell him goodbye. When World War II was beginning, Lester Sumrall had to go back to America and went to say goodbye to

Wigglesworth. Tears filled Wigglesworth's eyes. He loved being able to pass on to a young man what he had learned.

None of us are above our Master.

> But when they persecute you in this city, flee ye into another: for verily I say unto you, Ye shall not have gone over the cities of Israel, till the Son of man be come.
> The disciple is not above his master, nor the servant above his lord.
> It is enough for the disciple that he be as his master, and the servant as his lord. If they have called the master of the house Beelzebub, how much more shall they call them of his household?
>
> MATTHEW 10:23-25

Most of us have faced so little persecution compared to what our brothers and sisters have faced in Bible days or are faced with today in the Middle East or in communist countries. People call it persecution today when someone unlikes them on Facebook. They call it persecution when someone walks out of their meeting. We must toughen up in this hour. You can only fly at the altitude of criticism that you can take. We have not been beheaded for The Gospel's sake.

Maybe we should count our trophies not by the crowds or accolades but by how many bones were broken at the last place we preached or how many times we were thrown in prison. People wanted to kill Charles Finney, and they tried to run him off but could not. I heard the story of a young, twenty-year-old woman pastoring in Siberia. She had been given only the Book of Acts and the Book of John to read and study. She did not have a whole Bible. When the people who first gave her The Gospel of John returned, they found that she had a church of one thousand people. However, they noticed that she had a black eye and was bleeding. They asked what happened. She said, "I just came out of prison, and I got beat up." The others were horrified. She asked them why they were surprised by her persecution, and she opened the Book of Acts and read to them about how the apostles were beaten. She pointed to it and said, "It's here. That's how I knew it was all right, and I was honored to have this happen for the sake of The Gospel." That is pretty radical.

When you read *Fox's Book of Martyrs*, you realize what true persecution is. We have become so spoiled in America, the land of the free. I believe that the lockdowns of 2020 and 2021 have brought some people out of denial. We can no longer bury our heads in the sand and think that these extreme measures will not be implemented. We better toughen up and keep our eyes on Jesus. Those who aren't hungry enough for God to serve Him in easier times will certainly not be able to serve Him when things become worse.

Some backslide and lose their hunger for God because they are afraid of change. Revival brings change. Where there is fire, there is light, and light reveals things. My pastor says that when the light comes on, the cockroaches flee. We must not be afraid of the fire but must let it do its mighty work. It is important that we let The Holy Spirit finish what He comes to do. Revival and walking with God require us to make adjustments. We don't like the iron sharpening iron process. In the middle of adjustments and correction, we need to cry out, "Holy Ghost, help me not to become offended, but help me to change."

Sometimes, you will hear revivalists talk about "doing carpet time." By that, I am referring to waiting in the presence of God. Many times, people fall under the power of The Holy Spirit because the body cannot contain that much power without a reaction, much like the reaction to electricity. That is why we will need a glorified body in Heaven. Many people in The Bible fell because of the power of God. They still do today.

The Hebrew word for glory is *kabod*, meaning weight. People are overcome by the weight of God, forcing them to the floor.

> Abram fell into a deep sleep, and a thick and dreadful darkness came over him.
>
> GENESIS 15:12 (NIV)

The Hebrew Word *radam* means to be in or fall into a deep sleep. When God entered into a covenant with Abram, the same word is used for putting him down and to sleep as was used for putting Adam to sleep when he made Eve.

We see another Biblical example with King Saul.

> And he stripped off his clothes also, and prophesied before Samuel in like manner, and lay down naked all that day and all that night. Wherefore they say, Is Saul also among the prophets?
>
> 1 SAMUEL 19:24

King Saul lay in a prone position with God speaking through him for close to a twenty-four-hour period.

> This was the appearance of the likeness of the glory of the Lord. When I saw it, I fell facedown,
>
> EZEKIEL 1:28 (NIV)

> And the glory of the Lord was standing there, like the glory I had seen by the Kebar River, and I fell facedown.
>
> EZEKIEL 3:23 (NIV)

> As he came near the place where I was standing, I was terrified and fell prostrate.
>
> DANIEL 8:17 (NIV)

DESPERATE HUNGER GETS GOD'S ATTENTION

In another divine encounter with an angelic being, Daniel says, *"When I heard the sound of his words I then was lying stunned (radam) on the ground and my face was toward the ground"* (Daniel 10:9).

> When the disciples heard this, they fell facedown to the ground, terrified. But Jesus came and touched them. "Get up," he said. "Don't be afraid."
>
> MATTHEW 17:6-7 (NIV)

> The guards were so afraid of him that they shook and became like dead men.
>
> MATTHEW 28:4 (NIV)

As Judas and the soldiers came to arrest Jesus, they had an interesting encounter.

> When Jesus said, "I am he," they drew back and fell to the ground.
>
> JOHN 18:6 (NIV)

We are talking about hundreds of soldiers who fell backward to the ground at the same time.

When Paul was apprehended on the road to Damascus by a light from Heaven, he says:

> I fell to the ground and heard a voice say.
>
> ACTS 22:7 (NIV)

At the Transfiguration, people fell under the mighty power of God.

> The guards were so afraid of him that they shook and became like dead men.
>
> MATTHEW 28:4 (NIV)

> It came even to pass, as the trumpeters and singers were as one, to make one sound to be heard in praising and thanking the Lord; and when they lifted up their voice with the trumpets and cymbals and instruments of musick, and praised the Lord, saying, For he is good; for his mercy endureth for ever: that then the house was filled with a cloud, even the house of the Lord;
> So that the priests could not stand to minister by reason of the cloud: for the glory of the Lord had filled the house of God.
>
> 2 CHRONICLES 5:13-14

The Bible does not say that they fell but indicates they couldn't perform their services or functions or duties because of the cloud. They were immobilized somehow. Again, *kabod*, means a weight. They were overcome by great weight that forced them to the floor.

When God is doing something in and upon a person, God is doing spiritual surgery on that person. If a surgeon performed an appendectomy on you, you would want to let him finish it. After he removed your appendix and was getting ready to clean you out and stitch you up, you would not say, "That's good enough, Doc. You got most of it. I'm busy. I have to get up now because I have things to do. I'll just hold it together. You don't even have to stitch it up." You would be in serious trouble. Why let him do most of it and then not let him finish the surgery?

Christians tend to do the same thing spiritually. If God comes and lays heavily upon me so that my legs cannot even stand in His presence, why would I fall on the floor and bounce back up in seconds? He is doing this for a reason. He wants to take out some things that have plagued us and caused us to be bound. He wants to cauterize your wounds by the fire of The Holy Spirit. He wants to pour in the "healing balm of Gilead." Don't settle for half of what He wants to do in you.

I have made it a practice to stay on the floor longer than I think I may need to. I remember one time in Palmer, Alaska, at the end of my meeting, God did spiritual surgery on me. I preached, prayed for everyone, and finished the meeting. Most of the congregation was on the floor, and as I watched what The Holy Spirit was doing, I wanted my own touch. I asked a friend, who flowed in the anointing, to pray for me. I fell out beside the others who were still on the floor. After a few minutes, I became conscious of others around me talking. I knew that I could now get up. However, I thought to myself, "What am I going to do if I get up right now? I will only go home and go to bed. What if I were to lay here a few more minutes and allow God to go deeper? The only thing that will be different in the natural realm is that I will go to bed a little while later. But, perchance, if God is not quite through with me yet and wants to do something deeper, I will never be the same." So, I decided to linger in His presence. A few minutes later, a second wave of His glory swept over me. I was out in The Spirit for quite some time. They carried me out of my own meeting. I was caught up in His Spirit until the next day. It was glorious and life-changing.

The spiritually hungry person will crave the presence of God and spend time in His presence, both alone and corporately. We will not get up in a hurry but will learn to yield to whatever He wants done. He will pluck out every root of bitterness and unforgiveness. You must humble yourself and say, "If I have to stay here all night, I will until I get past the obstacles, financial setbacks, and disappointments because I am hungry for God and revival. I am hungry to see nations shaken, lives changed, people saved and healed." Never forget that what it takes to get, it takes to keep.

When I am in a meeting where the power of God is, I always cry out, *"Lord, go deeper this time than ever before. Don't let me leave the same way that I came. Lord, take me higher. Wind, blow through me. Holy Spirit rain, drench me. Fire, burn out the chaff and dross. Lord, heal me of anything that would hold me back from more of You or anything that is unpleasant to You."*

Pride kills hunger.

> Likewise, ye younger, submit yourselves unto the elder. Yea, all of you be subject one to another, and be clothed with humility: for God resisteth the proud, and giveth grace to the humble.
> Humble yourselves therefore under the mighty hand of God, that he may exalt you in due time.
>
> 1 PETER 5:5-6

God resists the proud.

> But he giveth more grace. Wherefore he saith, God resisteth the proud, but giveth grace unto the humble.
>
> JAMES 4:6

You cannot receive from God when He is resisting you. It is only the humble who can receive from God. When you are humble, God lifts you up.

> Humble yourselves in the sight of the Lord, and he shall lift you up.
>
> JAMES 4:10

That is one of the reasons that little children can receive easily. They simply believe and receive. They don't argue with God.

I held a revival in Long Beach, Mississippi, several years ago. It was a one-week revival that lasted six weeks. Sixteen states and fourteen denominations were represented in that revival. We saw outstanding miracles and a great harvest of souls.

One evening, as I was praying for people, a man stopped me as I was about to lay hands on him. He said, "Before you pray for me, I will tell you what I told God tonight. My wife is always getting touched in a big way, but I never receive anything. I told The Lord tonight that He better touch me or I am through with God. Do you understand me?" I said, "Well, I can't imagine what would keep you from receiving from God with an attitude like that." He needed to be brought up short. He had to make an adjustment in his heart and attitude before he could receive.

There is a big difference between threatening God and refusing to be denied. When I tell people to make a demand on the anointing, we are not telling them that God owes them something or that they are to make a demand on Him in a threatening and blackmailing way. The demand needs to be kept on His Word and His anointing, not because we deserve it.

SIX

HUNGER WILL CAUSE YOU TO EXPERIENCE HIM

Everyone in the world today, or in past church history, who has been used greatly, has had a supernatural encounter with The Holy Spirit. They can all go back to that encounter. You can't imitate an encounter. The man or woman with experience is never at the mercy of a man with only an argument. No one can argue with a person who has had an encounter with The Holy Spirit. Divine encounters will change everything about you—your walk, your preaching, your look, your talk, and your desires until you become unrecognizable.

It's too late to argue with me about my experiences in God. This is what I would tell anyone. "You've come too late to tell me He doesn't prosper me. I was in poverty, and now I am walking in the blessing of The Lord. You've come too late to tell me God doesn't baptize us in The Holy Ghost and fire. I have been baptized in The Holy Ghost, and I speak in tongues. You've come too late to tell me that God does not heal. I am supposed to be dead, according to the doctors, but I was healed by the power of God. You've come too late to tell me that God doesn't use women in ministry. I'm a woman, and I have been used now for over thirty years."

DR. DEBBIE RICH

> O taste and see that the Lord is good:
>
> PSALM 34:8

God wants us to taste of His goodness and to experience Him, not just describe properties about Him. We are not asked to just know facts about Him. He asked us to come up to His table and taste. We are to experience Him for ourselves.

My favorite steak is a rib-eye. It is extremely flavorful and tender because it is marbled with fat. I don't personally enjoy a dry piece of sirloin. Fat is what gives meat or anything else its flavor. I have eaten rib-eye steak many times. When I describe it to people who have never had it, they end up eating it for themselves. A person who has never had the privilege of eating a rib-eye steak cannot relate to what I am talking about unless I describe what they are missing. I must make it real to them. I tell them, "It is the most flavorful cut of steak in the world. When I slice into it with my knife, the juices run. I couple it with a big, baked potato slathered in rich fat, butter, and sour cream, and there is nothing that can compare to it." When I describe it, my eyes light up, and there is a big smile on my face. The people can see how much I enjoy it. They know that I have personally indulged and am speaking from experience. Even when I am in countries where they have never tasted a rib-eye steak, people have developed an appetite for one due to my description.

However, if I said in a monotone voice, "Rib-eye steak is from a cow. It is beef. It is mostly made up of protein and fat. An eight-ounce steak contains six hundred and sixty-one calories. It has nutritional value. It will fill up your stomach. There, would you like to have a steak?" Most would not even relate to that clinical description. It does not tempt them at all.

Yet, that is the way many preachers (even Pentecostal ones) describe the goodness of God and the manifestations of The Holy Spirit. When they go soul-winning (only because their church told them this is the day that each person must knock on ten doors), they go door to door with a frown on their face. When someone opens the door, they begin to clinically describe their need for salvation. "Do you know Jesus as Savior? No? You're going to Hell. Do you want what I have?" The person sees this depressed person asking them if they want what he or she has. They usually answer, "No, I don't." "O.K. You're going to Hell, but I tried. I have nine more houses to go to." Or, they might clinically try to describe what they have never tasted of themselves or have forgotten how good He is because it has been years since they tasted and had an actual experience with The Holy Spirit. He might say, "I will tell you how you must get saved. Jesus lived in Heaven, came to earth, died on the cross, and ascended back to Heaven. If you believe that, say this prayer. If you don't, you're going to Hell." No one wants anything that person has because there is no life in them.

Only the man or woman, boy or girl, who has personally tasted of God's goodness can provoke others to taste. God is a big God. His glory speaks of weight. How big is God? I don't know, but I know there is not a scale big enough to weigh Him. He is infinite, omniscient, and omnipresent. He is Alpha and Omega, The Beginning and The End. Oil is one of the symbols of The Holy Spirit. Oil is fat and thick and is the lubrication for everything we need.

The prophet Isaiah said:

> And it shall come to pass in that day, that his burden shall be taken away from off thy shoulder, and his yoke from off thy neck, and the yoke shall be destroyed because of the anointing.
>
> ISAIAH 10:27

> And it shall be in that day that the burden of [the Assyrian] shall depart from your shoulders, and his yoke from your neck. The yoke shall be destroyed because of fatness [which prevents it from going around your neck].
>
> ISAIAH 10:27 (AMPC)

That is even more descriptive. It is the fat of God that destroys the yoke in people's lives. Many things are a tight yoke around people's necks—addiction, lust, temper, and many other destructive characteristics are making people's lives almost unbearable. The person wants to move in a certain direction, but that enslaving yoke pulls them wherever it wants. However, when they get under the anointing, it paints a layer of the fat of God around their neck. It causes a slippery spiritual lubrication to put up a barrier between the yoke and their neck. Every time they are under the anointing, that neck gets another layer of the thick fat of God. When they get enough of the anointing, the yoke snaps and is completely destroyed because of the fat of God collecting around their neck.

Many times, people sing Christian songs about the anointing breaking the yoke. It is, of course, alright to sing that. However, technically, it is not completely true. Something broken can be put back together again. The Bible does not say that the anointing breaks the yoke but that it destroys it. It annihilates it like a bomb. It cannot be put back together again. That is good news.

The word anoint means to paint, to smear, to rub in as with oil. God takes His big paintbrush, dips it into His thick fat oil, and starts painting us layer after layer. That is a good reason to get your arms up in a prayer line. I want God to paint me everywhere and not miss anything. I want Him to get the trim and to paint me everywhere.

When God paints your neck with layer after layer of His thick anointing, the yoke gets looser and looser until it is destroyed. By that time, your neck is painted with God's fat. It is a fat neck. God wants us to have fat necks instead of fat heads. We have too many people running around with multiple degrees from cemeteries (I mean seminaries) and no anointing. Their heads are quite fat, but their necks are still skinny. They drone on and on, and no one gets anything except some notes, Greek and Hebrew words, and definitions. The yoke still hangs on. I would rather have a kindergartner, full of The Holy Ghost, lay hands on me any day of the week.

We established that fat is what gives meat its delicious flavor. What gives God His flavor? Once again, it is the spiritually heavy, fat Shekinah (glory). When it comes to the things of God, it is not the time to be on a spiritual diet. Yet, many act like they are. They are on some kind of God-lite or God Zero diet.

I have been on many diets through the years. Once, I tried the low-fat diet. There is nothing worse than going through a buffet line at a restaurant when you are on a low-fat diet. I can always see others who are doing that. They look totally depressed. You hear, "I'll have meat, no skin, please, potatoes, no gravy, bread, no butter, salad, no dressing, and of course, no delicious dessert." Sometimes, you feel that you would be better off to eat the plate and throw the food away. Nothing has any worthwhile taste.

I see Christians doing the same thing spiritually. "I will have enough healing to make it through one night's sleep but no real healing, please. I want just enough joy to not take my life, but not enough that I act crazy. I don't want so much that I can't tell if I am still on the earth or have gone onto Heaven. I sure don't want that joy unspeakable and full of glory kind. I want only enough joy to barely bring my frown up in the corners of my mouth to a neutral half-smile. I don't want that excessive fat joy where you might be carried out of the meeting with Rivers of Living Water bubbling out of me. I want just enough salvation to squeeze into Heaven by the skin of my teeth but not enough to really be a disciple or have anyone know that I belong to Jesus. I may want to speak in tongues once so that I can say I have been baptized in The Holy Spirit, but I don't want so much that I actually live in The Spirit and not in the flesh. I want a little strength but not enough to actually overcome anything." People want just enough of God to live, but they don't want to eat of the thick, fat, heavy oil of God. My Bible says that Jesus came to give us life and life more abundantly (John 10:10). Low-fat God is not the abundant life.

I don't want a little Holy Ghost but a big Holy Ghost. I don't want God-lite. I want the thick, fat, deep, wide, heavy anointing in every area of my life. I don't want the one little piece of carrot or broccoli of God. I want the chicken fried steak smothered with gravy, kind of God. I want the hot fudge sundae version of God.

The Bible speaks of God having a table spread before us.

> Thou preparest a table before me in the presence of mine enemies: thou anointest my head with oil; my cup runneth over.
> Surely goodness and mercy shall follow me all the days of my life: and I will dwell in the house of the Lord for ever.
>
> PSALM 23:5-6

> ...they that seek the Lord shall not want any good thing.
>
> PSALM 34:10

Once you know what He's offering on the table, right in the presence of your enemies, you can eat as much as you want. It is the only place we are allowed to be gluttons. This Psalm is not talking about death, even though people like to use it at funerals. We will have no enemies in Heaven. It is talking about eating of God's good things right here on earth while demons are howling and people are throwing rocks. I shall not want any good thing. My God knows how to put on a good spread. I'll have a cake of peace (not a piece of cake), a big steak of The Word of God marbled with His fat, a side of joy for my strength, and I will drink of the new wine until I am satisfied and filled. I will experience all of God for myself. *I will have personal experience to describe to people until they want to indulge themselves.*

The anointing is truly tangible and transmittable. That means it can leave a person and go into another person. John G. Lake compared the anointing to electricity. He said, "Just like electricity flows, so the anointing flows." Electricity was on the earth long before men discovered what it was or how to harness it. Just because some do not know about the anointing, how it operates and functions, how to conduct it, or how to transmit it, does not mean that it is not real. Just like there are electricians, there are anointing tech people. We must teach about the anointing until everyone understands how to operate in it.

Mark 5 is probably the greatest passage on the transference of anointing. The woman with the issue of blood prepared herself. She pressed in, she kept saying, and she touched Him with expectancy and faith. The moment that she touched Jesus, He recognized that virtue, the anointing and power of God, had left Him. He felt it physically as well as spiritually. It is a real substance. It can be felt. His clothes were saturated with the anointing. She only had to make contact with His clothing.

It is so important that we realize that there are people who are anointing carriers and know how to transmit that anointing. When we position ourselves to get where they are, we can receive of the anointing that they are carrying. We can participate in The Holy Ghost download that they participate in.

You read earlier a small portion of Dr. Rodney Howard-Browne's testimony, "God, come down here and touch me, or take me home to be with You, but I have to have more of You." Others may press in with desperate effort, like the woman with the issue of blood. Someone may yell out loud like Bartimaeus did. You may call out for fresh fire and fresh oil like I did in Alaska. The way in which you call out is not as important as the fact that you press in, period. God likes us showing Him how hungry and thirsty we are.

One of the reasons that you need a Holy Ghost encounter is that you can't stay in your natural mind and understand the things of the Spirit. You will never understand spiritual things with your natural mind. Paul contrasts natural thinking and Holy Spirit understanding:

> As for myself, brethren, when I came to you, I did not come
> proclaiming to you the testimony and evidence or
> mystery and secret of God [concerning what He has done
> through Christ for the salvation of men] in lofty words of
> eloquence or human philosophy and wisdom;

> For I resolved to know nothing (to be acquainted with nothing, to make a display of the knowledge of nothing, and to be conscious of nothing) among you except Jesus Christ (the Messiah) and Him crucified.
>
> 1 CORINTHIANS 2:1-2 (AMPC)

Paul was trained to be an orator of orators. He said that he was a Pharisee of Pharisees. He knew how to argue anyone into a corner with his intellectual ability and his knowledge of the Scriptures. He had used this ability in the past but now knew that he must persuade people by the anointing of The Holy Ghost.

> And I was in (passed into a state of) weakness and fear (dread) and great trembling [after I had come] among you.
> And my language and my message were not set forth in persuasive (enticing and plausible) words of wisdom, but they were in demonstration of the [Holy] Spirit and power [a proof by the Spirit and power of God, operating on me and stirring in the minds of my hearers the most holy emotions and thus persuading them].
>
> 1 CORINTHIANS 2:3-4 (AMPC)

Paul's words were not of men's wisdom but were words that brought about great demonstration of The Holy Spirit. I was holding revival in a church on the West Coast many years ago. We had two great revivals there, but unfortunately, the people began to get flaky and would not receive correction. I warned them, and they would not listen. Eventually, the place blew up and no longer exists. They told me that they didn't want me to preach, just get people on the floor for the entire meeting. They told me that 1 Corinthians 2:4 says that Paul didn't preach anymore but only had demonstrations of The Holy Spirit. I told them that they were most definitely wrong. Paul said he still preached. His words were in demonstration of The Holy Spirit.

It seems that we will always have both the religious, who want no demonstration of The Holy Spirit, and the flaky, who will not preach The Word. Both are equally wrong. The Word must be first. God only confirms His Word. However, He does confirm His Word with signs and wonders following and with the demonstration of The Holy Spirit.

Paul talks about stirring the holy emotions in the minds of his hearers. Our emotions were created for more than just the excitement of a football game or your favorite sport. They were created for more than the birth of your first child. We are three-part beings, and God wants to touch all three parts: spirit, soul (the area of your mind, will, and emotions), and body.

When we receive a Holy Ghost impartation, all three parts will be touched in a profound way. It is never surprising to me that someone cries, laughs, shouts, jumps, or shakes. It only surprises me that our heads don't blow off when God fills us. He is a big God, and when He fills us, our faces and our emotions will be notified. That's why I find it hard to believe when religious people, who look like old grouches, tell me that they have joy. They say that they don't have to laugh when they have joy. I beg your pardon. If you get enough of it, your face will be notified.

I don't care how stoic someone is, what the color of their skin, their culture or upbringing; when they have enough of the power of God going through them, their emotions will follow suit.

> So that your faith might not rest in the wisdom of men
> (human philosophy), but in the power of God.
>
> 1 CORINTHIANS 2:5 (AMPC)

We have too many people who base their faith only on human wisdom. Humans can fail us. We don't need human opinions and thoughts but God's. God's thoughts and ways are higher than men's. He will give us His

Word and then back it up with mighty signs and wonders, so that people will know that there is a God in the Heavens.

> Yet when we are among the full-grown (spiritually mature Christians who are ripe in understanding), we do impart a [higher] wisdom (the knowledge of the divine plan previously hidden); but it is indeed not a wisdom of this present age or of this world nor of the leaders and rulers of this age, who are being brought to nothing and are doomed to pass away.
> But rather what we are setting forth is a wisdom of God once hidden [from the human understanding] and now revealed to us by God—[that wisdom] which God devised and decreed before the ages for our glorification [to lift us into the glory of His presence].
>
> 1 CORINTHIANS 2:6-7 (AMPC)

God is not into mystery anymore. He is into revelation. However, you have to be spiritual to have the mystery unveiled. God had a plan from before the earth was formed to use the church to show the Devil how stupid he is and how brilliant God is. It is an honor to be part of that glorious church that is being used in this hour to show forth God's wonderful plan. He reveals and makes known to us His plan as we yield ourselves to His Spirit. The more that we do that, the more of His plan will be revealed to us. Then, we are in a better position to flow with His Spirit and fulfill our assignment.

> None of the rulers of this age or world perceived and recognized and understood this, for if they had, they would never have crucified the Lord of glory.
>
> 1 CORINTHIANS 2:8 (AMPC)

The Devil and his cohorts had no idea that instead of putting away their problem, they were multiplying it. They thought they were putting the Son of God to death. They were not. He laid down His life. They could not have killed Him. He could have called the angels of Heaven to help Him. They also thought that when He was dead, God's plan would be thwarted, and humanity would have no hope. They could not figure out that instead of one anointed man walking around, manifesting the glory of God, now all born-again people would have that ability. Now, there are millions of Christians walking around, anointed like Jesus was anointed. The enemy of our souls cannot figure out God's plan for us. He knows some things and is good at what he knows, but he is not a creator, and he is limited. We have access to The Creator, The Author, and The Finisher of our faith. We can tap into our Holy Spirit resources, and The Spirit of God will show us things to come, bring things back to our remembrance, teach us, comfort us, defend us, and use us.

> But, on the contrary, as the Scripture says, What eye has not seen and ear has not heard and has not entered into the heart of man, [all that] God has prepared (made and keeps ready) for those who love Him [who hold Him in affectionate reverence, promptly obeying Him and gratefully recognizing the benefits He has bestowed].
>
> 1 CORINTHIANS 2:9 (AMPC)

Verse nine is often used at funerals and grave-side services to comfort people, as Psalm 23 is also used. Again, any Scripture can be used at any time to bring comfort and hope to people. However, neither of these passages are referring to death but rather to the here and now. The context of 1 Corinthians 2 is living in the Spirit now. It contrasts the spiritual and natural life. The Apostle Paul is saying to us that people have no idea of the things God has reserved for us. The only way that we can taste them, see them, or hear them is by The Spirit of God. We must stay hooked up to The Spirit of God and not try to reason spiritual things with our limited minds.

We talk to God, spirit to Spirit, not mind to mind. Only a spiritual person can understand these things.

Unfortunately, many born-again people, and even some who have been baptized in The Holy Spirit, quit pursuing God and spiritual things a long time ago and are only living on spiritual memories. They have become spiritually dull and dormant and can no longer understand spiritual things. They must get hungry all over again and have a new Holy Ghost encounter.

> Yet to us God has unveiled and revealed them by and through His Spirit, for the [Holy] Spirit searches diligently, exploring and examining everything, even sounding the profound and bottomless things of God [the divine counsels and things hidden and beyond man's scrutiny].
>
> 1 CORINTHIANS 2:10 (AMPC)

Verse 10 speaks of sounding the profound and bottomless things of God. The word sounding makes me think of a submarine. I have watched enough movies with submarines to realize just a little about sounding. It seems that there is some sort of sonar device that puts out a sound or a ping to ask how deep the submarine is. The same system sounds back with a ping. It is saying "This is how deep you are, but you can still go deeper." Our spirits send out a signal to God asking if we can go deeper. His response is always, "Yes, you are this deep, but you can go deeper still." This is a matter of deep calling unto deep.

> For what person perceives (knows and understands) what passes through a man's thoughts except the man's own spirit within him? Just so no one discerns (comes to know and comprehend) the thoughts of God except the Spirit of God.
> Now we have not received the spirit [that belongs to] the

> world, but the [Holy] Spirit Who is from God, [given to us] that we might realize and comprehend and appreciate the gifts [of divine favor and blessing so freely and lavishly] bestowed on us by God.
>
> 1 CORINTHIANS 2:11-12 (AMPC)

We did not receive our salvation or any other spiritual gift from man. They were given to us by The Holy Spirit, and they must continue to come that way and be appreciated and understood by The Holy Spirit. Our minds do not house The Holy Spirit. Our spirits do. We are always checking out everything that happens in this world by the spirit of God. That is how we know how to conduct ourselves, what to do in any situation, etc.

> And we are setting these truths forth in words not taught by human wisdom but taught by the [Holy] Spirit, combining and interpreting spiritual truths with spiritual language [to those who possess the Holy Spirit].
> But the natural, nonspiritual man does not accept or welcome or admit into his heart the gifts and teachings and revelations of the Spirit of God, for they are folly (meaningless nonsense) to him; and he is incapable of knowing them [of progressively recognizing, understanding, and becoming better acquainted with them] because they are spiritually discerned and estimated and appreciated.
>
> 1 CORINTHIANS 2:13-14 (AMPC)

These verses make it plain how the natural mind and the natural man cannot begin to understand spiritual things. If you try to understand spiritual things with your mind, you will become frustrated. You will also judge wrong, and you will call things of The Holy Spirit folly, as many do in our revival meanings. Many people think that people expressing themselves with holy emotions is meaningless nonsense. If they are thinking with their natural minds, the Bible makes it clear that they are incapable of understanding these things. They are only spiritually discerned and appreciated.

> But the spiritual man tries all things [he examines, investigates, inquires into, questions, and discerns all things], yet is himself to be put on trial and judged by no one [he can read the meaning of everything, but no one can properly discern or appraise or get an insight into him].
>
> 1 CORINTHIANS 2:15 (AMPC)

You will never understand a spiritual person or a spiritual minister by natural reasoning. Don't even try. If you only think naturally, and the other person thinks the thoughts and purposes of God, it will always be confusing to you. You won't understand their faith, vision, or their actions. Don't even try. You will end up judging things that you know nothing about. That is dangerous.

> For who has known or understood the mind (the counsels and purposes) of the Lord so as to guide and instruct Him and give Him knowledge? But we have the mind of Christ (the Messiah) and do hold the thoughts (feelings and purposes) of His heart.
>
> 1 CORINTHIANS 2:16 (AMPC)

If we will stay in the Spirit, we will think like Christ and have His understanding in all things. The way that you continue in The Spirit, instead of in the natural, is to be continually filled with The Holy Spirit.

> And do not get drunk with wine, for that is debauchery; but ever be filled and stimulated with the [Holy] Spirit. Speak out to one another in psalms and hymns and spiritual

DESPERATE HUNGER GETS GOD'S ATTENTION

> songs, offering praise with voices [and instruments] and making melody with all your heart to the Lord,
>
> EPHESIANS 5:18-19 (AMPC)

You and I must have continuous Holy Ghost impartations and encounters.

You must expect more than a good meeting and prepare yourself ahead of time. Everyone in the Bible who had a Holy Ghost encounter did some things to get ready. Blind Bartimaeus took off his beggar's garment ahead of time before he was healed. Naaman was told to go to the muddy Jordon and dip seven times. The man in the Bible who was blind was told to "Go wash in the pool of Siloam."

One man was told to pick up his bed and walk. We've read that we might have to take off the roof for our friends. You must make a demand on the anointing. It can't be a casual touch. Jesus is looking for someone desperate enough to show Him how desperate you are. Let God hit you so hard that He knocks the "S" off your name like He did with Saul, who became Paul. Paul had a Jesus encounter on the Damascus Road.

We need to expect the unexpected, the sudden-lies of God like they experienced on the Day of Pentecost.

> When the Day of Pentecost had fully come, they were all with one accord in one place. And suddenly there came a sound from heaven, as of a rushing mighty wind, and it filled the whole house where they were sitting. Then there appeared to them divided tongues, as of fire, and one sat upon each of them. And they were all filled with the Holy Spirit and began to speak with other tongues, as the Spirit gave them utterance.
>
> ACTS 2:1-4 (NKJV)

We must become desperate and humble for revival. We should say, "God, come and do whatever You want to do. I won't stop or hinder You. I won't put You in a box. I will yield to You." However, when you tell God that, you must be careful that you really mean it because He will take you up on it.

Some will object to the demonstration of The Holy Spirit and try to remind us that all things must be done decently and in order, but whose order are we talking about? Are we talking about the second chapter of Acts order or the order of a graveyard?

We see that on the day that the church was birthed, many manifestations accompanied the impartation. First, some sort of a tornado came through the building. The AMPC says in verse 2, *"When suddenly there came a sound from heaven like the rushing of a violent tempest blast, and it filled the whole house in which they were sitting."* That is quite the manifestation. I don't think one person could be left sitting and quietly praying after a violent tempest blast has just come through the room. Next, they had cloven tongues of fire above their heads. How would you react if you knew that it was above your head and you could see it above the heads of all of the others in the room? Again, it would be impossible to remain sitting with no reaction. Verse 4 in the AMPC says, *"And they were all filled (diffused throughout their souls) with the Holy Spirit and began to speak in other (different, foreign) languages (tongues), as the Spirit kept giving them clear and loud expression [in each tongue in appropriate words]."* To be diffused throughout your soul is not an everyday occurrence. *Diffuse* is a term that means to spread out over a large area. God spread His power over a large area of the people's souls, their emotions. Then, they began to speak in languages that they had never learned. There is no way that all of that would not affect the emotions. They became so loud that they could be heard all over Jerusalem. That is what caused the people from many nations to run into the building to observe what was taking place. How loud would a congregation have to get to be heard all over the city?

If manifestations of The Holy Spirit, accompanied by holy emotions, were not found in church history or in the Bible itself, we would need to throw these experiences out. However, when we find them both in the Bible and throughout church history, we realize that God has always been touching His people and giving them divine encounters. Let's look at both historical and Biblical precedents of manifestations of The Holy Spirit where people's holy emotions were stirred.

Jonathan Edwards says of the Great Awakening, which took place in North Hampton, New Hampshire (1725-1760), "Many have had their religious affections raised far beyond what they had ever been before; and there were some instances of persons lying in a sort of trance, remaining perhaps for a whole twenty-four hours motionless, and with their senses locked up; but, in the meantime, under strong imaginations, as though they went to Heaven and had there a vision of glorious and delightful objects. It was a very frequent thing to see outcries, faintings, convulsions, and such like, both with distress, and also admiration and joy. It was not the manner here to hold meetings all night, nor was it common to continue them till very late in the night; but it was pretty often so, that there were some so affected and their bodies so overcome, that they could not go home, but were obligated to stay all night where they were."

In the second Great Awakening, at a country place named Sodom in the state of New York, Charles Finney gave one address in which he described the condition of Sodom before God destroyed it. "I had not spoken more than a quarter of an hour, when an awful solemnity seemed to settle upon them; the congregation began to fall from their seats in every direction, and cried for mercy. If I had had a sword in each hand, I could not have cut them down as fast as they fell. Nearly the whole congregation were either on their knees or prostrate, I should think, in less than two minutes from the shock that fell upon them. Every one prayed who was able to speak at all." Similar scenes were witnessed in many other places.

We see instances of people shaking under the power of God. George Fox, founder of the Quakers, after a life-changing experience with the Holy Spirit, said, "The Lord's power began to shake them, says he, and great meetings we began to have, and a mighty power and work of God there was amongst people, to the astonishment of both people and priests." Later, he says, "After this, I went to Mansfield, where there was a great meeting of professors and people; here I was moved to pray; and the Lord's power was so great, that the house seemed to be shaken." Describing his meetings at Ticknell, England, he says: "The priest began trembling himself; and one of the people said, 'Look how the priest trembles and shakes, he is turned Quaker also.'" Shaking has to do with holy fear and great power. When enough power goes through you, you will shake, like someone who is being electrocuted.

We have many Bible verses about joy. Galatians 5:22 lists joy as one of the fruits of the spirit.

> But the fruit of the Spirit is love, joy, peace, longsuffering, gentleness, goodness, faith.
>
> GALATIANS 5:22

> For the kingdom of God is not meat and drink; but righteousness, and peace, and joy in the Holy Ghost.
>
> ROMANS 14:17

> Whom having not seen, ye love; in whom, though now ye see him not, yet believing, ye rejoice with joy unspeakable and full of glory.
>
> 1 PETER 1:8

> Our mouths were filled with laughter...
> Those who sow with tears
> will reap with songs of joy.
>
> PSALM 126:2 AND 5 (NIV)

> A time to weep and a time to laugh...
>
> ECCLESIASTES 3:4 (NIV)

DESPERATE HUNGER GETS GOD'S ATTENTION

"I am coming to you now, but I say these things while I am still in the world, so that they may have the full measure of my joy within them."

JOHN 17:13 (NIV)

In thy presence is fullness of joy…

PSALM 16:11

Restore unto me the joy of thy salvation…

PSALM 51:12

And the ransomed of the Lord shall return, and come to Zion with songs and everlasting joy upon their heads: they shall obtain joy and gladness, and sorrow and sighing shall flee away.

ISAIAH 35:10

To appoint unto them that mourn in Zion, to give unto them beauty for ashes, the oil of joy for mourning, the garment of praise for the spirit of heaviness; that they might be called trees of righteousness, the planting of the Lord, that he might be glorified.

ISAIAH 61:3

He that believeth on me, as the scripture hath said, out of his belly shall flow rivers of living water.

(But this spake he of the Spirit, which they that believe on him should receive: for the Holy Ghost was not yet given; because that Jesus was not yet glorified.)

JOHN 7:38-39

...for the joy of the Lord is your strength.

NEHEMIAH 8:10

He that sitteth in the heavens shall laugh: the Lord shall have them in derision.

PSALM 2:4

A merry heart does good, like medicine...

PROVERBS 17:22 (NKJV)

And the disciples were filled with joy, and with the Holy Ghost.

ACTS 13:52

And there was great joy in that city.

ACTS 8:8

And he brought forth his people with joy, and his chosen with gladness.

PSALM 105:43

DESPERATE HUNGER GETS GOD'S ATTENTION

> Rejoice in that day and leap for joy...
>
> LUKE 6:23 (ESV)

> Let the saints be joyful in glory: let them sing aloud upon their beds.
>
> PSALM 149:5

> Thou wilt shew me the path of life: in thy presence is fulness of joy; at thy right hand there are pleasures for evermore.
>
> PSALM 16:11

> Therefore Sarah laughed within herself, saying, After I am waxed old shall I have pleasure, my lord being old also?
>
> GENESIS 18:12

Both Abraham and Sarah experienced joy when God told them they would have a child in their old age. Abraham named Isaac "he laughs" (Isaac). Joy and laughter present God's sovereign activity to heal the barrenness of His people.

Psalm 126: *"Our mouths were filled with laughter...those who sow in tears will reap in joy."* I have experienced that myself. After sowing for many years in tears, I have experienced great joy and laughter.

> A time to weep and a time to laugh...
>
> ECCLESIASTES 3:4 (NIV)

I had the privilege of ministering in New Zealand in 1996. I was there for two weeks. I ministered on both the North and South Islands. While on the North Island, I was asked to do a women's conference. Many women were healed from the inside out. Some of them had been victims of rape and incest, and God completely set them free. They received great "joy unspeakable and full of glory." The next week, I was on the South Island in a city called Christchurch, where I was in a church for revival. We had about five hundred people one evening. The pastor told me that we had many denominations represented. The joy of The Lord was engulfing the place, except for one section of the congregation. Much to my surprise, The Lord told me that it was the Pentecostal section that was being so religious and stiff. Then he told me just what to do.

I announced that I was going to call up women who had been touched previously at the women's conference on the other island. I called up five of them and asked them to testify. Each one responded in exactly the same way. Their faces glowed; they opened their mouths, burst out laughing, and fell out on the floor laughing. I ended up calling up about fifteen to twenty of them, and they all reacted the same way. By this time, I could see that the Pentecostals were even angrier. The Spirit of God spoke to me by His still voice on the inside again and told me what to do. I said, "Some of you are thinking that it would not be God for the evangelist to ask people to testify and then they can't testify." I saw some of them nod their heads in agreement with that statement. I went on to ask the question, "How many of you grew up singing the song *It is Joy Unspeakable and Full of Glory?*" They all raised their hands. I explained what that song was about.

The author of that song had experienced what The Apostle Peter was talking about when he said in 1 Peter 1:8, "*...ye rejoice with joy unspeakable and full of glory.*" He was trying to say in the song that it is too much, too powerful, too overwhelming to put into words. One of the verses says, "*I have found the joy no tongue can tell, how its waves of glory roll; it is like a great o'erflowing well, springing up within my soul.*" The problem is that another generation comes along that does not have the same experience. They only have the song. People continue to sing it but have no idea what it is about. They think they do. They sing the words with the right melody and maybe clap a little to the beat but with a frown on their face and no experience within.

DESPERATE HUNGER GETS GOD'S ATTENTION

I went on to explain to the crowd that these ladies knew from experience what the rest were only singing. They testified. They just didn't use words. I could hear everything that they said. It was clear. "I would love to tell you what He did for me, but it is too overwhelming. When I go to tell it, I step right back into the experience that I had when He touched me. I cannot talk. I can only express the joy because it is 'joy unspeakable and full of glory.' The language of joy is laughter."

Finally, the Pentecostals understood that they had only been singing the song of someone else's experience. Great joy broke out among them, and we had church in a big way. Now they had an experience for themselves.

> And the ransomed of the Lord shall return, and come to Zion with songs and everlasting joy upon their heads: they shall obtain joy and gladness, and sorrow and sighing shall flee away.
>
> ISAIAH 35:10

> ...for the joy of the Lord is your strength.
>
> NEHEMIAH 8:10

Many people have no strength because they have no joy. You cannot have lasting strength without lasting joy. If you want more strength, yield to God's wonderful joy.

These are some of the historical precedents of joy. Jonathan Edwards said, "It was very wonderful to see how a person's affections were sometimes moved, when God did as it were suddenly open their eyes, and let into their minds a sense of the greatness of His grace, the fullness of Christ, and His readiness to save... Their joyful surprise has caused their hearts as it were to leap, so that they have been ready to break forth into laughter, tears often at the same time issuing like a flood, and intermingling a loud weeping. Sometimes they have not been able to forebear crying out with a loud voice, expressing their great admiration. The manner of God's work on the soul, sometimes especially, is very mysterious."

Also, Charles Finney spoke about having to bury his head in a fireplace with a cloth over his face because he could not quit laughing uncontrollably when God touched him. In his book *Demonstrations of The Spirit's Power*, he said, "My heart was so overflowing with joy at such a scene, that I could hardly contain myself. A little way from where I stood was an open fireplace. I recollect very well that my joy was so great, that I could not help laughing in a most spasmodic manner. I knelt down and stuck my head into that fireplace and hung my pocket handkerchief over my head, lest they should see me laugh; for I was aware that they would not understand that it was irrepressible, holy joy that made me laugh. It was with much difficulty that I refrained from shouting, and giving glory to God."

This is how I got healed from years of heartache and abuse. When I first called out for fresh oil, the joy of The Lord came to my life and into our church, the prison ministry, and every village that I went to minister in. There were many nights that I was carried home from my own meetings. Many times, I was still laughing with joy that was unspeakable. Sometimes, I was crying and speaking in other tongues at the same time. I was caught up in that wonderful heavenly realm. In those moments, the Spirit realm is more real to people than the natural realm.

When I attended Dr. Rodney Howard-Browne's meetings in Anchorage, I received even more joy. I didn't think for one moment that I had enough. This is an ongoing relationship with The Lord, and I endeavor to continue to be filled every day.

Laughter is the language of joy. There is no such thing as joy without laughter.

Some people who claim that they have joy need to notify their face. Even in the world, no one claims joy without laughter. Many have a difficult time receiving joy because they are trying to reason with their heads. God needs to give some people a head bypass surgery so that He can drop into their hearts.

Overwhelming laughter has characterized many of our meetings from the beginning. Sometimes, it takes place during worship, sometimes at the end of the service, or in the prayer line. Joy can take place, even in the middle of preaching God's Word. Some say that it is interrupting the message. However, it would not be the first time because we see that happening in the Bible.

> While Peter yet spake these words, the Holy Ghost fell on all them which heard the word.
> And they of the circumcision which believed were astonished, as many as came with Peter, because that on the Gentiles also was poured out the gift of the Holy Ghost.
> For they heard them speak with tongues, and magnify God.
>
> ACTS 10:44-46

While Peter was yet preaching, The Holy Spirit dared to fall on them, and they began to speak in other tongues. It happened while he was still preaching. The Holy Spirit didn't say, "Peter, I know that you have been fasting and praying and have additional points for this message. Please let me know when you are finished so that I can confirm My Word with signs following." No, He basically was saying by demonstration, "You have preached enough. The people are ready to receive, and I am going to show them right now what you are preaching about."

If people understood what is available through this wonderful joy, they would endeavor to receive it. Isaiah 12:3 says, *"Therefore with joy will you draw water from the wells of salvation."* Many people's buckets are broken, and they cannot draw up all that salvation has purchased for them in the *sozo* life, the God-kind of life. That Greek word for life includes preservation, wholeness, health, peace of mind, and prosperity.

We live far below our rights in defeat, discouragement, and depression. It's not part of God's plan. The Comforter will deliver to you whatever Jesus purchased through His death, burial, and resurrection. When God can get

His people filled with The Holy Ghost, they can receive His benefits more easily.

We must stop allowing things on the outside to affect our lives. Instead, we must learn to let that joy bubble up on the inside. We can start rejoicing whenever we decide to. Smith Wigglesworth said, "When I get up in the morning, I never ask Wigglesworth how he is. I take him to the Bible and show him how he is." We can learn a lot from that great man of God.

We must learn to laugh at problems. The worst insult that you can give the Devil is to laugh at him instead of responding to him. Can you imagine a meeting in Hell and the Devil says to his demons, "I thought you were told to stop that Christian." The demons reply, "We tried, but he or she just laughs like we didn't do anything. Our weapons are useless against him. He seems to have joy, no matter how many times he is shot with one of our bullets."

> Restore unto me the joy of thy salvation; and uphold me
> > with thy free spirit.
> Then will I teach transgressors thy ways; and sinners shall be
> > converted unto thee.
>
> PSALM 51:12-13

David asked God to restore the joy of his salvation. If you have lost yours, simply ask God to restore it. If your joy is restored, you'll see sinners converted. We still need joy today to reach sinners.

I have observed that the more joyful our meetings are, that more people get saved. We see a lot of problems when joy is lost.

> Be ye ashamed, O ye husbandmen; howl, O ye vinedressers,
> > for the wheat and for the barley; because the harvest of
> > the field is perished.
> The vine is dried up, and the fig tree languisheth; the pomegranate tree, the palm tree also, and the apple tree, even

> all the trees of the field, are withered: because joy is withered away from the sons of men.
>
> JOEL 1:11-12

A teacher by the name of Mark Brazee, who was touched in Dr. Rodney Howard-Browne's meetings, says in his book *Blood, Fire, and Vapor of Smoke*, "The vine represents the church, the fig tree represents Israel, and other fruit-producing trees represent the gentiles. If we are not producing, it is because we have lost our joy. The vine is a picture of the church that has been grafted in. We see here that all three are barren because joy has been lost. When joy is restored to the church, it will affect all of the other groups."

What happened on the day of Pentecost in the move of The Holy Ghost never offended anyone. It actually got their attention. Being religious for two thousand years hasn't gotten the church anywhere. With the first outpouring of joy, the world was changed. Joy will still change the church and touch our world.

Joy brings about times of refreshing.

> Repent ye therefore, and be converted, that your sins may be blotted out, when the times of refreshing shall come from the presence of the Lord.
> And he shall send Jesus Christ, which before was preached unto you.
>
> ACTS 3:19-20

Peter joins together the times of refreshing with the return of Jesus. He says that before Jesus comes for us, there will be a great refreshing to the church. So, this is not some side issue but a sign of the times. We have now seen this joy go from nation to nation and continent to continent on a worldwide scale.

This great outpouring of the Holy Ghost is part of God's last-day eschatological calendar.

> But, beloved, be not ignorant of this one thing, that one day is with the Lord as a thousand years, and a thousand years as one day.
>
> 2 PETER 3:8

Peter is talking about the return of Jesus to the Jewish mind. He knew that they would reflect to the Old Testament. In Hosea 6:2-3, the prophet Hosea was talking about the latter rain. It says, *"After two days will he revive us: in the third day he will raise us up, and we shall live in his sight. Then shall we know, if we follow on to know the Lord: his going forth is prepared as the morning; and he shall come unto us as the rain, as the latter and former rain unto the earth."*

This is talking about the catching away of the church. After two days, or two thousand years, we should expect a great reviving.

To revive means to bring back or restore to life. Revival is for the church, not the world. You can't have a RE-vival until you have had a vival. The move of God began to gain momentum on a worldwide scale in about 1995. History says that Jesus was born about 5 B.C. Now, it is two thousand years since His first coming. After two days or two thousand years, there will be a great reviving. As we move into the third day or the three thousand year period, He's going to raise us up to live with Him.

There's different equipment for different seasons. Farmers understand that they must use different equipment for the harvest. Revivalists also realize that. We must operate in signs, wonders, miracles, and the outpouring of the Holy Spirit.

DESPERATE HUNGER GETS GOD'S ATTENTION

> He that goeth forth and weepeth, bearing precious seed,
> shall doubtless come again with rejoicing, bringing his
> sheaves with him.
>
> PSALMS 126:6

The Church has been weeping and bearing seed, which is the Word of God. Some of it has been hard plowing. We have been planting and waiting. It has meant blood, sweat, and tears for the church. However, when you get into harvest season, there's rejoicing. When you see people rejoicing, shouting, laughing, and being full of joy, you know we've stepped over from the weeping season to the rejoicing season, and Jesus' return is just around the corner.

Church history is full of joy. Let's start with Jesus Himself. He displayed great joy. People say that Jesus never expressed Himself that way. They are wrong.

> In that hour Jesus rejoiced in spirit, and said, I thank thee, O
> Father, Lord of heaven and earth, that thou hast hid
> these things from the wise and prudent, and hast
> revealed them unto babes: even so, Father; for so it
> seemed good in thy sight.
>
> LUKE 10:21

The word for *rejoiced* implies twirling and dancing. Besides, everyone who Jesus touched did display great joy. They went walking, leaping, and praising God. Also, the Bible says in John 17:13, *"I am coming to you now but I say these things while I am still in the world so that they may have the full measure of my joy within them."*

Sometimes, people have so much joy that they are overcome and look and act drunk. One of the definitions of the word drunk, according to Webster's dictionary, is to be "overcome by any powerful emotion, drunk with joy, happiness, etc." We see this in several places in the Bible.

> ...I am like a drunken man,
> like a strong man overcome by wine,
> because of the Lord
> and his holy words.
>
> JEREMIAH 23:9 (NIV)

Being overcome with God's holiness seems to overpower a man's senses in much the same way that alcohol overpowers them.

> Others mocking said, These men are full of new wine.
> For these are not drunken, as ye suppose, seeing it is but the third hour of the day.
>
> ACTS 2:13 AND 15

This text infers they are acting drunk. They would not have been accused of drunkenness if they were only speaking different languages. A person who is drunk on alcohol cannot even speak their own language, let alone many that they never learned. They were acting drunk, laughing, crying, falling, slurred speech by some, unusual boldness, etc.

I remember the story Pastor Rodney Howard-Browne tells of a lady who got so touched at his meeting in Lakeland, Florida. When she left his meeting, she continued to listen to the altar call on the radio. She was so overcome by The Spirit of God that she began to swerve a bit on the highway. She saw the blue lights of a police car in her rear-view mirror. She pulled over but was laughing and crying. The policeman asked her to open her door. At first, she was laughing too much to get it open. He yelled, "What is wrong with you, Lady? Are you drunk?" She replied, "Yes, I'm drunk, but not on what you think." Eventually, she got the door open and stepped outside of the vehicle. He grabbed her elbow and immediately fell to the ground, laughing and crying. He confessed that he was the backslidden son of a Pentecostal preacher and knew that the power of God that was on her went into him. He repented and came back into a relationship with The

Lord while he was on the ground. She was indeed drunk but not on alcohol. She was overcome with the power of The Holy Spirit. She was overcome with wonderful joy.

The Bible makes an analogy between the new wine of The Holy Spirit and alcohol.

> And be not drunk with wine, wherein is excess; but be filled with the Spirit.
>
> EPHESIANS 5:18

It is in the Greek present tense: "keep on being filled with The Holy Spirit." Paul contrasts carnal drunkenness with spiritual filling. Given the tense of the Greek verb, he appears to also be making an analogy as well as a contrast. Being filled is similar in many ways to being drunk on wine. The difference is that the former is holy while the other is sinful.

Let's think about the reasons that people go to a bar with the determination to get drunk. Some are shy and wish that they could be more outgoing, the so-called life of the party. When a man gets under another influence, he is the one who dances on the table at 2:00 a.m. Some feel that they are easily bullied and too gutless to stand up for themselves and fight. However, when he gets under the influence of enough alcohol, he will initiate the fight first and say, "I won't take that anymore." Then, he makes a fist and hits the other one first. He feels much larger on the inside than he is. Some go to the bar because they are lonesome and looking for love in all the wrong places. He may think a woman is so ugly that she needs to wear a bag over her head, but when he is under the influence of unholy spirits (notice that another word for alcohol is spirits), he suddenly loves the one he used to hate. Some go to the bar looking for counsel. They end up telling a bartender about their financial woes, their marriage, and relationship problems. They end up being given advice by a man whose greatest achievement in life is serving whiskey over a bar counter. "Well, I'll tell you what I would do with that old lady of yours…" Some are financial tight-wads who want to get free, but they do so under the wrong influence. They may say, "It's on the house. I'll pay for everybody." He finds out the next day that he spent a month's wages on alcohol. Others need fellowship and just want to go where they feel like they have friends and family.

The person who turns to alcohol or drugs may end up losing his family, finding himself in the wrong bed with a snaggle-toothed woman who he didn't even want to be with. He may end up losing all of his money and not even realize how it happened. He wakes up the next morning, vomiting over a porcelain throne, and has great regret. He may lose his health with a diseased liver or ulcers. He may even end up in jail because of a DWI (driving while intoxicated) or committing a crime that he would never have done if not under the wrong influence.

The Bible makes it clear that alcohol is a terrible counterfeit of what we really should desire to be filled with. When you step under the influence of The Holy Spirit, everything will be according to the will of God. The timid person will find boldness. The person who can't get along with anyone and is critical of people will now be saying, "I don't know what's been wrong with me. Now, I am filled with the love of God and love everyone." The one under the influence of The Holy Spirit may find himself saying while operating under a gift of faith, "I'll pay for the entire crusade." When a person is filled with The Holy Spirit, he will no longer let the Devil bully him. He will say, "I am a thousand times bigger on the inside, and I know who I am in Christ Jesus. I now know how to stand up and use the weapons of my warfare and fight. Devil, you will no longer cause havoc in my life or my house. I'm not afraid of you anymore." The person under the influence of The Holy Spirit receives divine counsel and guidance and has access to know all things. He receives healing instead of losing his health. He prospers instead of going into financial ruin. Everyone should desire to have that empty place filled with The Holy Spirit instead of filling it with a counterfeit.

> No man putteth a piece of new cloth unto an old garment,
>   for that which is put in to fill it up taketh from the
>   garment, and the rent is made worse.
> Neither do men put new wine into old bottles: else the

DESPERATE HUNGER GETS GOD'S ATTENTION

bottles break, and the wine runneth out, and the bottles perish: but they put new wine into new bottles, and both are preserved.

MATTHEW 9:16-17

Finis Dake says this in Dake's Annotated Bible: "Old wineskins weren't good for any liquid especially wine, because of fermentation (violence and turbulence) caused it to burst. They have to be soaked in water to soften them. Then they must be greased with oil or butter to prevent leaking and evaporation. In keeping the old customs of Matthew 9:14-15, the two systems of Jewish religion and Christianity can't be mixed. To patch the old with the new wine would make things worse and to combine the two systems would be destruction to both. The old covenant must make way for the new. The new cannot be part of the old because of the new life and freedom is impossible to have with the old."

We can't just reform the old system. In order to get new wineskins, the animal has to die. That is why many churches that say they want a move of God need to get rid of old religious practices that are not part of the freedom of The Holy Spirit or what we find in The Bible. You cannot sing funeral songs or songs of doubt and unbelief and have a move of God. I have heard my pastor, Dr. Rodney Howard-Browne, explain to pastors why they cannot continue in some of their flaky doctrines and have the move of God at the same time. Often, they nod and then continue as before. I have witnessed that the move of God stops, and they return to their pre-revival days.

We see people not only laughing with joy but also weeping in revival. Sometimes, people cry when they are touched. That is a common occurrence when God shows up. Crying is a natural response to the move of the Holy Spirit. It comes as a result of the Holy Spirit bringing conviction. Sometimes, it is a cleansing cry. Others may have a gut-wrenching wail. Sometimes, the cry accompanies feelings of joy. Once again, we have Biblical precedents and church historical precedent.

> ...all the people had been weeping as they listened to the words of the Law.
>
> NEHEMIAH 8:9 (NIV)

> Because your heart was responsive and you humbled yourself...and tore your robes and wept in my presence, I have heard you...
>
> 2 CHRONICLES 34:27 (NIV)

> When the people heard this, they were cut to the heart...
>
> ACTS 2:37 (NIV)

John Wesley said in 1739 that there was another remarkable case of conviction of sin in Bristol. He had just expounded on Acts 4 on the power of the Holy Spirit. "We then called upon God to confirm His Word," says he. "Immediately one that stood by (to our no small surprise) and cried aloud, with the utmost vehemence, even as the agonies of death. It was a frequent occurrence for people to cry aloud or fall down as if dead in the meetings, so great was their anguish of heart, caused, no doubt, by the Holy Spirit convicting them of sin."

You may shake when you have a Holy Spirit encounter. These manifestations are all part of holy emotions. We see it many times in the Bible. Sometimes, the shaking has to do with holy fear. Other times, it has to do with how much power is going through a person and their body's response to it.

> And I, Daniel, alone saw the vision, for the men who were with me did not see the vision, but a great trembling fell upon them, and they fled to hide themselves.
>
> DANIEL 10:7 (ESV)

DESPERATE HUNGER GETS GOD'S ATTENTION

> "Should you not fear me?" declares the Lord.
> "Should you not tremble in my presence?"
>
> JEREMIAH 5:22 (NIV)

In speaking of his prophetic experience, he says:

> My heart is broken within me;
> all my bones tremble...
>
> JEREMIAH 23:9 (NIV)

> I heard and my heart pounded,
> my lips quivered at the sound;
> decay crept into my bones,
> and my legs trembled...
>
> HABAKKUK 3:16 (NIV)

> And for fear of him the keepers did shake, and became as dead men.
>
> MATTHEW 28:4

> ...the place where they were meeting was shaken...
>
> ACTS 4:31 (NIV)

> ...the devils also believe, and tremble.
>
> JAMES 2:19

When John G. Lake compared the anointing to electricity, he was very accurate. When a person grabs ahold of a live wire flowing with electricity, they usually shake. When enough of the anointing of The Holy Spirit is flowing through a person, they also may shake. If the molecules in the walls of a building can shake with God's power, it does not surprise me that a human may shake when God's power saturates him or her. Acts 4:31: *"The place where they were meeting was shaken."*

People may even experience a Holy Spirit trance. In Acts 10:10, while Peter was on the roof of Simon the Tanner's house, it says that *"he fell into a trance."* Strong's Greek word for trance is *ekstasis* and means a displacement of the mind, i.e., bewilderment, *ecstasy*. It means to be amazed, amazement, astonishment. Dr. Thayer, in The Hebrew Greek Dictionary, says it means: (1) any casting down of a thing from its proper place or state, displacement, (2) A *throwing* of the mind out of its normal state, and (3) Although he is awake, his mind is drawn off from all surrounding objects and wholly fixed on things divine that he sees nothing but the forms and images lying within, and thinks that he perceives with his bodily eyes and ears realities shown him by God.

The word amazement means the state of one who is thrown into a state of blended fear and wonderment. The same word is used again in Mark 16:8: *"And they went out quickly, and fled from the sepulcher: for they trembled and were amazed: neither said they any thing to any man; for they were afraid."* Vine's dictionary says that *ekstasis* means to amaze. It was said of any displacement, and especially concerning the mind, of that alteration of the normal condition by which the person is thrown into a state of surprise or fear or both; or again, in which a person is so transported out of his natural state that he falls into a trance. Webster's dictionary says that ecstasy is the state of being overpowered with emotion, especially joy, being beside oneself with feeling.

> He became hungry and wanted something to eat, and while the meal was being prepared, he fell into a trance.
>
> ACTS 10:10 (NIV)

This speaks of Peter entering into a trance.

DESPERATE HUNGER GETS GOD'S ATTENTION

> "I was in the city of Joppa praying, and in a trance I saw a vision. I saw something like a large sheet being let down from heaven by its four corners, and it came down to where I was."
>
> ACTS 11:5 (NIV)

> "When I returned to Jerusalem and was praying at the temple, I fell into a trance."
>
> ACTS 22:17 (NIV)

Paul went into a trance after his conversion.

This is a condition in which ordinary consciousness and the perception of natural circumstances were withheld, and the soul was susceptible only to the vision imparted by God. (Vine's Expository Dictionary of Biblical Words)

> It is not expedient for me doubtless to glory. I will come to visions and revelations of the Lord.
> I knew a man in Christ above fourteen years ago, (whether in the body, I cannot tell; or whether out of the body, I cannot tell: God knoweth;) such an one caught up to the third heaven.
> And I knew such a man, (whether in the body, or out of the body, I cannot tell: God knoweth;)
> How that he was caught up into paradise, and heard unspeakable words, which it is not lawful for a man to utter.
>
> 2 CORINTHIANS 12:1-4

Paul describes an amazing experience where he didn't know if he was in or out of his body. He was *caught up in paradise*, where he heard inexpressible things that he was not permitted to tell. It implies he was awake when the revelation came and was in some sort of trance-like state. The Apostle John says in Revelation 1:17, *"When I saw him I fell at his feet as though dead."*

We have already talked about Jonathan Edwards of the Great Awakening. In his *An Account of Revival of Religion in Northampton 1740-1742*, he says, "Many have had their religious affections raised far beyond what they had ever been before; and there were some instances of persons lying in a *sort of trance*, remaining perhaps for a whole twenty-four hours *motionless*, and with their *senses locked up*; but in the meantime under strong imaginations, as though they went to Heaven and had there a vision of glorious and delightful objects. It was a very frequent thing to see outcries, faintings, convulsions, and such like, both with distress and also admiration and joy. It was not the manner here to hold meetings all night, nor was it common to continue them till very late in the night; but it was pretty often so, that there were some so affected and their bodies so overcome, that they could not go home, but were obligated to stay all night where they were." He also said, "Nothing of religious significance ever took place in the human heart if it wasn't deeply affected by such Godly emotions."

Maria Woodsworth-Etter went into Holy Ghost trances, and people in her meetings also went into Holy Ghost trances. Many times, while she was ministering, she would freeze in a trance. She sometimes would stay in this trance-like state for long periods of time, even hours. When she came out of the trance, she shared with her audience visions that she had just seen. Often, these visions were of Heaven and Hell. The newspapers began calling her the "Trance Evangelist." Many accused her of using hypnotism. But she told them that the trances in her meetings were by the power of God.

Commenting on these trances, in 1885, a newspaper reporter for the *Cincinnati Enquirer* wrote: "I have endeavored to give a true and impartial account of the very remarkable revival of religion at the Methodist Episcopal Church in this city, and I am impressed with the magnitude of the undertaking. Scores have been stricken down at these meetings, and whatever form the limbs or body chanced to assume, in that position, immovable as a statue, they remained – sometimes the hand uplifted far above the head, the eyes open wide, and not a muscle of the entire body moved; they were as immovable as in death."

There was a young girl in Pastor Rodney's meetings in South Africa many years ago who stepped into a Holy Ghost trance. When her mother attempted to grab her by the elbow to take her home, her mother was struck to the floor by the power of God. It was a true sign and wonder. Her life was transformed, and she became a soul-winner and is in the ministry today. Many have been born again as a result.

When I attended Pastor Rodney Howard-Browne's campmeeting in Louisville, Kentucky, in the early nineties, there was an elderly man who also stepped over in a Holy Ghost trance. Pastor Rodney pointed at where he was, and as we looked, there was the man with one foot off the ground and his arm outstretched, but he was not blinking or moving. He stayed like that for quite some time. It would be almost impossible for any person to maintain their balance in that position, let alone an elderly man. A holy hush came over the audience as that sign and wonder occurred.

I was holding meetings in a place called Hungry Horse, Montana, in an Assembly of God church. They were glorious meetings. One evening, as the power of God was falling all over the congregation, a ten-year-old girl stepped over in a Holy Ghost trance. She was standing in the middle aisle of the church when suddenly we noticed that she was not blinking or moving, her face glowing. This went on until after the meeting. It was a sign and wonder to everyone.

Another manifestation of The Holy Ghost is dancing and rejoicing. People dance for many reasons. They dance because the harvest is coming in, and people are getting saved. They dance because God has been good to them. They dance because they have been rescued from Hell. They dance because there is such a joy that they can't hold their legs and feet still.

Kenneth E. Hagin told a story many times of an unusual and special manifestation of The Holy Ghost. He knew of a man that they called "Old Dad

Smith." He came with his daughter, Inez. He literally danced people to the altar. Brother Hagin said that he had never seen anything like that before. He said to his daughter, who played the fiddle, "Inez, strike me up a tune." She began to play, and this man began to dance. Kenneth Hagin said that they watched him dance off the end of the platform, and he continued to dance in the air. People began to weep and run to the altar. We have Biblical examples of dancing.

> Now his elder son was in the field: and as he came and drew nigh to the house, he heard musick and dancing.
>
> LUKE 15:25

The father was celebrating his lost son coming home, coming back into the fold.

> And David danced before the Lord with all his might; and David was girded with a linen ephod.
>
> 2 SAMUEL 6:14

It does not say that David danced in The Spirit or that The Holy Spirit picked up his feet and forced him to dance. He picked up his own feet and decided to dance.

The Holy Spirit is not a Devil and does not take over our bodies. It says that David danced with all of his might. He made the decision and put effort into it. His wife, Michal, hated it. She was a lot like her daddy, Saul. They were both full of pride. David basically said, "If you don't like it, honey, you better stay home next time because you haven't seen anything yet. When I get in the presence of God, I am not self-conscious, people-conscious, or Devil-conscious. I am only God-conscious, and He is going to know how much I love His presence." We have other verses about dancing.

DESPERATE HUNGER GETS GOD'S ATTENTION

> Thou hast turned for me my mourning into dancing: thou
> hast put off my sackcloth, and girded me with gladness.
>
> PSALM 30:11

Anyone who has been forgiven, has received of God's great grace and mercy, or has been touched by Him in any way has reason to dance. I am one who has had my mourning turned into dancing. When you are healed up from abuse, poverty, and rejection, you will want to dance. When you are supposed to be dead, but God has healed you, you will want to dance.

> Let them praise his name in the dance: let them sing praises
> unto him with the timbrel and harp.
>
> PSALM 149:3

Just as a person can decide to sing at any time, you can decide to dance at any time.

I remember a time when I was a student at Rhema Bible Training Center in Broken Arrow, Oklahoma. Reverend Kenneth Hagin was having a camp meeting. Thousands of people were there for the event. I was sandwiched in a section in the bleacher stands where we had no extra room to stretch out. At some point in the praise part of the service, a person on my left and a person on my right began to dance. I was clapping but certainly not dancing.

When I was growing up in a Pentecostal church, no one did any dancing unless they did some kind of spontaneous dance that we called "dancing in The Holy Ghost." We were taught that since dancing was something done in the world, and much of it is sensuous in the way bodies move and couples interact, no one should dance unless God supernaturally moves your feet for you and you are overcome. We heard about Charismatics who moved their legs on their own, and we even made fun of that. We called it "the Charismatic bunny hop."

Now, I was witnessing that first-hand and becoming totally disgusted. I thought to myself, "These charismatics are so fleshly, so carnal. They should not be dancing on their own. They should wait for some spontaneous Holy Ghost dance." Besides, I was irritated that they were bumping into me as they danced. While I was thinking about how much these people beside me were "in the flesh," The Holy Spirit spoke to me on the inside. I heard, "Debbie, why are you clapping your hands?" I responded, "I am happy and keeping beat to the music, Lord." He went on to talk to me about this. "Did I move your hands for you, or did you just decide to move them because you are happy and like that song?" "Lord, I just decided to move them and cooperate with The Holy Spirit." He said, "Well, that's what they decided to do, but they are not just moving their hands. They are moving their feet too and praising me twice as much as you are. You are judging them for praising me, which shows that you are in the flesh, not them. You are concerned that they are in the flesh, while I am concerned that you are in the flesh." I learned a valuable lesson that day.

Some people take off running when The Holy Spirit is stirring their most holy emotions. The fire gets in their feet, and they sense the urge to take off running in the meeting. Some see themselves running to the nations and then act it out.

I remember a night in Lakeland, Florida, at one of Dr. Rodney Howard-Browne's camp meetings. Hundreds of people took off running at the same time. Many were answering the call to the nations. Others had the fire of God all over them until it went down to their legs and feet. In Helsinki, Finland, in March of 2023, the same thing happened. It was a European minister's conference, and I was the preacher. I was only a few minutes into preaching when the fire of God hit all of their feet at the same time. I had never experienced anything like it to that degree before. Hundreds of European pastors (who are usually fairly stoic) shot out of their chairs at the same time and began to run around the building. It went on for over fifteen minutes before they stopped and went back to their seats. When it happened, I was talking about the body of Christ rising up in Europe to take the continent. It became real to them. It looked like a spiritual army running to war.

Sometimes, people get a glimpse of something no one else has seen or heard. They may see in their spirit that they are running to the nations. They may see that God is about to give them the victory over a certain situation.

We do have Biblical precedent for running. Elijah heard the sound of the abundance of rain in 1 Kings 18:41. *"And Elijah said unto Ahab, Get thee up, eat and drink; for there is a sound of abundance of rain."* Then, in 1 Kings 18:46, *"And the hand of the Lord was on Elijah; and girded up his loins, and ran before Ahab to the entrance of Jezreel."* It was a thirty-mile race, and Elijah beat King Ahab, who was on a horse.

There are many unusual things that can happen when revival is burning. I have heard and read about such things in church history. I have even heard of such things fairly recently. In some places, fire departments were called because people saw fire above the church building where the revival was taking place. Sometimes, people not only cry but may wail because it feels like physical fire is on them. We don't know what God is doing in people, and you better be careful not to judge when their holy emotions are being stirred.

I've seen people do cartwheels in my meetings. A young lady in Omaha, Nebraska, started doing them up and down the aisle. When I asked what was going on, I was told that she had one of the worst cases of rheumatoid arthritis that the medical profession had ever seen. Her mother and aunts had died from it. This young lady had small children and was told that she would die of it. She received her healing in my meeting and was so overcome that she wanted to do something she had not been able to do in years. Thus, the somersaults and cartwheels. I certainly let her continue. In Tulsa, Oklahoma, a man was healed of severe back pain and stood on his head. Again, when I found out the reason, I allowed it, and the people rejoiced.

In the Welsh revival, people who tried to resist The Holy Spirit couldn't bend their elbows to get their beer mugs off the counter. In Charles Finney's revivals, it was recorded that horses bucked people off in front of the church. God can do anything. I am believing that cars can stop or run out of gas in front of our revival meetings.

I was holding a revival in Roswell, Georgia, many years ago. There was a lady who kept blinking. She asked out loud why she saw snow in the atmosphere. I realized that she was looking at a physical manifestation of the glory of God.

We have Biblical precedent for the glory cloud of God being in manifestation.

> And it came to pass, when the priests were come out of the holy place: (for all the priests that were present were sanctified, and did not then wait by course:
> Also the Levites which were the singers, all of them of Asaph, of Heman, of Jeduthun, with their sons and their brethren, being arrayed in white linen, having cymbals and psalteries and harps, stood at the east end of the altar, and with them an hundred and twenty priests sounding with trumpets:)
> It came even to pass, as the trumpeters and singers were as one, to make one sound to be heard in praising and thanking the Lord; and when they lifted up their voice with the trumpets and cymbals and instruments of musick, and praised the Lord, saying, For he is good; for his mercy endureth for ever: that then the house was filled with a cloud, even the house of the Lord;

DESPERATE HUNGER GETS GOD'S ATTENTION

> So that the priests could not stand to minister by reason of the cloud: for the glory of the Lord had filled the house of God.
>
> 2 CHRONICLES 5:11-14

> Now when Solomon had made an end of praying, the fire came down from heaven, and consumed the burnt offering and the sacrifices; and the glory of the Lord filled the house.
> And the priests could not enter into the house of the Lord, because the glory of the Lord had filled the Lord's house.
> And when all the children of Israel saw how the fire came down, and the glory of the Lord upon the house, they bowed themselves with their faces to the ground upon the pavement, and worshipped, and praised the Lord, saying, For he is good; for his mercy endureth for ever.
>
> 2 CHRONICLES 7:1-3

In chapter five, the priests cannot perform their functions, and in chapter seven, they can't even get into the building. I remember one night in my prison ministry in Palmer, Alaska, when the glory of God was filling the room. Hardened criminals were weeping under conviction; some fell out of their seats, one crawled out of the room, and suddenly I couldn't see. As I looked out, it was as though I was looking at the thickest fog that I had ever seen. I was so overcome that I could not speak or move. I just let God continue to do His mighty work. It was a night that can never be forgotten. We had many saved and baptized in The Holy Ghost that night.

I have heard others speak of the glory cloud in such a light way that it is hard not to vomit. They laugh, giggle, and supposedly take pictures. If the glory of God manifested in their midst for real, they could not be walking around taking pictures and doing a commentary. Today, there are smoke machines in churches and many other things that could try to imitate the real. That's why we need the fear, honor, and awe of God to come back to the church. These things are holy. They are not to be taken lightly. God is holy. His presence, manifestations, and the work that He does on the human heart are extremely holy.

There was a man in one of Pastor Rodney's meetings who actually rolled up and down the stairs. That would be an impossible feat without The Holy Spirit. It was a sign and wonder to the congregation. When God is profoundly touching people, we never know what the outward manifestation will look like. In one of my revival meetings in Nome, Alaska, the pastor was on the floor laughing, crying, giving messages in tongues and interpretation, and prophesying. When the power of God hit him, his entire body arced, his face turned red, and blood vessels broke in his face. It looked like he was being electrocuted. His associate pastor, Andy, had what looked like sunburn marks on his face. They were both touched in a glorious way.

People fell out of trees in Jonathan Edward's meetings and during the second great awakening in Kentucky. People sat up in trees to hear the sermon because the crowds were so large, and there were no microphones in that day. As God began to touch them, the power of God hit them, and some fell to the ground but were not hurt.

One of the greatest revivals that I ever had was in the nation of Ukraine. In the evening services, we had about fifteen hundred people. In the mornings, the pastor asked me to share in the Bible school. They rented a separate building for that, and it usually held seventy-five people. However, they crowded one hundred twenty people in the room while I was there. It was an upper room. God likes the upper rooms, and He seems to like the number of one hundred twenty. It all seemed much like it must have been on the day of Pentecost.

While I was teaching, the power of God saturated the place. In the middle of teaching, all of the people began to run around the building for quite some time. They all stopped suddenly at the same time, as though a conductor were telling them when to start and when to stop. Then, they all began to laugh in the joy of the Holy Ghost for about twenty minutes or so.

Again, they stopped at the same time and began to weep. They, again, stopped at the same time and began to sing in the Spirit, in other tongues. In the middle of that, I again heard the angels of Heaven join in with the worship. This is the second time I have heard this, the first being in Dr. Rodney Howard-Browne's meeting in Lakeland, Florida. All of this went on for about four hours. We found out later that there was a governmental office under that room. When the students ran and danced, it shook the plaster off the ceiling. The officials came up to see what was going on and temporarily confiscated our passports.

I have experienced other unique moments in ministry. One night in Soldotna, Alaska, I began to prophesy over many people in perfect rhyme while singing. In Prestonville, Kentucky, I found myself preaching what I thought was a disjointed message. I started in the call of God but suddenly found myself saying that I needed to take a side journey on the subject of healing. After some time, I said, "Now, I need to talk about grief for a few minutes." Later, I said, "I need to talk about something that has been taken out of context to persecute my pastor and explain what he meant about being 'A Holy Ghost Bartender.'" I saw the pastors looking at each other perplexed and thought, "They probably are wondering why this message is all over the place. I am wondering the same thing."

After the meeting, the host pastor said, "I've never witnessed anything quite like this. Did you see a man come in late to the meetings? He was just diagnosed with a terminal illness, and when he arrived, you began to talk about healing, and he received his healing today. You also spoke about grief right after a lady came in, also late, who just lost her fiancée in a motorcycle accident. Also, a woman came to the meeting who was not going to come back because she was up all night on the internet reading about your pastor, Dr. Rodney Howard-Browne. She read that he calls himself The Holy Ghost Bartender, and then she read others' critical comments. However, she decided to give it one more try and come today. When you walked in, you explained what that was all about, and she was happy again. We've never seen anyone operate in that kind of Word of Knowledge." It seems that God works in a unique way with me and changes my message to fit individuals.

Kenneth E. Hagin spoke often about a country preacher he knew in Texas who spit on people, and they were healed. He said it was a very unique gifting. He knew another preacher who witnessed a man's arm growing out from the shoulder when this minister spit on him. That does not mean that any of us can copy that or should even want to. We have no idea why God used him in such a unique way. However, once again, we see Biblical precedent for spitting for someone to be healed.

> And they bring unto him one that was deaf, and had an impediment in his speech; and they beseech him to put his hand upon him.
> And he took him aside from the multitude, and put his fingers into his ears, and he spit, and touched his tongue;
> And looking up to heaven, he sighed, and saith unto him, Ephphatha, that is, Be opened.
>
> MARK 7:32-34

The Bible speaks of people being struck dumb, struck blind, and falling dead in meetings. Some were eaten by bears. I believe that we are in an hour that, as God's glory picks up, we will see these things again. People cannot mock the power of God.

I will never forget an unusual occurrence in Spokane, Washington, years ago. I was going down a prayer line, praying for people. As I was about to pray for a man, The Holy Spirit spoke to me, "Ask that man if he is married to this woman." I was shocked. God had never asked me to do anything like that before. I knew that I had to obey. I asked him, and he was angry. "Of course, we are married. You already know that because we asked you for marital advice the other night." I replied that I had to obey God and ask. I went down the line to pray for the lady. (They had been separated in the prayer line.)

The Holy Spirit told me to ask her the same question, and I received the same answer. I was becoming embarrassed. I tried to move down the prayer line. I was asked by The Holy Spirit to go back to the man and ask again. I got the same reaction, except that he was angrier than before. I ended up having to ask both him and the woman three times each. The last time, he responded with a shocking answer. "All right, I consider her to be one of my concubines." I have never even heard of anyone using that phrase since Old Testament days. I began to shake under the power of God and felt something that I have never felt before or since, and I hope that I never do again. I said, "You have lied to both me and The Holy Ghost, and God is giving you two options. You can either fall on your knees and repent now or run out of here as fast as you can for your life." I was hoping that they would fall on their faces and repent. However, I am disappointed to tell you that he grabbed the woman, and they both ran out of the auditorium. It is not wise to lie to The Holy Ghost, especially in the middle of a glorious service.

In my Long Beach, Mississippi, six-week revival, one night especially comes to mind. People were being healed all over the place. A man who was scheduled to have his leg amputated the next day was healed. He had been in a terrible motorcycle accident. He began running all over the auditorium. A few minutes later, I looked up and could not see because of the brightness of flashes of light popping in front of my face all over the room. I remember thinking, "Who gave permission for reporters to come in and start taking pictures?" For seconds, I could not figure out what was going on. The flashes were so intense and bright that my mind could not compute. Then, suddenly, as I put my hands over my eyes, the pastor asked what was going on. Suddenly, we all realized that I was seeing the flash of angels all over the room, and once again, I could not speak for a while.

In 2018, I was having a campmeeting at my church in Washington State. It was called Northwest Ablaze. I was going down the prayer line and as I turned, I was face to face with what seemed to be the belt of a large angel that was glowing. He was so tall that my head was only at his waist level. I could see the white and the brightness of the robe and consciously stepped back as holy awe and fear flooded me. I was overcome by the sight. Everyone could tell that I had seen something glorious. I had to wait to finish the prayer line.

Please do not get the wrong impression. I have seen things like this only a few times, but they are indelibly impressed upon my spirit. We are not to ask for visitations. I am very aware of God's presence without needing to see or hear with my five senses. I do not want to entertain familiar spirits by seeking out experiences. Neither am I ashamed when Godly experiences happen. Again, these things are so very real and should not be taken lightly.

I hear of people taking all of these trips to Heaven and Hell and want to brag. It is so evident that they are lying or delusional. You can't experience any of these things and talk lightly about them. God doesn't work like that. He doesn't take people to Heaven or Hell on a weekly or even a yearly basis.

If we want God to show up in a big way and manifest Himself so that all will know that He is a big God, we must be careful how we act in the glory. We can't exaggerate or fabricate things. We must not disdain or criticize what He does. We can search the Scripture and try the Spirit like the Bereans did, but don't operate with a critical, skeptical attitude. We must stay hungry for more of Him while being grateful for what He has already done.

The hungry and the humble always receive first. God resists the proud.

Many times, you see children and simple people being touched first. They don't analyze and scrutinize. They don't worry about how they look or sound.

Make sure that you participate when God is moving. Do not look at your watch, text your friend, think about your grocery list, or the things that you need to do; I cannot over-emphasize that these things are not holy. Make room for the glory and respond to His glory.

Some would ask, "Why would God move on a person like this?" I will give you just a few examples of people's testimonies of the change that took place in their lives when they had a Holy Ghost encounter. What we saw was the outward manifestation of what was happening in the heart.

Some have been healed from the inside out when they received unspeakable joy. Sometimes, it is after losing mothers, mates, and even children. I remember a lady in Oregon City, Oregon, who had just buried her little girl from leukemia before I arrived to hold a revival. She and her husband came to the revival, even though the funeral had taken place only about a week previously. One night, I left my rental car at the church and rode with the pastors to a restaurant after the meeting. When they brought me back later to pick up my car, we saw the husband carrying his wife to the car, drunk in The Holy Ghost. She was laughing with "joy unspeakable and full of glory." The sight made the pastors cry for joy. They made the comment that only supernatural joy could do that.

When people see others being carried out, laughing with joy, they may make judgments that are wrong. We have no idea what is going on with a person when they are having a Holy Ghost encounter. When we get filled on the inside, there is no more room for problems. The anointing imparts spiritual deposits in the lives of many that will be seen in the days to come.

I want to teach you how to yield to The Holy Spirit. Again, John Wesley said, "I just light myself on fire for God, and people come to watch me burn." Wigglesworth said, "If The Holy Spirit does not move, I move Him." They were both saying, in different ways, that they know that God wants to move all of the time, so they initiate yielding to Him.

Be very attentive to the moving of The Holy Spirit. One of my Bible school teachers said that we students should always pay attention and try to ascertain what we think The Holy Spirit is going to do next. Be ready in season and out of season. However, make sure that in the process, you don't start thinking that you know more than the person conducting the service. Do not become critical. Don't think, "He or she is taking this service the wrong way." When you are relaxed and sitting in the service, you are in a very different place than the minister who is up there trying to get it right for everyone. It is easy for you to sit and judge when you are not the one responsible. Do not be like the armchair quarterback when he is watching football on television. Some holler, "What is wrong with you? I could have caught that." What a ridiculous statement! The person hasn't exercised in years, has a beer belly, and has never caught a football. Somehow, he thinks he could do it better than the professional, however.

Do not be the last one to flow with The Holy Spirit. Be the first to flow. Someone else may need you to start the flow. When you yield, it could start a revival for the entire area. Do not decide to jump in after the fact.

People who are not skeptical usually get more from God. The Bible says in Isaiah 1:19, *"If ye be willing and obedient, ye shall eat the good of the land."* There is an old argument of how much is up to the sovereignty of God and how much is up to the will of man. Theologically, we are talking about Arminianism versus Calvinism. There is a middle ground there. God has made man with a free will. Throughout history, we can see that God moves when people cry out, pray, get in faith, press in, repent, and yield. Everyone who has been impacted by a move of God could have been touched sooner. They had a Holy Ghost encounter when they got hungry enough to have one. Some had to travel to receive a tangible touch. Others continued to call out to God in their own way right where they were.

The definition of yieldedness, according to Strong's Concordance, is to give or present yourself. The word yield means to give up possession. This is part of making Jesus your Lord. It is part of surrendering your all. If you have a hard time yielding to the Holy Spirit, many times pride is involved. It will keep you from receiving other things from God. Ask Him to search your heart and reveal to you anything that should not be there. Ask Him what needs to be changed, and then allow Him to do spiritual surgery on you.

The yield sign helps people to understand what yielding is. When you see the sign, you don't dare take your foot off of the accelerator pedal, shut off the car, put it in the parking gear, and come to a stop. If you do, you'll cause an accident (which is what many pastors and board members have done). To yield at the entrance of the interstate means that you have to stay more alert than ever, keep your foot on the accelerator, keep your hands on the wheel, continue to steer the car, and concentrate. You must look to see what the traffic is doing. You must perceive what you need to do. You may have to speed up or slow down in order to blend in with what the majority are doing. They have the right-away. In our case, The Holy Spirit has the right-of-way, not us. It's not about my favorite top-ten song list, the way I like to yield, or my favorite sermons. It's all about what He wants to do for the sake of His people.

Yielding is a learned process. It gets easier with practice. A good clue is that if a bunch of others are running, dancing, or laughing with joy, you don't have to be a rocket scientist to know what God's doing. Don't resist Him or even sit in neutral gear. You didn't get saved like that. You decided out of your heart and your own will, and then you made your body agree with your will. You told your arms to lift to answer the altar call. Then, you told your legs to walk up to the altar, and then you told your mouth to ask Jesus to forgive you of your sins and to confess Him as Lord.

People yield to the enemy or the flesh on a regular basis, but we must make the decision to yield only to The Word of God and the leading of The Holy Spirit.

> Neither yield ye your members as instruments of unrighteousness unto sin: but yield yourselves unto God, as those that are alive from the dead, and your members as instruments of righteousness unto God.
>
> ROMANS 6:13

> Do not continue offering or yielding your bodily members [and faculties] to sin as instruments (tools) of wickedness. But offer and yield yourselves to God as though you have been raised from the dead to [perpetual] life, and your bodily members [and faculties] to God, presenting them as implements of righteousness.
>
> ROMANS 6:13 (AMPC)

> Know ye not, that to whom ye yield yourselves servants to obey, his servants ye are to whom ye obey; whether of sin unto death, or of obedience unto righteousness?
>
> ROMANS 6:16

> I speak after the manner of men because of the infirmity of your flesh: for as ye have yielded your members servants to uncleanness and to iniquity unto iniquity; even so now yield your members servants to righteousness unto holiness.
>
> ROMANS 6:19

Smith Wigglesworth said, "It is better to miss God than to grieve Him." I read the book *Blood, Fire, and Vapor of Smoke* by Mark Brazee. He told the story about how he got tired of grieving The Holy Spirit. He felt the nudge in his meeting to tell two people in his service to step out in the aisle and dance in The Holy Ghost and that they would be healed as they obeyed God. Two elderly men stepped out in the aisle, and he thought, "Oh no, of all the people to step into the aisle," but they began to dance and then run and were totally healed.

> In the last day, that great day of the feast, Jesus stood and cried, saying, If any man thirst, let him come unto me, and drink.
> He that believeth on me, as the scripture hath said, out of his belly shall flow rivers of living water.
>
> JOHN 7:37-38

This tells us that we actually have to drink, not just come to where the water is, or put the water in our mouth. Jesus did not say to sit back and see what happens. He told us that we have a responsibility to drink.

DESPERATE HUNGER GETS GOD'S ATTENTION

Drinking involves several things: moving our mouth and throat muscles, forming our lips to be able to drink, and swallowing.

People like to use the cop-out that The Holy Ghost is a gentleman and will never make you do anything that you don't want to. Yes, I have said in this book that we have free will, and usually, The Holy Spirit wants our total cooperation. However, there are exceptions to the rule. I believe it has to do with the fact that God looks into the heart and sometimes knows that those putting up the greatest resistance on the outside are actually hungry. We see that with the Apostle Paul when he was still Saul on the Damascus Road. He was persecuting the church when he met up with The King of Kings and The Lord of Lords. Jesus blinded Paul on the Damascus road against his will.

I remember hearing the testimony of Pastor Rick Shelton of St. Louis, Missouri. He talked about going to a Rodney Howard-Browne meeting extremely skeptical. He didn't think the joy was necessary or real. He didn't even want to be seen at his meeting but went one night because his wife wanted to attend. He suddenly saw the cameras focusing on him, and he didn't want anyone to know that he was there. He decided to dive to the floor to avoid the cameras. However, God had a surprise in store for Pastor Rick. He was immediately and suddenly drunk in The Holy Ghost. That impartation changed him, his ministry, and his church forever.

Don't think that you're necessarily safe to resist. You might just be sitting in the wrong seat, and God decides to show you how big He is. Ananias and Sapphira didn't have much to say about their outcome. What about Zachariah being struck dumb when John the Baptist was born or the boys being eaten by bears after mocking Elisha? Then there is Elymas, the sorcerer, who was struck blind. God is God and does what He wants.

> ...I say, 'My purpose will stand,
> and I will do all that I please.'
>
> ISAIAH 46:10 (NIV)

He overrode Balaam in Numbers 23 and caused him to prophesy against his will. He overrode Saul and his men in I Samuel 19 and caused them to prophesy instead of killing David.

I have witnessed people being stuck to the floor in a meeting for hours. Some were not able to speak in English for days. I remember a man in my meeting in Montana who was extremely stoic, but his wife fell out of her seat each night with great joy. He looked straight ahead with a frown as if he didn't know her and hoped that no one would notice. After several nights of that, I was standing close to the couple, preaching. Suddenly, I reached out and put my hand on his head and said, "Sir, this isn't just for your wife. It is for you also." Much to my surprise, he fell out of his chair and hit the floor beside his wife, laughing and crying. The church could not believe it.

I called both of them up to testify the next evening. She was joyful, as always. He looked like he was back to being stoic and uncomfortable. When I asked him what happened, he said in a very serious voice, "Well, you all know that my nickname is Mr. Excitement. (I did not know that, but the congregation burst out laughing. It was obvious that he had the reputation of not showing emotion, so they called him that name in teasing.) He went on to say, "Many of you know that my wife gets, well, you know how she gets, but I didn't think I could ever get anything like that. But last night, when Debbie laid her hands on me..." We heard no more for seconds, for there was a great pause. Then he looked shocked, lifted his head, and shouted, "Well, there it is again." He fell straight over backward and began to roll and laugh. I don't think that he yielded, but God knew that deep down, he wanted what God wanted for him.

It may take some time to get what you want. There may be several factors in that. Remember the story of Evangelist Richard Moore that I talked about earlier? We don't know why it took him four and one-half months to receive, but he did not give up, did not get angry with God, and did not get bitter.

Here are some real practical ways to yielding. Hang out with yielders, not criticizers. Continue to rub shoulders with joyful, thankful, and hungry people who love everything that The Holy Spirit does. Use tools, such as good worship music and revival videos, that you can watch in your home and the car. Practice yielding at home where you are not self-conscious. Be open to The Holy Spirit as you pray and read His Word and worship. Pray in The Spirit daily. Sing in the Spirit with other tongues. Worship God in The Spirit. Keep your attitude right. Ask God to remove any barriers that would hold you back from yielding. When something is even just funny naturally, laugh. Don't hold back and worry about what others think. Trust your emotions. Fast, as the Spirit leads you, to become more sensitive to The Holy Spirit. When you are in a corporate service, trust The Holy Spirit on the inside of you, and simply step out and do what you are getting the leading to do. Don't seek manifestations, but seek the Manifestor, Jesus. On the other hand, expect signs, wonders, and manifestations. These will happen as The Holy Spirit works with us. The reality of these things will convince people that Jesus Christ is the same yesterday, today, and forever.

A man in Nome, Alaska, was backslidden for many years. When he saw the power of God fall as he had never seen before, he was convinced that he needed to come back to Jesus. These signs are to make us wonder. After the man rolled up and down the stairs in Pastor Rodney's meeting, hundreds came running to the altar. Signs and wonders should always point people to Jesus. Most of all, continue to hunger and thirst for Him, and He will continue to give you Holy Spirit encounters.

People who think we should go the Seeker-Sensitive way argue that people are offended by signs, wonders, and the moving of The Holy Spirit. They want revival, but no one offended or upset. They want to control it. In the old revivals, as we have proven, there was quaking, running, falling, laughing, and singing. In every revival, there has been a rock of offense. Azusa Street had tongues. We have been fed a lie about people being offended.

We see many things in the Bible that are stranger than the things we see today. A prophet married a prostitute, and Ezekiel prophesied, lying on his side. King Saul lay on his side without his clothes, prophesying. Some had donkeys talk to them. Elijah called fire down from Heaven. Jesus spoke to fig trees and cursed them, walked on water, spoke to the wind and waves, and spit on a blind man. He also fed thousands with a little boy's lunch and turned water into wine. Jonah was swallowed up by a big fish. The children of Israel had the Red Sea open for them. Elijah was caught up to Heaven in a whirlwind with a chariot of fire. Philip was translated, and the hundred and twenty had a tornado blow through the building with tongues of fire above their heads. Naaman, the leper, had to dip in the muddy Jordan River to be healed. Elisha found a borrowed axe head by the anointing of The Holy Ghost. Ezekiel prophesied to dead bones and watched them come back together. Enoch never died but was taken to Heaven. The Three Hebrew children were protected in the fiery furnace. Daniel was protected in the lion's den, as God shut the mouths of the lions. Prophets and their assistants saw angels around them at war. Some entered into a trance. Moses was supernaturally sustained during long fasts. We see people raised from the dead and funerals stopped. Jacob wrestled with God and ended up with a limp. Cain was marked so that people would recognize what he did.

Signs and wonders are nothing new. It is time for things to get out of hand and for us to get free from religion. People who get upset are more in the flesh than those who yield. It is so important that you keep your eyes on Jesus. The Holy Spirit can only be as real through you as He is to you. God told my pastor, "The men and women who I am using in the world today aren't anything special. I've touched them, and they've touched Me."

We cannot use the excuse that some don't understand what is happening. God's chosen people missed Jesus. The Pharisees called Jesus Beelzebub, a term for the Devil. The disciples didn't understand the mission of Jesus and thought that He came to set up an earthly kingdom. The Jews didn't understand that God's heart was for all nations. They were shocked that God would offer the Gospel to Gentiles. God took a murderer (Moses) and turned him into a great deliverer. He sent His Son to die so we could live. He caused The King of Kings to be born in a manger and has used nobodies to turn the world upside down. Jesus said that we must lose our life to gain it and that the first would be the last. None of these things make sense to the natural mind. They can only be discerned spiritually. We have finite minds, but God is infinite and beyond us. When we encounter the supernatural, we encounter the fear of the unknown. It is good to have a reverential fear, but it is not good to fear manifestations of The Holy Spirit or the moving of The Holy Spirit.

Some will not let God move because it might cause division. When the supernatural meets up with the natural, there will be division. When free people meet up with religious people, there will be division. Jesus even prophesied it.

> "A man's enemies will be the members of his own household."
>
> MATTHEW 10:36 (NIV)

> If any man come to me, and hate not his father, and mother, and wife, and children, and brethren, and sisters, yea, and his own life also, he cannot be my disciple.
>
> LUKE 14:26

> Think not that I am come to send peace on earth: I came not to send peace, but a sword.
> For I am come to set a man at variance against his father, and the daughter against her mother, and the daughter in law against her mother in law.
> And a man's foes shall be they of his own household.
>
> MATTHEW 10:34-36

Godly division is Biblical. Jesus caused division wherever He went. The Pharisees and Sadducees were angry with Him whenever they met up. The rulers were angry with Him. Those who didn't want to repent were angry with Him. The inclusion of the Gentiles caused division in Acts 15. Paul rebuked Peter to his face in Galatians, chapter 2. Paul and Barnabas split up over the issue of taking John Mark with them on Paul's second missionary journey. Luke never tells us whether Paul or Barnabas was wrong. The Kingdom still advanced despite division in the ranks. John Wesley had bitter disputes with other godly men over issues of doctrine. Dowie opposed Mariah Woodsworth-Etter, and many so-called theologians have opposed me.

Godly division is found throughout the history of the church. The Great Awakening broke out in New Jersey in 1725 and was violently opposed by more traditional churches. G. Campbell Morgan called the Pentecostal Movement "the last vomit of Satan." The last move of God usually persecutes the present one. Lester Sumrall said that no denomination has ever made the change, only individuals.

Some complain and argue that it's so disorderly. Again, do we want the order of a graveyard or the second chapter of Acts' order? Until Christ returns, there will always be a mixture of the Spirit and the flesh. The disciples were rebuked for their mixed motives. They wanted positions and were competitive and hostile to each other and yet were trying to serve Jesus.

The Devil always tries to discredit what's true by infiltrating it with what's false. None of us get everything right one hundred percent of the time. However, a little wildfire is better than no fire at all. There are always plenty of wet blankets to put out the fire. We need Godly men and women who will bring correction in love. We need to have people in the body of Christ who will hold us accountable. We are still learning. We must build the fireplace around the fire, not the other way around. 1 Corinthians 14:40 says, *"Let everything be done in order."* That is talking about gifts of the spirit, not the presence of God showing up while the service is going on. We have an example of Peter preaching and The Holy Ghost interrupting him. The Holy Spirit fell on them while Peter was still speaking.

> While Peter yet spake these words, the Holy Ghost fell on all them which heard the word.
>
> ACTS 10:44

It's okay to have questions like the Bereans, but make sure your motive is right. Don't get mad like the man did in Long Beach, Mississippi, when he didn't get touched. Another man got angry with me when I suggested that he needed to get hungrier. He replied that he was tired and said that God understood that. No, He doesn't. Stir yourself up as Richard Moore did. Ask why you're afraid or offended. Don't run like the children of Israel did when Moses went up on the mountain because they knew they weren't in a position to meet up with God. Ask Jesus to open up the Scriptures to you as He did after the crucifixion with the disciples who had questions. In Acts 3:19, Peter told onlookers to repent so that times of refreshment would come from the Lord's presence.

Just get hungry and allow God to do anything that He wants to do in you and through you. You must not care about the opinions of others. You will stand before a holy God on that day in Heaven, and none of them will be standing with you.

SEVEN

THE COST OF CARRYING THE ANOINTING

Salvation is free, but God's glory will cost us everything. God is raising up a generation of men and women who will radically obey God, no matter the cost. These men and women will dare to believe God in the middle of the most trying circumstances. The power and presence of God are holy, and He will be able to entrust that to people who will remain pure before Him.

There are prices to be paid to carry the anointing. How badly do we want it? It is easier to say miracles are done away with, or this isn't the time to pay the price to have them again. We must decide to pay the price for carrying the anointing, even if everybody else backs out of revival.

Some of that price will involve holiness, time, money, laying down desires and hobbies, and forgiving people. It will involve praying, fasting, getting The Word of God into our spirits, and allowing God to change our appetites. It will require you to forget the past and not care what people say about you. It will change your habits, dreams, and desires until there is no compromise in you. Are you ready to lay down your everything? It may involve your reputation and your possessions. Are you ready to get radical for Jesus? You will be criticized, but it would be worse to get to Heaven and see what you could have done.

What causes manifestations like every bar in town closing as they did in church revival history? You must be willing to pay any price for it. Everything in your mind, flesh, and soul will beg to quit, but your spirit has to say, "Come on, The Spirit of The Lord is upon me, and if nobody understands me, I must get up and keep going." God's looking for water walkers, not dry boat sitters.

Many years ago, Pastor Rodney Howard-Browne preached a message that he called The Cost of The Anointing. It affected me more than any sermon that he ever preached until that time. I listened to it many times until it became my message. It was that real to me. I added some points to it. I told him that I was preaching it everywhere I went, and he thought that was wonderful. You are about to read part of that message.

> And it came to pass, when Jesus had finished all these sayings, he said unto his disciples,
> Ye know that after two days is the feast of the passover, and the Son of man is betrayed to be crucified.
> Then assembled together the chief priests, and the scribes, and the elders of the people, unto the palace of the high priest, who was called Caiaphas,
> And consulted that they might take Jesus by subtilty, and kill him.
> But they said, Not on the feast day, lest there be an uproar among the people.
> Now when Jesus was in Bethany, in the house of Simon the leper,
> There came unto him a woman having an alabaster box of very precious ointment, and poured it on his head, as he sat at meat.
> But when his disciples saw it, they had indignation, saying, To what purpose is this waste?
> For this ointment might have been sold for much, and given to the poor.
> When Jesus understood it, he said unto them, Why trouble

DESPERATE HUNGER GETS GOD'S ATTENTION

ye the woman? for she hath wrought a good work upon me.

For ye have the poor always with you; but me ye have not always.

For in that she hath poured this ointment on my body, she did it for my burial.

Verily I say unto you, Wheresoever this gospel shall be preached in the whole world, there shall also this, that this woman hath done, be told for a memorial of her.

Then one of the twelve, called Judas Iscariot, went unto the chief priests,

And said unto them, What will ye give me, and I will deliver him unto you? And they covenanted with him for thirty pieces of silver.

And from that time he sought opportunity to betray him.

Now the first day of the feast of unleavened bread the disciples came to Jesus, saying unto him, Where wilt thou that we prepare for thee to eat the passover?

And he said, Go into the city to such a man, and say unto him, The Master saith, My time is at hand; I will keep the passover at thy house with my disciples.

And the disciples did as Jesus had appointed them; and they made ready the passover.

Now when the even was come, he sat down with the twelve.

And as they did eat, he said, Verily I say unto you, that one of you shall betray me.

And they were exceeding sorrowful, and began every one of them to say unto him, Lord, is it I?

And he answered and said, He that dippeth his hand with me in the dish, the same shall betray me.

The Son of man goeth as it is written of him: but woe unto that man by whom the Son of man is betrayed! it had been good for that man if he had not been born.

Then Judas, which betrayed him, answered and said, Master, is it I? He said unto him, Thou hast said.

And as they were eating, Jesus took bread, and blessed it,
and brake it, and gave it to the disciples, and said, Take,
eat; this is my body.
And he took the cup, and gave thanks, and gave it to them,
saying, Drink ye all of it;
For this is my blood of the new testament, which is shed for
many for the remission of sins.
But I say unto you, I will not drink henceforth of this fruit of
the vine, until that day when I drink it new with you in
my Father's kingdom.
And when they had sung an hymn, they went out into the
mount of Olives.
Then saith Jesus unto them, All ye shall be offended because
of me this night: for it is written, I will smite the shepherd, and the sheep of the flock shall be scattered abroad.
But after I am risen again, I will go before you into Galilee.
Peter answered and said unto him, Though all men shall be
offended because of thee, yet will I never be offended.
Jesus said unto him, Verily I say unto thee, That this night,
before the cock crow, thou shalt deny me thrice.
Peter said unto him, Though I should die with thee, yet will I
not deny thee. Likewise also said all the disciples.
Then cometh Jesus with them unto a place called Gethsemane, and saith unto the disciples, Sit ye here, while I go
and pray yonder.
And he took with him Peter and the two sons of Zebedee,
and began to be sorrowful and very heavy.
Then saith he unto them, My soul is exceeding sorrowful,
even unto death: tarry ye here, and watch with me.
And he went a little farther, and fell on his face, and prayed,
saying, O my Father, if it be possible, let this cup pass
from me: nevertheless not as I will, but as thou wilt.
And he cometh unto the disciples, and findeth them asleep,
and saith unto Peter, What, could ye not watch with me
one hour?

Watch and pray, that ye enter not into temptation: the spirit indeed is willing, but the flesh is weak.

He went away again the second time, and prayed, saying, O my Father, if this cup may not pass away from me, except I drink it, thy will be done.

And he came and found them asleep again: for their eyes were heavy.

And he left them, and went away again, and prayed the third time, saying the same words.

Then cometh he to his disciples, and saith unto them, Sleep on now, and take your rest: behold, the hour is at hand, and the Son of man is betrayed into the hands of sinners.

Rise, let us be going: behold, he is at hand that doth betray me.

And while he yet spake, lo, Judas, one of the twelve, came, and with him a great multitude with swords and staves, from the chief priests and elders of the people.

Now he that betrayed him gave them a sign, saying, Whomsoever I shall kiss, that same is he: hold him fast.

And forthwith he came to Jesus, and said, Hail, master; and kissed him.

And Jesus said unto him, Friend, wherefore art thou come? Then came they, and laid hands on Jesus and took him.

And, behold, one of them which were with Jesus stretched out his hand, and drew his sword, and struck a servant of the high priest's, and smote off his ear.

Then said Jesus unto him, Put up again thy sword into his place: for all they that take the sword shall perish with the sword.

Thinkest thou that I cannot now pray to my Father, and he shall presently give me more than twelve legions of angels?

But how then shall the scriptures be fulfilled, that thus it must be?

In that same hour said Jesus to the multitudes, Are ye come

> out as against a thief with swords and staves for to take
> me? I sat daily with you teaching in the temple, and ye
> laid no hold on me.
> But all this was done, that the scriptures of the prophets
> might be fulfilled. Then all the disciples forsook him, and
> fled.
> And they that had laid hold on Jesus led him away to
> Caiaphas the high priest, where the scribes and the
> elders were assembled.
> But Peter followed him afar off unto the high priest's palace,
> and went in, and sat with the servants, to see the end.
> Now the chief priests, and elders, and all the council, sought
> false witness against Jesus, to put him to death;
> But found none: yea, though many false witnesses came, yet
> found they none. At the last came two false witnesses.
>
> MATTHEW 26:1-60

Most people know nothing of the price. They act like they are standing in a line in a supermarket, picking out what they want. However, it involves more than standing in a line. It is all about change. How much will this cost me? It will cost everything: your reputation, friendships, and associations. Are you prepared to go there? Jesus said you must take up your cross and follow Him.

> And there went great multitudes with him: and he turned,
> and said unto them,
> If any man come to me, and hate not his father, and mother,
> and wife, and children, and brethren, and sisters, yea,
> and his own life also, he cannot be my disciple.
> And whosoever doth not bear his cross, and come after me,
> cannot be my disciple.
> For which of you, intending to build a tower, sitteth not
> down first, and counteth the cost, whether he have suffi-
> cient to finish it?

> Lest haply, after he hath laid the foundation, and is not able to finish it, all that behold it begin to mock him,
> Saying, This man began to build, and was not able to finish.
> Or what king, going to make war against another king, sitteth not down first, and consulteth whether he be able with ten thousand to meet him that cometh against him with twenty thousand?
> Or else, while the other is yet a great way off, he sendeth an ambassage, and desireth conditions of peace.
> So likewise, whosoever he be of you that forsaketh not all that he hath, he cannot be my disciple.
> Salt is good: but if the salt have lost his savour, wherewith shall it be seasoned?
> It is neither fit for the land, nor yet for the dunghill; but men cast it out. He that hath ears to hear, let him hear.
>
> LUKE 14:25-35

Unfortunately, Americans hang around a church for only a few years and then they are gone. There is no commitment. Will you still be in revival five years from now?

> "And 'a man's enemies will be those of his own household.' He who loves father or mother more than Me is not worthy of Me. And he who loves son or daughter more than Me is not worthy of Me. And he who does not take his cross and follow after Me is not worthy of Me. He who finds his life will lose it, and he who loses his life for My sake will find it.
> He who receives you receives Me, and he who receives Me receives Him who sent Me."
>
> MATTHEW 10:36-40 (NKJV)

> And Jesus answered and said unto them, Take heed that no man deceive you.
> For many shall come in my name, saying, I am Christ; and shall deceive many.
> And ye shall hear of wars and rumours of wars: see that ye be not troubled: for all these things must come to pass, but the end is not yet.
> For nation shall rise against nation, and kingdom against kingdom: and there shall be famines, and pestilences, and earthquakes, in divers places.
> All these are the beginning of sorrows.
> Then shall they deliver you up to be afflicted, and shall kill you: and ye shall be hated of all nations for my name's sake.
> And then shall many be offended, and shall betray one another, and shall hate one another.
> And many false prophets shall rise, and shall deceive many.
> And because iniquity shall abound, the love of many shall wax cold.
> But he that shall endure unto the end, the same shall be saved.
> And this gospel of the kingdom shall be preached in all the world for a witness unto all nations; and then shall the end come.
>
> MATTHEW 24:4-14

People take offense so easily. Pastor Rodney has had preachers so touched in his meetings, but now they won't even say where they got that touch from. They are afraid that his name will bring discredit to them. Yet, they wanted to use his name when they thought it could help them. I've had the same thing happen to me. Some who were on my board, and were some of my best friends in the world, now won't return a phone call. When Jesus performed with signs, wonders, and miracles, the crowds flocked around Him. But the moment the commitment part was preached, they were gone.

> From that time many of his disciples went back, and walked no more with him.
> Then said Jesus unto the twelve, Will ye also go away?
> Then Simon Peter answered him, Lord, to whom shall we go? thou hast the words of eternal life.
>
> JOHN 6:66-68

Jesus explained that they needed to drink His blood and eat His flesh. It says that many disciples left Him that day. So, He asked the twelve if they were going to leave also.

We're in a war. We don't usually emphasize it because of people who already make the Devil too big. When Reinhard Bonnke spoke at The River University Bible School graduation, he said to the graduates and people sitting in the audience, "God has shown me that this will ultimately cost people their lives."

It is worth it if we are flowing in the Holy Ghost with the anointing, but not if we are only in religion and tradition.

People are touched by revival today, and later, we can't even find a trace of it. They have flaked out and are into weird doctrines and contraptions. They are trying to pull devils out of the atmosphere and into gold dust and rubies falling from Heaven. Some are pouring oil on the streets to anoint the city. They are into dove feathers falling in the meeting and calling it The Holy Spirit. The Holy Spirit is not a dove and certainly does not molt. They are casting devils out of mailboxes and blowing shofars to clear the atmosphere. It is a bunch of mumbo-jumbo that has nothing to do with revival.

This is not about just getting the anointing but keeping it. You can't have both the real and the counterfeit. You must make a decision. For some pastors, it might mean clearing out eighty percent of what they preach. They might have to repent and say, "I've been preaching the biggest bunch of crap." Why are people drinking pure water in revival and then going back to drinking swamp water? If we want the true riches, we have to get rid of the junk. We can't have both.

> Now it came to pass, when Jesus had finished all these sayings, that He said to His disciples, "You know that after two days is the Passover, and the Son of Man will be delivered up to be crucified."
>
> MATTHEW 26:1-2 (NKJV)

In verse two, Jesus tells them that He is about to be betrayed and die. They've seen miracles, people raised from the dead, healed, and delivered. Judas witnessed these things. He must have thought, "No problem. No one can touch Him. I've seen Him go right through the crowd when they wanted to throw Him over a cliff. No one can take Him." The disciples thought (when He was talking about dying), "Maybe He's going through a difficult time and is discouraged."

When we look out at people in the congregation on a typical Sunday, perhaps we should ask, "What have you come here for today? To look or partake?" I wonder if angels are watching how we respond during the service and give us report cards on how we respond.

Heaven knows if you're a Peter, who will later deny your involvement with The Lord, or a Judas, who will sell the anointing. Lucifer was the original trafficker of the anointing, and people are still doing that today. I heard recently about people saying that you could give a certain amount to be guaranteed against the coronavirus. These people have no business in the ministry. They are not even saved. Maybe someone in the congregation is a Thomas, a doubter. Three of Jesus' disciples, one-third of them, were deniers, betrayers, and doubters.

Maybe people should weigh if they want to get in the line, for there is a cost. In the middle of the battle, you may want to strangle the person who brought you revival because they did not tell you of the cost involved. You may say, "I lost all of my friends."

DESPERATE HUNGER GETS GOD'S ATTENTION

> Then the chief priests, the scribes, and the elders of the people assembled at the palace of the high priest, who was called Caiaphas, and plotted to take Jesus by trickery and kill Him.
>
> MATTHEW 26:3-4 (NKJV)

The chief priests were the religious leaders. They are always the greatest opposition to revival and the move of The Holy Spirit. They are always criticizing the minister's methods. It would be no different if Jesus were here today. We also still have the scribes. Sometimes, those are the editors of major Christian magazines today. They are sometimes as bad as the news media with their reports. Thank God that the Gospels weren't written by scribes.

Caiaphas was the high priest. You can't go any higher than the high priest. We still have them today. They are the religious system that sets itself in power and place. They won't come against you or attack you as long as there is no anointing. You better not manifest the anointing, demonstrate, or get people set free. If you do, they will come against you. If you go to where the anointing is flowing and come back changed, they'll ask where you have been.

Several years ago, Evangelist Richard Moore held a revival in Columbus, Georgia. When we arrived, we found out they did not have a pastor. He had left, and the administrator was acting as Pastor along with the board. He was hungry for revival and had invited Pastor Rodney to come. Pastor Rodney suggested that Richard and I go first, and he would come on the weekend. We were having a great revival, even though no one on the board attended Richard and my meetings. They did come for Pastor Rodney, I think, out of curiosity. Some acted as if they liked it, especially when the Pastor called them out to pray for them. However, when he left, Richard and I were to continue the meeting. Before we could have another service, the board asked us to meet with them on charges of heresy. We were in shock and called Pastor Rodney. He told us to tell them, "We are not under your jurisdiction or the jurisdiction of the Assemblies of God. We are under the cover of Revival Ministries International. You refused to come to our meeting, and now we refuse to go to your meeting." We left, and the accountant resigned and started his own church, which is thriving years later. He has built three buildings because of the growing congregation.

It is interesting how church politics try to fence revivalists in and refuse the move of The Holy Ghost, even though their denominations were birthed out of a move of God.

I went through something similar in Alaska. I held revival meetings in many churches that were part of The Assemblies of God. We had outstanding revivals, and the pastors could have me in because they were large enough churches to be considered sovereign. However, they still received letters from headquarters suggesting that they should not invite any non-Assembly of God credentialed ministers. Some of those pastors showed me the letters but continued to have me in. They even recommended me to their other pastor friends. Eventually, some of them wanted me to become credentialed by their denomination and arranged a meeting in Anchorage with the superintendent. At the beginning of the meeting, he handed me an article written by the secretary of their denomination in Springfield. This article massacred Pastor Rodney. I didn't even finish reading it. I was too angry and told them nicely that I would keep my present credentials. He smiled and said, "I thought you would say that. Have a nice day."

> But they said, "Not during the feast, lest there be an uproar among the people."
> And when Jesus was in Bethany at the house of Simon the leper, a woman came to Him having an alabaster flask of very costly fragrant oil, and she poured it on His head as He sat at the table. But when His disciples saw it, they were indignant, saying, "Why this waste? For this fragrant oil might have been sold for much and given to the poor."
>
> MATTHEW 26:5-9 (NKJV)

Have you noticed that people with a black heart never announce it? They like to cover it with religious lingo. "We just care about the poor and those who are suffering, those who have the virus, and those who don't understand revival."

> But when Jesus was aware of it, He said to them, "Why do you trouble the woman? For she has done a good work for Me. For you have the poor with you always, but Me you do not have always. For in pouring this fragrant oil on My body, she did it for My burial. Assuredly, I say to you, wherever this gospel is preached in the whole world, what this woman has done will also be told as a memorial to her."
> Then one of the twelve, called Judas Iscariot, went to the chief priests and said, "What are you willing to give me if I deliver Him to you?" And they counted out to him thirty pieces of silver.
>
> MATTHEW 26:10-15 (NKJV)

It is plain in verse seven that the spirit controlling Judas manifested at offering time. This is what they most often do. That is why there are so many church splits over finances. This is also why we spend so much time on this subject. When people complain about how much time we take to teach people about giving or how much a minister is blessed when we could be ministering to the poor instead, I say, "Hello, Judas. You must be a descendant of him because you got so upset about us teaching people how to pour oil on Jesus' feet."

Didn't Judas handle the anointing as well? Didn't he walk with Jesus and lay hands on people? He was with Jesus for three and a half years and yet set Him up for thirty pieces of silver. People may be using the anointing today and selling it tomorrow for a few cents.

The Bible says that Jesus told them that some of them would get offended. It is amazing what causes people to leave church and sometimes leave God.

They get offended at an usher, the parking attendant, or from waiting in line for the restroom. What will it take to offend you? God will use people to purposely offend your mind to reveal your heart. Offense and betrayal go hand in hand.

> Now before the feast of the passover, when Jesus knew that his hour was come that he should depart out of this world unto the Father, having loved his own which were in the world, he loved them unto the end.
> And supper being ended, the devil having now put into the heart of Judas Iscariot, Simon's son, to betray him;
>
> JOHN 13:1-2

When did the Devil put into Judas Iscariot's heart the thought of betraying Him?

It happened in John 12 over an offering. The Bible says that Judas was a thief. He held what was in the bag and was dishonest about the money. Mary broke an alabaster box of spikenard, a year's salary over Him, and wiped His feet with her hair. Then Judas said, "Why was it not sold and given to the poor?" He must have thought that Jesus would agree with him and thank him for being the one on His board with all of the wisdom to point out how this should have been used. However, Jesus said, "Leave her alone. She has done this for My burial. You'll always have the poor with you, but you won't always have Me." The other disciples joined in by calling her offering a waste. Which part were they calling a waste? Was it a waste to serve and bless Jesus? The entire group got caught up in this. There are still carnal-minded Christians today. There are still people who quote what Judas said as though Jesus said it instead. They need to be careful before they say anything like that because they are sitting in the chair of Judas. That is very dangerous. We hear people talking about how it's a waste that preachers get blessed, fly business class, drive a nice car, or live in a nice house. They think large offerings are a waste. Then, they always bring up that we only should give to the poor.

DESPERATE HUNGER GETS GOD'S ATTENTION

> And supper being ended, the devil having now put into the heart of Judas Iscariot, Simon's son, to betray him;
>
> JOHN 13:2

The Bible tells us here that the Devil had already put the offense and betrayal into the heart of Judas. It happened when he took issue with Jesus about the money. Judas became obsessive that Jesus would allow such a waste on Himself.

I heard the great Greek scholar Rick Reiner teach on this subject. He explained that it is so important that we see how the Devil puts this into the heart of the people. The word devil in Greek is *diablos*, and it means to strike and strike multiple times. So, when we see the word devil, it is a job description. The Devil continues to penetrate in a weak moment until he gets through. When Judas got offended over money, that door was opened. Then, he sat around the supper table at the Last Supper and pretended to be in covenant with Jesus when he had already broken covenant in his heart. When you are deceived, you think what you are doing is right, or you know it's wrong, and you don't care.

Mark 4 talks about five things that the Devil uses to steal the seed of The Word of God. Offense is at the top of the list.

> Then took Mary a pound of ointment of spikenard, very costly, and anointed the feet of Jesus, and wiped his feet with her hair: and the house was filled with the odour of the ointment.
>
> JOHN 12:3

When Mary gave that sacrificial offering, Satan finally penetrated Judas's mind. He had been trying to bombast his mind for a long time.

It may be that Judas had a weakness in his character that the Devil knew about. Until that time, he may have been able to resist, but Satan finally found a way to penetrate the mind of Judas. He was one of the twelve disciples and a close one at that. He was the treasurer, and he and Jesus talked every day about the money. They would have had a very close relationship. When the Devil wants to hurt you, he uses those closest to you. It is never the parking lot attendant but the people closest to you who eat at your table.

Judas could have come back to Jesus and repented, even in that state, but did not. God's plan is always for restoration. Judas was called, and Jesus wanted to mold him into a usable vessel. What would have happened if he had done that instead of taking the road to suicide? But, instead, he went out and hung himself.

The Bible says in James 3:16, *"Where there is strife, there is confusion and every evil work."* We must make sure that we close the door to the enemy and not allow him to continue to pull our strings. If we are not careful, we will end up taking ourselves out. At some point, we must be like the prodigal son and say, "What I'm doing is wrong." Don't blame it on anyone else. Just get on your knees, repent, and cry out to God.

Think about what was going on in the ministry of Jesus. All the demons of Hell were trying to stop Him. Judas was in such a key position to help, but the Devil took him out. He could have repented, but pride stops it every time. Pride is involved in every Christian failure. It goes before a fall. We must not run from Jesus when we sin but to Him.

Judas betrayed Jesus with a kiss, which is the ultimate betrayal. It was reserved for only those for whom you had the deepest affection. Judas regularly called Jesus *diadosulas*, which is the Greek word for master or teacher. However, he did not call Him Lord. He recognized that Jesus was a great teacher who operated in great authority, but there was some area of surrender that Judas was never willing to give.

Judas saw Jesus walk out of the midst of people trying to kill Him before. He had been stealing from the bag, and probably thought that this would be a quick fix. He thought, "I'll take the thirty pieces of silver and put it back in the bag before anyone knows that I took it. I don't like the Pharisees anyway. I know Jesus will walk through them." He also thought Jesus was gonna raise up the kingdom of Israel at that time.

When he came to the garden of Gethsemane, he betrayed Jesus with a kiss. Jesus had been struggling before He ever went to the cross. He was a bloody mess, and right in the midst of that, Judas came with about six hundred men to arrest Him. Judas didn't think they could take Him because he told them something where they thought they needed that many soldiers. Judas was shocked when they arrested Jesus and that Jesus went with the soldiers.

If you and I are going to be carriers of the anointing, we will have to wade through the Iscariots, the doubters, and the Peters. I remember when Pastor Rodney was having a campmeeting, someone called the fire department in Tampa and told them that we were overcrowded. They were trying to get Pastor Rodney in trouble. The fire department came and saw that what they were told was not true. That was someone inside the meeting, pretending to be a friend of the revival and Pastor Rodney. These things can and will happen right in the middle of some of the greatest meetings.

Verse 15 says that they covenanted together to kill Him for thirty pieces of silver. People will do that to stop us when we carry the anointing. They will pay each other to silence our mouths, to lie and tell stories about us. In Africa, a few years ago, a particular denomination paid two point five million dollars to out-of-work evangelists to spread lies about a man of God who had great miracles in his meetings. They became jealous of him. The only way to stop the anointing is to ruin the reputation of the anointed vessel or kill him.

During the COVID-19 virus scare, I was pastoring in Washington State. I was given a cease and desist order to stop me from preaching and to stop us from meeting. I refused. Later, I found out that it was a jealous pastor who turned us in and badgered them to stop me. It was also jealous pastors who stood with a sheriff in Hillsborough County to denounce Pastor Rodney when he kept his church open. They quoted Scripture to show how he was in defiance of The Word of God, which of course, he was not.

Most people do not realize that many men and women of God receive death threats and lawsuit notices almost daily. Who would ever think that pulling people out of wheelchairs would cause people to want to kill you? Benny Hinn has spoken of having five to seven lawsuits filed against him at one time from people who say they didn't get healed. Yet when we ask, "Who wants the anointing?" people come running without knowing what they are asking for. Do you want double portion anointing? It may involve double the persecution. Are you able to handle that? Do you want fifteen lawsuits a day and death threats?

We won't have it any different than Jesus did. It wasn't just happening in Jesus' ministry. It is still happening today. If we move in the anointing, we will face these things. Are you prepared for this? There could be a Maria Woodsworth-Etter reading this book or a Kathryn Kuhlman, Aimee Semple-McPherson, John G. Lake, or a Rodney Howard-Browne out there somewhere. However, you had better count the cost.

John Alexander Dowie, whom you read about earlier in this book, was arrested over one hundred times for practicing medicine without a license. Ministers are not made out of that caliber today. When they get their first or second arrest, they will probably say, "I'm not praying for the sick anymore. This shouldn't have happened to me." Really? We need to look at Paul and Silas or Peter in jail. What about John the Baptist, who lost his head, or James, the Apostle, who was martyred, along with most of the disciples? People say, "That can't happen in America!" It just did with my pastor and others being arrested in the good ole U.S.A., the land of the free. If they could lock us up right now, they would. What happened with COVID-19 was just a test, and a whole lot of the church failed miserably.

There is a Homeland Security law that warns about us conservatives and calls us radical extremists. They put us in the same category as terrorists. If they could kill Pastor Rodney, they would, but the hand of The Lord is upon him.

Several years ago, a senator from Iowa attacked five major ministries and viciously went after them for tax evasion. Thank God for the protection that has been afforded to us by Him and by the constitution of the United States of America.

The Bible says in Matthew 26:16, *"So from that time he sought opportunity to betray Him."* There will be people coming in very close for one purpose. That purpose is to betray you and to try to destroy you. You want a double dose of the anointing, yet you get offended at the church parking lot attendant or an usher? Then, you don't have what it takes. You'll be either a Judas, a Thomas, or a Peter.

Some people think we should keep this on the lighter side. Then, I have to ask you, "Why are people falling out of the ministry every day?" There are people who are saying, "I didn't know it was going to be like this." They think there's something wrong with them because no one warned them. We need to tell them that there is nothing wrong with them. They just need to go home and read their Bible.

> Now on the first day of the Feast of the Unleavened Bread the disciples came to Jesus, saying to Him, "Where do You want us to prepare for You to eat the Passover?"
> And He said, "Go into the city to a certain man, and say to him, 'The Teacher says, "My time is at hand; I will keep the Passover at your house with My disciples."
> So the disciples did as Jesus had directed them; and they prepared the Passover.
> When evening had come, He sat down with the twelve. Now as they were eating, He said, "Assuredly, I say to you, one of you will betray Me."
> And they were exceedingly sorrowful, and each of them began to say to Him, "Lord, is it I?"
> He answered and said, "He who dipped his hand with Me in the dish will betray Me.
>
> MATTHEW 26:17 23 (NKJV)

While Jesus was at the table with twelve of his closest followers, he said, "One of you will betray me." They all said, "Surely, it's not me." We should not live suspiciously but realize that everyone has the potential to betray or deny.

Verse 22: *"And they were exceedingly sorrowful, and each of them began to say to Him, "Lord, is it I?"* They were exceedingly sorrowful. How do you betray Jesus? You betray Him when you say, "I used to believe in laying on of hands and in the operation of the gifts of Spirit, but that brought too much offense. I used to have that joy, but it caused too much trouble."

The ministry of Jesus consisted of healings, miracles, signs, wonders, and casting out devils. If we don't follow Him and go after those things, we're betraying Him. Jesus told Peter that He would build His church upon the revelation that He is the Christ, the anointing, The Anointed One. He went on to say that *"the gates of hell shall not prevail against it"* (Matthew 16:13-19).

We are looking for a group of people that will be raised up by God, anointed, and will go out with the fire of God. This group will not betray and will not backslide. They will be nation-shakers. Why does the military have boot camps?

So that when you get into the battle, you will not be killed. We must have training, or people will be killed spiritually. We can't afford to lose people in the body of Christ.

Be careful how you treat fallen ministers.

> Brethren, if a man be overtaken in a fault, ye which are spiritual, restore such an one in the spirit of meekness; considering thyself, lest thou also be tempted.
>
> GALATIANS 6:1

America is full of these fallen ministers. Yet, in the military, if there are three casualties, it is considered a tragedy, as it should be. They are buried

DESPERATE HUNGER GETS GOD'S ATTENTION

in Arlington Cemetery. Yet, in the body of Christ, the attitude is, "Good, he's out of the way now, and maybe I can move up."

> The Son of Man indeed goes just as it is written of Him, but woe to that man by whom the Son of Man is betrayed! It would have been good for that man if he had not been born."
> Then Judas, who was betraying Him, answered and said, "Rabbi, is it I?"
> He said to him, "You have said it."
>
> MATTHEW 26:24-25 (NKJV)

Verse 25: Judas... knew it was him who was in the deception.

> And as they were eating, Jesus took bread, blessed and broke it, and gave it to the disciples and said, "Take, eat; this is My body."
>
> MATTHEW 26:26 (NKJV)

Verse 26 is betrayal attendant—it's the not from the parking lot—one that you eat with. It could take you to Calvary.

> Then He took the cup, and gave thanks, and gave it to them, saying, "Drink from it, all of you. For this is My blood of the new covenant, which is shed for many for the remission of sins. But I say to you, I will not drink of this fruit of the vine from now on until that day when I drink it new with you in My Father's kingdom."
> And when they had sung a hymn, they went out to the Mount of Olives.
> Then Jesus said to them, "All of you will be made to stumble because of Me this night, for it is written:
> 'I will strike the Shepherd,

And the sheep of the flock will be scattered.'"

MATTHEW 26:27-31 (NKJV)

Pastors and other ministers have actually told Dr. Rodney Howard-Browne, "I know this is a move of the Holy Ghost, but I have to decide how many friends I'm going to lose." That is so unbelievable to hear that a Christian, let alone a minister of The Gospel, would know this is a move of God but purposefully deny it for the sake of expediency.

> "But after I have been raised, I will go before you to Galilee."
> Peter answered and said to Him, "Even if all are made to stumble because of You, I will never be made to stumble."
> Jesus said to him, "Assuredly, I say to you that this night, before the rooster crows, you will deny Me three times."
> Peter said to Him, "Even if I have to die with You, I will not deny You!"
> And so said all the disciples.

MATTHEW 26:32-35 (NKJV)

If you walk away from the anointing, you walk away from Jesus. If you become seeker-sensitive or give into religion and tradition, you are betraying the very one who gave His life for you. If you back off the power of God to appease people, you are not worthy of Him. You better stay hooked up to the anointing. Our very lives will depend on it.

When we watch videos of the services of several years ago, we can see how many have backed out of revival. We have learned the hard way and have cried out, "God, what did we do wrong that more are not staying in revival the way they once were?" Then, we came to the revelation that all we have to do is to read the Gospels: Matthew, Mark, Luke, and John. It has nothing to do with us. It has to do with only one word: anointing. When you say,

"All have left me, all have forsaken me," He'll say, "I'm with you. I'll never leave you or forsake you."

Pastor Rodney went into churches for weeks to help them. As a result, minister friends were touched powerfully. They tripled in their finances and were able to buy beautiful homes and cars, but now they won't even return a phone call. The Bible says in Luke 6:26, "*Beware when all men speak well of you.*" Today, they will celebrate you, and tomorrow they will crucify you. They'll be the first ones to put the nail in your hand.

Some didn't want the anointing. They only wanted it to attract the people and to get their tithes and offerings up. When they could not control it, they did not want it. The move of God is not you controlling it, but it controlling you. You are never going to know what's in you until you're squeezed.

> Peter answered and said unto him, Though all men shall be offended because of thee, yet will I never be offended.
>
> MATTHEW 26:33

He was too sure of himself. He didn't know what was in him until some pressure was applied.

> Then cometh Jesus with them unto a place called Gethsemane, and saith unto the disciples, Sit ye here, while I go and pray yonder.
> And he took with him Peter and the two sons of Zebedee, and began to be sorrowful and very heavy.
> Then saith he unto them, My soul is exceeding sorrowful, even unto death: tarry ye here, and watch with me.
> And he went a little farther, and fell on his face, and prayed, saying, O my Father, if it be possible, let this cup pass from me: nevertheless not as I will, but as thou wilt.
> And he cometh unto the disciples, and findeth them asleep,

> and saith unto Peter, What, could ye not watch with me one hour?
> Watch and pray, that ye enter not into temptation: the spirit indeed is willing, but the flesh is weak.
> He went away again the second time, and prayed, saying, O my Father, if this cup may not pass away from me, except I drink it, thy will be done.
> And he came and found them asleep again: for their eyes were heavy.
> And he left them, and went away again, and prayed the third time, saying the same words.
> Then cometh he to his disciples, and saith unto them, Sleep on now, and take your rest: behold, the hour is at hand, and the Son of man is betrayed into the hands of sinners.
>
> MATTHEW 26:36-45

Gethsemane is a place where you, as an individual, are going to have to go. Don't think God's against you. It's a place where you lay everything on the altar. Kathryn Kuhlman said that "she remembers the place and time where she died a thousand deaths." The closer you get to eternity, the lonelier it will be. What's the cost? Everything you have, are, and ever will be.

Do you love rejection? Gethsemane is not a place to take your friends. They will fall asleep on you. If you haven't been there already, you will have to go there. The disciples wouldn't even understand what He was praying about. When people ask, "Can I pray with you?" "No, you can pray for me, but not with me." The disciples couldn't pray with Him. It wasn't their burden; it wasn't their cross. You can't pray where you're not going, and you can't pray what you're not carrying.

Don't try to take a person with an anointing and try to figure them out. You can't. Some of the greatest meetings that people have ever been in have been during some of the greatest turmoil. Evangelist Richard Moore rented a neutral venue in Houston, Texas, a number of years ago to hold a revival. They were glorious meetings. Pastor Rodney even came in and did one night for us. Richard told me that he had never seen the anointing on me that strong before. Others commented the same. What no one but Richard knew was that by the end of the week, I was going through some of the worst personal Hell of my life. I had been betrayed and lied to, and I was not sure how God was going to bring me out. He did, with His big hand, grace, and mercy. I had to press in that week as never before, and as a result, the anointing was strong. My total dependency was on God. Nothing in me wanted to even go out into the meeting every morning and night, but I pressed through, and God met me there.

In America and much of the Western world, there seems to be a lack of commitment. If someone betrays someone, that person just goes to another church with no regard for anyone. I can't do that. I am compelled by God and am on a mission. I can't do just what I want to do because years ago, I prayed a prayer, laid my life on the altar, and said, "I'll go where You want me to go, say what You want me to say, and do what You want me to do." I don't care if everyone deserts me or if I'm never invited to a conference. I must stay with the fire of God. I will stick with His purpose and plan for my life.

We are going after a nation-shaking revival, and we can't just go for anything. We have to stay with the unction.

> Then He said to them, "My soul is exceedingly sorrowful, even to death. Stay here and watch with Me."
>
> MATTHEW 26:38 (NKJV)

At Gethsemane, Jesus took with Him Peter and the two sons of Zebedee. He was sorrowful and heavy with the burden, the weight for souls, the harvest. When you are like that, it is all that you see. It grabs ahold of you and dominates your thought life. If people took your sweat and put it under a microscope, it would shout revival, souls, signs, wonders, and miracles. It would scream that America must be shaken, people saved, healed, delivered, blessed, and broken free from poverty.

> ..."O My Father, if it is possible, let this cup pass from Me; nevertheless, not as I will, but as You will."
> Then He came to the disciples and found them sleeping, and said to Peter, "What! Could you not watch with Me one hour? Watch and pray, lest you enter into temptation. The spirit indeed is willing, but the flesh is weak."
> Again, a second time, He went away and prayed, saying, "O My Father, if this cup cannot pass away from Me unless I drink it, Your will be done." And He came and found them asleep again, for their eyes were heavy.
> So He left them, went away again, and prayed the third time, saying the same words. Then He came to His disciples and said to them, "Are you still sleeping and resting? Behold, the hour is at hand, and the Son of Man is being betrayed into the hands of sinners. Rise, let us be going. See, My betrayer is at hand."
>
> MATTHEW 26:39-46 (NKJV)

The disciples were sleeping. They were not bad people. They just didn't see what He saw. When you have a vision and a dream and nobody wants to see it, don't get upset. They can't see it except by revelation.

When my pastor, Dr. Rodney Howard-Browne, went to New York City in 1999 to conduct the largest soul-winning crusade since Billy Graham in the fifties, he went to the garden alone, so to speak. Yes, a large part of our church went to be a part of the soul-winning and help in other areas. I joined him for a week of it. However, the ministry friends that he thought would support him, at least with encouragement and prayer, told him that he was making one of the biggest mistakes of his life. They told him that he should not have had to borrow money to do the crusade, yet they borrowed for their fancy buildings. He was borrowing for souls. Some mocked him and hoped that he would fail. Very few whom he had helped through the years supported him in any way. He said that it is tough when you are in your greatest battle, and your friends are sleeping. However, God came through, and almost fifty thousand souls were saved as a result of his going to the garden alone. Some of those people worked in the Twin Towers and are now in eternity. Thank God that he went.

We cannot judge ministry by a crowd. The crowds are here today and gone tomorrow. Pastor Rodney said that in the years 1994–1995 alone, he laid hands on three hundred thousand people. He laid hands on everyone who came for prayer, but in retrospect, he thinks that perhaps he should have only laid hands on about ten thousand of them. Why? Because the price, the cost, is too high. He wonders if he should have said to some, "Get out of the line, Judas. You want this for the wrong reasons." However, he wanted everyone to have a chance to get under the anointing. He didn't want to be suspicious of anyone and allowed all of them to be touched by God.

When Jesus came back, He found the disciples asleep again. Sometimes, people ask this question, "If people are being anointed, how come so few stay?" Have we made it too easy? In the early Pentecostal meetings, they taught people to have tarrying meetings. They made you pray until you received the fire. People weren't allowed to leave until they were baptized with The Holy Ghost. Maybe we should have more of those kinds of meetings today.

You have to get the anointing, even if it means that you have to put yourself on the altar ten thousand times. Press into God. Tell your friends and family, "That's it. If you want to see me, you'll have to come looking for me because, for the next thirty days, I'm switching off my cell phone and emails and pressing into God."

That is, unless you want to just be a nominal Christian. But if you want God to use you, you must get extremely serious. There can be no more sitting on the fence. It means no compromise. The Lord wants and demands total commitment and total sell-out.

In the story of the rich young ruler, we find someone professing to be hungry, but we find out quickly that he is not hungry enough.

> And, behold, one came and said unto him, Good Master, what good thing shall I do, that I may have eternal life?
> And he said unto him, Why callest thou me good? there is none good but one, that is, God: but if thou wilt enter into life, keep the commandments.
> He saith unto him, Which? Jesus said, Thou shalt do no murder, Thou shalt not commit adultery, Thou shalt not steal, Thou shalt not bear false witness,
> Honour thy father and thy mother: and, Thou shalt love thy neighbour as thyself.
> The young man saith unto him, All these things have I kept from my youth up: what lack I yet?
> Jesus said unto him, If thou wilt be perfect, go and sell that thou hast, and give to the poor, and thou shalt have treasure in heaven: and come and follow me.
> But when the young man heard that saying, he went away sorrowful: for he had great possessions.
>
> MATTHEW 19:16-22

At first glance, most people would think that this was an evangelist's dream coming true. Jesus didn't have to go to him. The rich young ruler approached Jesus. Jesus didn't have to give an altar call. The man told Him that he wanted eternal life. He wanted salvation. Most people that I know would have led him in the sinner's prayer on the spot. However, Jesus looked into his heart and knew that commitment was not there, and the man was only making a pretense of hunger. He wasn't willing to give up everything and follow Jesus. You cannot follow Him halfway. He asks for everything.

The man walked away sad. I am sure he will be a lot more sad than that when he meets with God on judgment day. He will never know how blessed he would have been if he had given his life to Christ. Jesus never asks for anything without blessing back many times. But it is always about the heart. He searches the heart to see where the blockages are. I often hear from people who are not committed, "God knows my heart." I want to say, "Yes, He absolutely does. That is the problem. You don't see it, but He does."

In Luke 14, we see that Jesus was not accepting excuses.

> Then said he unto him, A certain man made a great supper, and bade many:
> And sent his servant at supper time to say to them that were bidden, Come; for all things are now ready.
> And they all with one consent began to make excuse. The first said unto him, I have bought a piece of ground, and I must needs go and see it: I pray thee have me excused.
> And another said, I have bought five yoke of oxen, and I go to prove them: I pray thee have me excused.
> And another said, I have married a wife, and therefore I cannot come.
> So that servant came, and shewed his lord these things. Then the master of the house being angry said to his servant, Go out quickly into the streets and lanes of the city, and bring in hither the poor, and the maimed, and the halt, and the blind.
> And the servant said, Lord, it is done as thou hast commanded, and yet there is room.
> And the lord said unto the servant, Go out into the highways and hedges, and compel them to come in, that my house may be filled.
> For I say unto you, That none of those men which were bidden shall taste of my supper.
> And there went great multitudes with him: and he turned, and said unto them,
> If any man come to me, and hate not his father, and mother, and wife, and children, and brethren, and sisters, yea, and his own life also, he cannot be my disciple.

> And whosoever doth not bear his cross, and come after me, cannot be my disciple.
> For which of you, intending to build a tower, sitteth not down first, and counteth the cost, whether he have sufficient to finish it?
> Lest haply, after he hath laid the foundation, and is not able to finish it, all that behold it begin to mock him,
> Saying, This man began to build, and was not able to finish.
> Or what king, going to make war against another king, sitteth not down first, and consulteth whether he be able with ten thousand to meet him that cometh against him with twenty thousand?
> Or else, while the other is yet a great way off, he sendeth an ambassage, and desireth conditions of peace.
> So likewise, whosoever he be of you that forsaketh not all that he hath, he cannot be my disciple.
>
> LUKE 14:16-33

Earlier, in Luke 9, Jesus would not even accept the excuse of a man going to his father's funeral.

> And it came to pass, that, as they went in the way, a certain man said unto him, Lord, I will follow thee whithersoever thou goest.
> And Jesus said unto him, Foxes have holes, and birds of the air have nests; but the Son of man hath not where to lay his head.
> And he said unto another, Follow me. But he said, Lord, suffer me first to go and bury my father.
> Jesus said unto him, Let the dead bury their dead: but go thou and preach the kingdom of God.
> And another also said, Lord, I will follow thee; but let me first go bid them farewell, which are at home at my house.

DESPERATE HUNGER GETS GOD'S ATTENTION

> And Jesus said unto him, No man, having put his hand to the plough, and looking back, is fit for the kingdom of God.
>
> LUKE 9:57-62

We aren't going to make it easy for people. I can't make that commitment for you. I'm concerned you'd be killed in the battle if you signed up under false expectations. You can choose the easier way of no anointing and nobody will know. Everyone will love you, and you'll be accepted and be a prophet with honor.

There's not one person on the planet today who hasn't been through the winepress. If you haven't been, the anointing will never flow. The problem is that we all think we're the only ones going through it at the time.

It is easy to get touched with the anointing and revival, but whether you stay in or not is another thing. There's nothing more precious than the anointing. If you don't like speaking in tongues, if you are against people casting out devils, and if you are against the laying on of hands for the sick to be healed, you are against Jesus. That means you are of the spirit of the antichrist. We cannot be for anything less than the four Gospels. To believe in the Gospel is to be full Gospel, not half Gospel and half tradition, half joy and half depression, half faith and half doubt and unbelief. Again, if you are against what Jesus did, you are against the ministry of Jesus. If you're for Him, you are for His anointing. You cannot preach the cross with no power! You must preach it with power and anointing.

I knew a woman minister years ago who told me this story of a nurse who wanted to be a missionary. She had a great job working for a well-known physician. This doctor claimed to be an atheist. One day, she approached him and said, "Doctor, I love working for you, but I feel that God has called me to be a full-time missionary in the foreign field. What do you think that I should do?" This atheist had a surprising and yet profound answer for her. He understood more about how a Christian is supposed to live than most people who claim to be Christians realize today. He asked her a series of questions. "Do you believe that the only way to Heaven is Jesus? Do you believe that without Christ, you're going to Hell? Then, you can't live like other people can? You can't spend money like others do." Wow! He hit the nail on the head.

Jesus had to die to many things before He ever went to Gethsemane and Calvary. He died to reputation, family, what people thought, persecution, and being misunderstood. We have to as well. Again, we are not above our master. Are you hungry enough to pay the price to carry the anointing? I assure you, it is worth any price.

EIGHT

GET HUNGRY ENOUGH TO GET YOUR DREAMS BACK

Have you had some dreams die? You may feel that too much has happened, too much time has transpired, and it now looks impossible. You can be revived again and dream again.

> Wilt thou not revive us again: that thy people may rejoice in thee?
>
> PSALM 85:6

I know that it may look like it's all over, but it's not. Even when it looks like nothing is happening, God has not forgotten about you. It may look and sound totally hopeless to you, as well as to everyone around you. But I promise that if you get hungry enough, you are going to get it all back. Revival means coming back to life again. That tells me that something has died and needs to be resurrected.

In the story of Lazarus in John 11, we read of Jesus raising Lazarus from the dead. It looked pretty hopeless. He was dead four days and already stinking. Some of the Jews in that day had a superstition that the spirit hovered close to the body for three days after a person died. However, on the fourth day, the spirit departed. I believe that God purposely waited four days to destroy that superstition. Your dreams and callings may be so dead that they are stinking. Everyone around you is crying and having a funeral for what looks hopelessly dead. People remind you daily of how it is all over for you. Your head, condemnation from the enemy, and terrible regrets taunt you with what could have and should have been. You feel that every vision, business idea, book, invention, and life goal can never be retrieved. But this is going to be a turning point in your life. When you become spiritually hungry and thirsty for God again, watch out. You are about to hear, LAZARUS COME FORTH!

With Ezekiel's vision, found in Ezekiel 37:1-10, we see another example of dead bones living again. Those who had been dead stood up on their feet again and marched throughout the land. An army came alive when the Holy Spirit came upon them, and God breathed into their nostrils.

Everything is built on the resurrection power of Christ Jesus. He is the resurrection and the life. You've been through Hell, but you are still here, reading this book, because deep down inside, you know that God can do it again. You have been through the furnace of affliction, but you are here. Every fight that you're in is a faith fight. You will be an overcomer by the blood of the Lamb and by your testimony. You must say, "Come Hell or high water, I will get through this. I will contend, I will fight, and I will get it all back, plus some. Devil, you will regret the day that you touched my life or my family. I'm coming out of it." You have to be radical to come out of it!

My God did it for me, and He is no respecter of persons. He'll do it again for you. When I was writing my autobiography *Resurrected, Overcoming Death, Destruction, and Defeat*, I realized that my qualification was mostly that I am hungry for more of God. In the last chapter, I reflected on the wonderful places that God has allowed me to go and all of the wonderful things that I have been allowed to do. It is somewhat ironic that as I am finishing this book, I am sitting in Zimbabwe, Africa, viewing elephants at a waterhole with the sunset behind them. I have been on the road ministering for about two months without a break.

DESPERATE HUNGER GETS GOD'S ATTENTION

Two weeks ago, I was ministering in Cape Town, South Africa, and decided that I was closer to Victoria Falls than I have been in years and needed to see this indescribable wonder of the world. I allowed myself a one-week vacation. My team and I saw Victoria Falls and went on a safari in Botswana, where we saw lions, elephants, crocodiles, hippos, smaller monkeys, baboons, wart hogs, many varieties of the venison family, a unique lizard, mongoose, and lots of different kinds of birds. I have been in four African nations this week. I have now had the privilege of visiting fifty-three nations in my life. We have witnessed to many tour guides and taxi drivers on this trip. I talked to one tour guide about what God has done for me, and his eyes filled with tears. I gave him an abbreviated version of my testimony, and he told us how his wife left him more than once, and he continued to forgive her, but she ran off again. My testimony greatly encouraged him to go on. I found out that he does crusades, and God directed me to sow into his ministry.

I stand in awe at how much God has blessed me. I also stand in awe at the grace of God in my life and how many times He has rescued me from total destruction. I believe that His great mercy, grace, and power would never have reached me if I ever quit being hungry and chose to feel sorry for myself. I knew that what He did once, He could and would do again if I humbled myself and pressed into Him.

We can't quit. We have to refire. You're either going to be hot or cold, or you will be vomited out at this hour. The only thing that cures lukewarmness is fire. Check your temperature. You have to get hot enough to create an atmosphere for God. Our God is riding a chariot of fire. In His temple, there was a blazing altar, not a refrigerator. You have been born in the fire, and you shall live and serve in the fire. The fire of God is a divine enablement. When you go forth with a burning enablement, our generation will be saved.

God will bypass millions to touch one person who is hungry and in faith. You must get to the place where you say, "I'm gonna die if I don't have You." Keeping your heart hungry will propel you to a level of fire in The

Holy Ghost that will cause you to receive everything else from God. Just pray, "Lord, I'll do my part and trust you to do your part."

Never blame God. If you stop, it's not because anything stopped you. You quit because you weren't hungry enough. When the trials come, just get up and swing the bat twice as hard the next time. Say to the enemy, "You're going to pay for this one. Everywhere I go, I'll plunder Hell and populate Heaven. This won't cause me to quit. You'll regret the day that you touched me because I am hungry for Jesus. He's going to do things for me that He won't do for others."

You may have circumstances breathing down your neck that are telling you it's all over, but you have to get desperate all over again. If you fall, keep getting back up, no matter what mistakes you have made. Be that Holy Ghost beach ball and smack the Devil in the face on your way up.

I will ask you one last time. Are you hungry enough to get through anything when it starts to look impossible? When it looks like it's not worth it, that's when you will find out how hungry you are. It comes down to you and God and no one else around you.

Are you after God or only after the ministry and popularity? Are you after Him or after what you can get from Him? He will freely give us all good things and has promised life more abundantly, but that's not my motive for serving Him. We must hunger for Him, not just what He will do for us.

Are you ready to lay down everything? He's waiting to show you what He wants to do with you and for you. However, He's waiting to hear from you. Get hungry for God. If you are hungry, get hungrier. Get thirsty. If you are thirsty, get thirstier. When you do, God will do things for you that He won't do for others.

ABOUT DEBBIE RICH

Known as a fiery preacher who flows in the Holy Spirit while ministering the Word of God, Dr. Debbie Rich is an international teacher, evangelist, and revivalist who has carried the fire of revival to over fifty nations.

Dr. Debbie received her Ph.D. in Theology from Life Christian University following her graduation from Rhema Bible Training Center in Broken Arrow, Oklahoma. She also attended Open Bible College in Des Moines, Iowa.

As a pioneer missionary in the remote "Alaskan Bush," she traveled where few dared to go. Ministering in prisons, she saw inmates filled with the Holy Spirit after receiving Jesus as their Lord and Savior. Her ministry ignited a fire of revival across the state of Alaska as she boldly ventured into remote villages, towns, and cities where she felt called to go but had not been invited. While some local pastors initially opposed her efforts, many have since become long-time friends.

Dr. Debbie pioneered Faith Life Church and Word & Spirit Institute Northwest in the state of Washington. She teaches in Bible schools around the world.

Currently, she ministers out of Revival Ministries International in Tampa, Florida, with Pastors Rodney and Adonica Howard-Browne.

For Ministry Information Contact:

Dr. Debbie Rich Ministries
13194 US HWY 301 S,
Suite 107, Riverview, FL. 33578
Web Info: debbierichministries.org
E-mail: office@debbierichministries.org

facebook.com/debbierichministries
instagram.com/debbierichministries
youtube.com/debbierichministries

www.ingramcontent.com/pod-product-compliance
Lightning Source LLC
Chambersburg PA
CBHW021145160426
43194CB00007B/696